First World War
and Army of Occupation
War Diary
France, Belgium and Germany

17 DIVISION
52 Infantry Brigade
Manchester Regiment
12th Battalion
5 July 1915 - 31 March 1919

WO95/2012/2

The Naval & Military Press Ltd
www.nmarchive.com
Published in association with The National Archives

Published by

The Naval & Military Press Ltd

Unit 10 Ridgewood Industrial Park,

Uckfield, East Sussex,

TN22 5QE England

Tel: +44 (0) 1825 749494

www.naval-military-press.com

www.nmarchive.com

This diary has been reprinted in facsimile from the original. Any imperfections are inevitably reproduced and the quality may fall short of modern type and cartographic standards.

© **Crown Copyright**
Images reproduced by permission of The National Archives, London, England, 2015.

Contents

Document type	Place/Title	Date From	Date To
Heading	WO95/2012/2		
Heading	17th Division 52nd Infy Bde 12th Bn Manchester Regt Jly 1915-Mar 1919		
Heading	52nd Inf. Bde. 17th Div. Battn. disembarked Boulogne from England 16.7.15. 12th Battn. The Manchester Regiment. July (15/30.7.15) 1915		
War Diary		05/07/1915	30/07/1915
Heading	52nd Inf. Bde. 17th Div. 12th Battn. The Manchester Regiment. August 1915		
War Diary		01/08/1915	31/08/1915
Heading	52nd Inf. Bde. 17th Div. 12th Battn. The Manchester Regiment. September 1915		
War Diary		01/09/1915	29/09/1915
Heading	52nd Inf. Bde. 17th Div. 12th Battn. The Manchester Regiment. October 1915		
War Diary		01/10/1915	31/10/1915
Heading	52nd Inf. Bde. 17th Div. 12th Battn. The Manchester Regiment. November 1915		
War Diary		01/11/1915	24/11/1915
Heading	52nd Inf. Bde. 17th Div. 12th Battn. The Manchester Regiment. December 1915		
War Diary		01/12/1915	31/12/1915
Map			
Heading	War Diary of 12th Bn Manchester Regt. 1st Oct. to 31st Oct. 1916 Vol 13		
Miscellaneous	12 Manchester Vol 6		
Miscellaneous	12th Manchester Vol II		
Miscellaneous	Manch R. Forwarded		
Miscellaneous	A Form. Messages And Signals.		
Miscellaneous	Headquarters 52 Inf. Bde.	17/09/1917	17/09/1917
Miscellaneous	War Diary		
Miscellaneous	17th Div. 52 Bde. 12th Manchester Vol: 4 Jan 1916		
War Diary		01/01/1916	15/01/1916
Miscellaneous	Officer To A Gs Office Base.	29/02/1916	29/02/1916
War Diary		01/02/1916	29/02/1916
Miscellaneous	Officer To A.G's. Office Base	03/04/1916	03/04/1916
War Diary		01/03/1916	31/03/1916
War Diary		01/04/1916	30/04/1916
War Diary		01/05/1916	31/05/1916
War Diary		01/06/1916	30/06/1916
Heading	52nd Inf. Bde. 17th Div. War Diary 12th Battn. The Manchester Regiment. July 1916		
War Diary	In The Field	01/07/1916	31/07/1916
Heading	52nd Brigade. 17th Division. 1/12th Battalion Manchester Regiment August 1916		
Heading	War Diary 12th Manchester Regt. August 1916. Vol 11		
War Diary		01/08/1916	31/08/1916
Heading	War Diary. of. 12th Manchester Regiment. From 1st September 1916 To. 30th September 1916. Volume. XV.		

War Diary	In The Field	01/09/1916	30/09/1916
War Diary	In The Field	01/10/1916	30/10/1916
Heading	War Diary of 12th Manchester Regt. From. 1st November to 30th November 1916. Volume 17.		
War Diary	In The Field	01/11/1916	30/11/1916
Heading	War Diary of 12th. Manchester Regt. From 1st. December. to 31st. December 1916. Vol 15		
War Diary	In The Field	01/12/1916	31/12/1916
War Diary	In The Field	01/01/1917	31/01/1917
Heading	War Diary of 12th The Manchester Regt. for February 1917.		
War Diary	In The Field	01/02/1917	28/02/1917
Heading	War Diary of 12th Manchester: Regt. from 1st March 1917. to 31st March 1917 Volume XXI		
War Diary	In The Field	01/03/1917	31/03/1917
Heading	War Diary of 12th Manchester Regt. From 1st April-30th April. Volume XXII		
War Diary	In The Field	01/04/1917	30/04/1917
Heading	War Diary of the 12th (S) Bn Manchester Regiment From 1/5/17 to 31/5/17 Vol XXIII		
War Diary	In The Field	01/05/1917	31/05/1917
Heading	War Diary of 12th Bn Manchester Regt From 1/6/17 to 30/6/17 Vol XXIV		
War Diary		01/06/1917	30/06/1917
War Diary	In The Field	01/07/1917	31/07/1917
Heading	War Diary of 12th Manchester Regt for Month of August 1917 Vol 23		
War Diary	In The Field	01/08/1917	31/08/1917
War Diary	In The Field	01/09/1917	30/09/1917
Operation(al) Order(s)	12th Manchester Regt. Operation Order No. 3.	14/09/1917	14/09/1917
Heading	War Diary 17/9/17		
Operation(al) Order(s)	12th Manchester Regt Operation Order No. 1 is cancelled and the following substituted:- Operation Order No. 1.	07/09/1917	07/09/1917
Heading	War Diary 8/9/17		
Miscellaneous	III Corps.	13/09/1917	13/09/1917
Miscellaneous	C Form (Original). Messages And Signals.		
Miscellaneous	B Form. Messages And Signals.		
Miscellaneous			
Miscellaneous	XVII Corps No. G. 5/11. 17th. Division.	24/09/1917	24/09/1917
Miscellaneous	17th. Division. A.S.C. 27.9.17	24/09/1917	24/09/1917
Miscellaneous	Lancashire Fusiliers.	17/09/1917	17/09/1917
War Diary	In The Field	01/10/1917	31/10/1917
Heading	War Diary of 12th (D.L.O.Y.) Bn. Manchester Regt. From 1st November 1917 to 30th November 1917 (Volume XXIX)		
War Diary	In The Field	01/11/1917	30/11/1917
War Diary	In The Field	01/12/1917	31/12/1917
Operation(al) Order(s)	Special Operation Order No. 1	10/11/1917	10/11/1917
Miscellaneous	Husk 80 with W. Diary.	11/11/1917	11/11/1917
Heading	War Diary of 12th (D.L.O.Y.) Bn. Manchester Regt. From 1st December 1917 to 31st December 1917 (Volume XXX)		
War Diary	In The Field	01/01/1917	31/01/1917

Heading	War Diary of 12th (D.L.O.Y.) Bn. Manchester Regt. From 1st February 1918 To 28th February 1918. Volume XXXII.		
War Diary	In The Field	01/02/1918	28/02/1918
Heading	52nd Inf. Bde. 17th Div. 12th Battn. The Manchester Regiment. March 1918		
Heading	War Diary of 12th. (D of L.Y.) Battalion Manchester Regiment. From March 1st. 1918. To March 31st. 1918. Volume XXXIII		
War Diary	In The Field	01/03/1918	31/03/1918
Miscellaneous	Operations of the 12th Battalion Manchester Regiment. 21st/25th March 1918.		
Heading	17th Division. 52nd Infantry Brigade War Diary 12th Battalion The Manchester Regiment April 1918		
Heading	War Diary of 12th. (D of L.Y.) Bn. Manchester Regiment. From April 1st. To April 30th. 1918. Volume XXXIV.		
War Diary	Field	01/04/1918	30/04/1918
Heading	War Diary of 12th Bn. Manchester Regiment. From May 1st to May 31st 1918. Volume XXXV		
War Diary	In The Field	01/05/1918	31/05/1918
Heading	War Diary. of 12th (D.L.O.Y.) Battn Manchester Regiment. From 1st June, 1918-30th June, 1918 Volume XXXVI		
War Diary	In The Field	01/06/1918	30/06/1918
Heading	War Diary of 12th (D.L.O.Y.) Bn. Manchester. Regt. From 1st July, 1918 to 31st July, 1918. Volume XXXVII		
War Diary	In The Field	01/07/1918	31/07/1918
Heading	52nd Bde. 17th Div. 12th Battalion, Manchester Regiment, August 1918.		
Heading	War Diary of 12th (D.L.O.Y.) Battalion Manchester Regiment. August 1st 1918-August 31st 1918. Volume XXXVIII		
War Diary	In The Field	01/08/1918	31/08/1918
Heading	War Diary of 12th (D. of L.Y.) Batt'n Manchester Regiment. from 1st September to 30th September 1918. Volume XXXIX.		
War Diary	?	01/09/1918	30/09/1918
Heading	War Diary of 12th (D.O.L.Y.) Battn Manchester Regiment from 1st October to 31st October 1918. Volume XL		
War Diary	In The Field	01/10/1918	31/10/1918
Heading	War Diary. of 12th. (D. of. L.Y.) Bn. Manchester Regt. From. 1.11.18. To. 30.11.18. Volume. XLI.		
War Diary		01/11/1918	30/11/1918
Heading	War Diary. of 12th (D. of L.Y.) Bn. Manchester Regt. Volume. XLI. From. 1st December 1918. To. 31st December 1918.		
War Diary		01/12/1918	31/12/1918
Heading	12th. (D. of L.Y.) Bn. Manchester Regt. War Diary From January 1st. 1919. to January 31st, 1919. Volume. XLII.		
War Diary Miscellaneous		01/01/1919	31/01/1919

Heading	War Diary of 12th (D.L.O.Y.) Bn. Manchester Regiment. for. 1st February 1919 to 28th February 1919. Volume XLIV.		
War Diary	Warlus France.	01/02/1919	28/02/1919
Heading	War Diary of the 12th (D.O.L.Y.) Bn. Manchester Regiment from 1st March 1919 to 31st March 1919 Volume. XLV.		
War Diary	Warlus France.	01/03/1919	31/03/1919

W095/20/2/2

17TH DIVISION
52ND INFY BDE

12TH BN MANCHESTER REGT
JLY 1915 - MAR 1919.

52nd Inf.Bde.
17th Div.

Battn. disembarked
Boulogne from
England 16.7.15.

12th BATTN. THE MANCHESTER REGIMENT.

J U L Y

(15/30.7.15)

1 9 1 5

WAR DIARY or INTELLIGENCE SUMMARY

Place	Date	Hour	Summary of Events and Information	Remarks and references to Appendices
	July 15th 1915		Battalion, strength 30 Officers and 945 Rank and File entrained at Winchester for service with Expeditionary Force in France. The following are the Officers who embarked.	

HEADQUARTERS Lieut-Colonel E.G. Harrison C.B. D.S.O.
Major W.P. Nash. Major and Adjutant E. McFarlane.
Lieut and Hon Q.M. G.J. Pitts and Lieut T. Boston Johnson R.A.M.C.

A. COMPANY. Capt. E.R. Thompson. Capt. J.E. Elam.
Lieut. W.E. Parrott. 2nd Lieut A. Allcott and Lieut C.N. Marsden.

B. COMPANY. Capt. R. Dawson-Hewitt. Capt. J.H.M. White.
Lieut M.J. Tuchmann. Lieut A.J. Moorhouse. Lieut T.C. Stott.
Lieut F. Fowler. 2nd Lieut C. Heingoley. and 2nd Lieut G.D. Dixon.

C. COMPANY. Capt. H. McHearn. Capt. W.M. Benton.
Lieut B. Du Val. Lieut J.L.D. French. 2nd Lieut W.J. Pope.
2nd A.K. Coules. 2nd Lieut R. Lunn, and 2nd Lieut H.M. Butler.

WAR DIARY
INTELLIGENCE SUMMARY

Army Form C. 2118

Place	Date	Hour	Summary of Events and Information	Remarks and references to Appendices
			D. COMPANY. Capt H. F. Boswell, Capt. J. H. Bett, Lieut. O. P. Gebhard and Lieut. D. H. Williamson. 2nd Lieut H. Buckley	
	July 15th 1915	12 MN	Embarked at FOLKESTONE	
	July 16th	2 AM	Disembarked at BOULOGNE and proceeded to OSTROHOVE Large Rest Camp.	
		8 PM	Left BOULOGNE by troop train, and arrived at ARQUES 4. A.M. 17th July, and marched to billets at WIZERNES	
	July 18th		Proceeded by march route to HAZEBROUCK and bivouacked outside Cathedral	
	July 19th		Proceeded by march route to GODEWAERSVELDE to billets	

Army Form C. 2118

WAR DIARY
INTELLIGENCE SUMMARY
(Erase heading not required.)

Instructions regarding War Diaries and Intelligence Summaries are contained in F. S. Regs., Part II. and the Staff Manual respectively. Title Pages will be prepared in manuscript.

Place	Date	Hour	Summary of Events and Information	Remarks and references to Appendices
	July 21st		Proceeded by march route to OUDERDOM and joined 2nd Army. Commanded by Lieut. General Sir H.C.O. PLUMER, K.C.B. Posted to V Corps by Lieut General Sir A.H.H. ALLENBY, K.C.B.	
	July 23rd		Attached for instruction in trench warfare, to LIVERPOOL SCOTTISH (T.F.) and sent platoons into trenches for instruction. Here we met 2nd Battalion Monmouth Regiment under Command of Major H.R. WESTON.	
	July 25th		In trenches for instruction of Officers and men.	trench instruction see map
	July 30th		Proceeded by march route to White Chateau 3 miles west of Hooge and bivouaced 48 hours.	

52nd Inf.Bde.
17th Div.

12th BATTN. THE MANCHESTER REGIMENT.

A U G U S T

1 9 1 5

Army Form C. 2118.

WAR DIARY
or
INTELLIGENCE SUMMARY. 12/Manchester Regt.
August 1915

(Erase heading not required.)

Place	Date	Hour	Summary of Events and Information	Remarks and references to Appendices
	Aug 1st		Relieved 1st Battalion Royal Scots Fusiliers. Relief completed by 3 a.m. of the 2nd inst without incident	
	Aug 2		Quiet day.	

WAR DIARY or INTELLIGENCE SUMMARY

(Erase heading not required.)

Army Form C. 2118

Place	Date	Hour	Summary of Events and Information	Remarks and references to Appendices
	Aug 3rd		Quiet day but for a few whiz-bangs	
	4th		Rather quiet with a little Artillery activity	
	5th		Quiet day	
	6th		Our Artillery more active than usual. Enemy shelled us with whiz-bangs, doing little damage.	
	7th		The Battalion began digging a V shaped ditch for barricades in front of our barbed wire and assembly pits near SNIPERS BARN. No attempt made by enemy to interfere. Hear that new troops have taken over enemy trenches	
	8th		Very quiet day	
	9th	2·45am	Our Artillery opened heavy bombardment on our left, directed on a frontage of 500 yards. Ordered to cause diversion while 6th Division attacked at HOOGE. Reports from	

WAR DIARY
or
INTELLIGENCE SUMMARY

(Erase heading not required.)

Army Form C. 2118

Instructions regarding War Diaries and Intelligence Summaries are contained in F. S. Regs., Part II. and the Staff Manual respectively. Title Pages will be prepared in manuscript.

Place	Date	Hour	Summary of Events and Information	Remarks and references to Appendices
	Aug 9th	9 am	Patrols were out that the enemy were seen leaving trenches on our front and making for BOIS QUARANTE. Heard the attack by 6th Division was successful	
	10th		Quiet day	
	11th		Very quiet day	
	12th		Normal small amount of shelling on both sides.	
	13th		Quiet day	
	14th		Quiet with the exception of a few heavy shells which fell well behind the reserve trenches.	
	15th		Quiet day; some Artillery activity in afternoon on both sides. Heavy rifle and machine gun fire during night	
	16th		Enemy fired rifle grenades on trench H 5.	

WAR DIARY
INTELLIGENCE SUMMARY

Army Form C. 2118

Instructions regarding War Diaries and Intelligence Summaries are contained in F.S. Regs., Part II. and the Staff Manual respectively. Title Pages will be prepared in manuscript.

Place	Date	Hour	Summary of Events and Information	Remarks and references to Appendices
	Aug 17		Very quiet day. Were relieved by the 9th Bn. Duke of Wellington Regt. Relief commenced at 8:00 pm but did not complete until 4:30 am of the 18th due mainly to fourteen bombardment by the enemy	
	18th		At Canada Huts rest camp 1 mile west of DICKIEBUSCH. Two Companys went to RENINGHELST for a bath	in rest camp during 19th & 20th
	21st		Went into Brigade Reserve dugouts about ½ mile west of the LA BRASSERIE Coys left at half hour intervals commencing at 3.15 p.m.	
	22nd		Battalion found all digging parties also covering parties for the whole time while in Reserve.	In Brigade Reserve during 23rd & 24th
	25th		In Brigade Reserve. Relieved the 9th Bn. Duke of Wellington Regt. in the trenches. Commenced relief at 4 p.m. completed by 9 p.m. without incident	

WAR DIARY
INTELLIGENCE SUMMARY

(Erase heading not required.)

Army Form C. 2118

Instructions regarding War Diaries and Intelligence Summaries are contained in F. S. Regs., Part II. and the Staff Manual respectively. Title Pages will be prepared in manuscript.

Place	Date	Hour	Summary of Events and Information	Remarks and references to Appendices
	Aug 26"		Quiet day	
	27"		Enemy hung hanged our front line also a little of every activity	
	28"		Our Artillery rather more active than usual.	
	29"		Exceptionally quiet day. Enemy V shaped trench in front of our line.	
	30"		Quiet day. Continued work on ditch in front of our line.	
	31"		Quiet day. Enemy dropped a few shells round Battalion Headquarters. One dropping on 1st Field Dressing Station	

52nd Inf.Bde.
17th Div.

12th BATTN. THE MANCHESTER REGIMENT.

S E P T E M B E R

1 9 1 5

WAR DIARY
or
INTELLIGENCE SUMMARY.   12/Manchester Regt.

(Erase heading not required.)

September 1915

Army Form C. 2118.

Instructions regarding War Diaries and Intelligence Summaries are contained in F. S. Regs., Part II. and the Staff Manual respectively. Title pages will be prepared in manuscript.

Place	Date	Hour	Summary of Events and Information	Remarks and references to Appendices
	Sept 1st		Enemy rather more active, throwing Rifle Grenades in our front line. Again shelled Battalion Headquarters but only damaged trenches	

WAR DIARY or INTELLIGENCE SUMMARY

Army Form C. 2118

(Erase heading not required.)

Place	Date	Hour	Summary of Events and Information	Remarks and references to Appendices
	Sept 2nd		Our Artillery rather active. Enemy again threw rifle grenades in our front line	
	3rd		Quiet and very wet. Continued work on Vaich in front of our lines.	
	4th		General quiet day. Very wet. Our Artillery very active at night. A draft of 15 men to B Company and 15 men to D Coy proceeded into trenches	
	5th		Relieved from the trenches by the 9th Duke of Wellington Regt.; relief completed by 8.15 p.m. Went into rest camp at LA CLYTTE	
	6th		In rest camp at LA CLYTTE	In rest camp during the 7th, 8th and 9th.
	10th		Relieved the 9th Battalion Northumberland Fusiliers in Reserve at RIDGEWOOD. Completed relief by 9 p.m.	In Reserve during the 11th, 12th, 13th, 14th, 15th

WAR DIARY or INTELLIGENCE SUMMARY

Army Form C. 2118

(Erase heading not required.)

Place	Date	Hour	Summary of Events and Information	Remarks and references to Appendices
	Sept 15th		Relieved the 9th Battalion Duke of Wellington's Regt in trenches. Relief commenced 1.30 pm completed 8 pm	
	16th		Quiet day. Aeroplane brought down by hostile rifle fire; landed near our dept at Lt CLYTTE. Aeroplane slightly damaged, but neither Pilot or Observer injured	
	17th		Quiet day	
	18th		Quiet day	
	19th		Quiet day. Enemy threw Trench Mortars and Rifle Grenades into our trench wounding the Commanding Officer Lieut-Col. E.J. Harrison C.B. D.S.O. in the leg by a splinter from a Trench Mortar	
	20th	9 am	The enemy fired a few Rifle Grenades, and followed them up with about 25 Trench Mortars	
		11.30 am	The enemy commenced again and this continued intermittently during the day until our Battalion came to our assistance	

WAR DIARY or INTELLIGENCE SUMMARY

Army Form C. 2118

Place	Date	Hour	Summary of Events and Information	Remarks and references to Appendices
	Sept 20th		Some of the projectiles apparently were Aerial Torpedoes as judging by peculiar noise made in passage and the force of explosion.	
	21st		Quiet day. Our patrols report that all was quiet with the exception of small parties working at their parapets. The enemy's chief occupation seems to be lobbing bombs just over their parapets. We never meet any patrols of theirs.	
	22nd	4 p.m.	Very quiet during the morning and early afternoon. Our artillery commenced a bombardment which did great damage to the enemy's front line and support trenches. The bombardment lasted 1 hour. About 6 p.m. the enemy commenced to whiz bang our support trench but the damage was practically nil.	
	23rd	4.45 p.m.	An enemy aeroplane travelled from EAST to WEST but did not come as far as their front line of trenches	

WAR DIARY
INTELLIGENCE SUMMARY
(Erase heading not required.)

Army Form C. 2118

Instructions regarding War Diaries and Intelligence Summaries are contained in F. S. Regs., Part II. and the Staff Manual respectively. Title Pages will be prepared in manuscript.

Place	Date	Hour	Summary of Events and Information	Remarks and references to Appendices
	Sept 23rd		It then dropped a red light and travelled back. Shortly afterwards it appeared again in exactly the same course, but this time dropped a green light. It appeared to be circling again a long way back	
	24th		Fairly quiet day. During yesterday scarcely a shot was fired from the enemy's lines, and very few during the night; the enemy have been throwing bombs from their trenches to just in front of their wire. Our Artillery bombarded the enemy's front line trenches with good results this lasted from 4 p.m. to 5 p.m.	
	25th	11 AM	Our Artillery bombarded the enemy's lines for 1 hour. Enemy reported to have retired to their second line of trenches after our dummy attack	
	26th		Very quiet	
	27th		Very quiet	

WAR DIARY
INTELLIGENCE SUMMARY

(Erase heading not required.)

Army Form C. 2118

Place	Date	Hour	Summary of Events and Information	Remarks and references to Appendices
	28.		Enemy threw a few rifle grenades into our trenches which were ineffective. Relieved by the 9th Batt" Duke of Wellington Regt. completed by 6.30 p.m. Went into rest camp at LA CLYTTE. Very wet night	
	29.		In Corps Reserve. A and B Coys baths at trains at LA CLYTTE. C and D Coys Physical Training and Route March. Very wet	

52nd Inf.Bde.
17th Div.

12th BATTN. THE MANCHESTER REGIMENT.

OCTOBER

1915

WAR DIARY or INTELLIGENCE SUMMARY

Army Form C. 2118

(Erase heading not required.)

Place	Date	Hour	Summary of Events and Information	Remarks and references to Appendices
	Oct 1st		In Corps Reserve. Battalion went for a route march in the morning. Received orders at 1 p.m. to relieve the 9th Battalion Northumberland Fusiliers in Brigade Reserve at RIDGEWOOD; relief to be completed by 4 P.M. Relief completed by 4 p.m. B Company in trenches O5. P5. O3. In Reserve at RIDGEWOOD. Quiet day.	
	Oct 2nd		Reserve. Quiet day.	
	3rd		In Reserve. Were relieved by SEELYS CANADIAN BRIGADE. The 52nd Infantry Brigade went into their billets at	
	4th		LA CLYTTE. The Battalion arrived at LA CLYTTE about 9.30 p.m. The Battalion were relieved by the 1st Regt. Canadian Cavalry Brigade, and the Regiment of the 1st Canadian Mounted Rifle Brigade (600 in squadron)	

WAR DIARY or INTELLIGENCE SUMMARY

Army Form C. 2118

(Erase heading not required.)

Place	Date	Hour	Summary of Events and Information	Remarks and references to Appendices
	Oct 5th		In close billets at LA CLYTTE. Left at 6 p.m. and proceeded into billets at GODEWAERSVELDE arriving at 11 p.m.	
	6th		In billets; rested.	
	7th		In billets. Battalion trained in grenade throwing	
	8th		In billets continued grenade throwing, also route marching and rifle exercises	
	9th		In billets. Same programme as the 8th.	
	10th		In billets. Commanding Officers inspection and Church Services. Training in Bomb throwing.	continued been during the 13th to the 22nd Oct.
	11th		In billets continued Bomb throwing	
	12th		In billets Battalion Head Quarters moved into the Town	
	22nd	2 pm	Left GODEWAERSVELDE and proceeded by march route to G.14 A8.7 2 miles W by S.W. of Vlamertinghe to Reserve.	

Army Form C. 2118

WAR DIARY
or
INTELLIGENCE SUMMARY

(Erase heading not required.)

Instructions regarding War Diaries and Intelligence Summaries are contained in F. S. Regs., Part II. and the Staff Manual respectively. Title Pages will be prepared in manuscript.

Place	Date	Hour	Summary of Events and Information	Remarks and references to Appendices
	Oct. 23rd		In Brigade Reserve.	continued on reserve from 23rd to 29 Oct
	29th		Proceeded to trenches at I 2 + D 1.1 10 miles distant. Relief completed without incident about 1.15 AM of the 30th inst	
	30th		Morning quiet. Enemy shelled supports during afternoon using high explosive shells.	
	31st		Quiet day.	

52nd Inf.Bde.
17th Div.

12th BATTN. THE MANCHESTER REGIMENT.

NOVEMBER

1915

WAR DIARY
INTELLIGENCE SUMMARY
(Erase heading not required.)

Army Form C. 2118

Instructions regarding War Diaries and Intelligence Summaries are contained in F. S. Regs., Part II. and the Staff Manual respectively. Title Pages will be prepared in manuscript.

Place	Date	Hour	Summary of Events and Information	Remarks and references to Appendices
	Nov 1st 1915	6 A.M.	Two of the enemy came over from their lines and gave themselves up proving to be Russians, who were taken prisoner at Warsaw and forced to work for the Germans on the Western Front behind the firing line, after being passed on. Heavy 24 hours continuous rainfall caused the firing line parapet to fall in necessitating much work on retrenching, practically in full view of the enemy. A few shells were dropped on the supports during the afternoon.	
	2nd		Morning quiet. Work of rebuilding firing line parapets and communication trenches continued. During the afternoon 30 to 40 shells were dropped in our outposts but were ineffective as regards casualties. Our artillery replied heavily and effectively.	
	3rd			
	4th	3.30 p.m.	Morning quiet. A little excitement was caused by a duel between rival aeroplanes. Our airman with his machine gun brought the duel to a successful issue bringing the German down who dropped into Zillebeke Lake.	

1875 Wt. W593/826 1,000,000 4/15 J.B.C. & A. A.D.S.S./Forms/C. 2118.

WAR DIARY
INTELLIGENCE SUMMARY
(Erase heading not required.)

Army Form C. 2118

Instructions regarding War Diaries and Intelligence Summaries are contained in F.S. Regs., Part II. and the Staff Manual respectively. Title Pages will be prepared in manuscript.

Place	Date	Hour	Summary of Events and Information	Remarks and references to Appendices
	May 5th 1915		Morning quiet. During the afternoon the enemy were driven out of the firing line, and our Artillery bombarded the enemy's front line trenches for 2 hours to which the enemy did not reply.	
	6th		Quiet day. Enemy aeroplanes very active during the afternoon	
	7th		Enemy artillery dropped a few shells into the outpost trenches causing a few casualties	
	8th	10 AM	A heavy bombardment of the enemy's front line commenced and continued till noon. the enemy retaliating vigorously. We were relieved by the 6th Bn Royal Scots Fusiliers and 6th Bn Kings Own Scottish Borderers. Relief completed by 11 pm. Moved to Rest Camp at 6 AM on the 9th inst	
	9th –		In Rest Camp 2 miles W by SW of Vlamertinghe G.17.A.6.7.	10th 11th 12th 13th 14th Still in Rest Camp.
	15th		Left Rest Camp and proceeded to trenches where we relieved the 4th Bn Yorks Regt. Relief completed by 11 pm. Battalion was shelled heavily while on the way to the trenches on the Vlamertinghe – Ypres Road	

Army Form C. 2118

WAR DIARY
or
INTELLIGENCE SUMMARY
(Erase heading not required.)

Instructions regarding War Diaries and Intelligence Summaries are contained in F. S. Regs., Part II. and the Staff Manual respectively. Title Pages will be prepared in manuscript.

Place	Date	Hour	Summary of Events and Information	Remarks and references to Appendices
	Nov 16th 1915		Enemy dropped a few shells and throughout in the vicinity of Battn Head Quarters; otherwise a quiet day.	
	17th		Enemy shelled our front line destroying parts of the parapets and causing several casualties. Owing to the bad weather all Trenches and Dugouts were flooded.	
	18th		Conditions in the trenches beyond description men covering almost waist deep in mud and water. Both our and the enemys artillery active. HOOGE being shelled during the afternoon.	
	19th		The Battalion was relieved by the 10th Bat. Loyal Lancashire and proceeded to our Rest Billets at Ouderdom.	
	20th		In Brigade Reserve at Ouderdom.	
	24th		Battalion moved into Rest Camp at Busse Boom. Physical exercises and Bayonet Drill Company Drill and Route Marching daily	21st 22" 23" too on Brigade Reserve 25. 26. 27. 28. 29 " 30 Nov. all in Brigade Reserve

1875 Wt. W593/826 1,000,000 4/15 J.B.C. & A. A.D.S.S./Forms/C. 2118.

52nd Inf.Bde.
17th Div.

12th BATTN. THE MANCHESTER REGIMENT.

DECEMBER

1915

WAR DIARY or INTELLIGENCE SUMMARY

Army Form C. 2118

(Erase heading not required.)

Place	Date	Hour	Summary of Events and Information	Remarks and references to Appendices
	Dec 1st 1915	4.0pm	Left rest camp and proceeded to trenches situated at I.24 and	
		10.0pm	relieved the 4th Bn Yorkshire Regt. Relief completed.	
	2nd		Enemy artillery very active bombarding our supports.	
	3rd		Enemy Artillery again very active to which our Artillery effectively replied. Trenches in a very bad condition. Wet day	
	4th		Very quiet and wet. Trenches had almost worst deep in water.	
	5th		Enemy Artillery very active. Relieved the 10th Bn Lancashire Fusiliers on the Ramparts at YPRES. Relief completed	
	6th	11.30pm	In reserve at the Ramparts. Enemy shelled YPRES heavily. Battalion found working parties at night	
	7th		In reserve at the Ramparts. Enemy again shelled YPRES heavily. Battalion again found working parties	
	8th		Still in reserve. Quiet day	
	9th	9.0pm	In reserve. Were relieved by the 6th & 8th Durhams. Relief completed. Proceeded to Rest Camp at Reninghurst.	
	10th 11th 12th 13th		In Rest Camp at Reninghurst. Left Rest Camp at Reninghurst and proceeded to Brigade Reserve at Ouderdom.	

WAR DIARY or INTELLIGENCE SUMMARY

Army Form C. 2118

Place	Date	Hour	Summary of Events and Information	Remarks and references to Appendices
	Dec 18th 1915		In Brigade Reserve at VLAMERTINGHE. Quiet day.	
		9.30am	Enemy commenced a heavy bombardment shelling the roads and district VLAMERTINGHE - YPRES. Our Artillery responded vigorously. Enemy used a large amount of gas shells.	
	19th	6.0am	As an attack was probable the Bn was ordered to "Stand to" and moved into reserve at KRUISSTRAAT + CANAL LINE S.E. of YPRES	
		7.30am	Enemy aeroplanes very active in rear of our lines	
		8.0 to 9.0am	Enemy aeroplanes dropped bombs on POPERINGHE	
		9.30am		
	20th		Bn moved from KRUISSTRAAT. D Coy and 2 Platoons of B Coy into support trenches PS1; The remainder of the Bn moved into the Ramparts at YPRES. Enemy continued shelling roads and throwing gas shells into YPRES	
	21st		Enemy threw a few Gas shells during the early morning otherwise quiet. Very wet	
	22nd		Bn left Ramparts and proceeded to trenches situated at C I 24 where we relieved the 10th Batt. Lancashire Fusiliers. Relief completed without incident	
		9.0pm		
	23rd		Morning quiet. Enemy threw a few shells in the neighbourhood of MAPLE COPSE during the afternoon	
	24th	12.9 noon to 12.15pm	Enemy dropped a few shells near Yeomanry Post. Otherwise quiet day	

Army Form C. 2118.

WAR DIARY
or
INTELLIGENCE SUMMARY
(Erase heading not required.)

Instructions regarding War Diaries and Intelligence Summaries are contained in F. S. Regs., Part II. and the Staff Manual respectively. Title Pages will be prepared in manuscript.

Place	Date	Hour	Summary of Events and Information	Remarks and references to Appendices
In the Field	Dec 27th 1915		Quiet day. Our Artillery threw a few shells in the rear of enemy's front line	
	Dec 28th	9.0 pm	Were relieved by the 7th East Yorks. Relief completed without incident and proceeded to Rest Camp at Brandhoek.	
	Dec 29th		In Rest Camp at Brandhoek. Battalion exercises daily in Gas Helmet drill including firing on the Range erected in the Camp. Bayonet Exercise and Platoon Drill.	
	30th		In Rest Camp at Brandhoek. Enemy aeroplane dropped 4 bombs on the camp, one not exploding.	
	31st		In Rest Camp. Quiet day.	

31 - 12 - 15

MWake(?) A/Lt Col
Comman'dg 12th Bn Manchester Regiment

1875 Wt. W593/826 1,000,000 4/15 J.B.C. & A. A.D.S.S./Forms/C. 2118.

Vol B

CONFIDENTIAL.

War Diary of
12th Bn Manchester Regt

1st Oct. to 31st Oct. 1916

17

12 Manchesters
Vol 6

12ᵈ Manchester

17 Vol II

Manch R.   5253728

"Forwarded"

F R Lindles
Captain
a/ Bde Major
19.9.17.   52nd Inf Bde

"A" Form.
MESSAGES AND SIGNALS.

Army Form C. 2121.
(In pads of 100.)

No. of Message ....

Prefix	Code	Words.	Charge.	This message is on a/c of:	Recd. at .... m.
Office of Origin and Service Instructions. Bylaw//		Sent At ...... m. To By		.... Service. (Sig. of "Franking Officer.")	Date From By

TO	HUMBLE.		

Sender's Number	Day of Month	In reply to Number	AAA
DN 3	10		

① HUMBLE	will	carry	out
a	counter	attack	on
the	post	lost	last
night	at	GRAVEL	FARM
at	11	pm	to-night
② Ref	map	issued	to HUMBLE
No 12	platoon	will	move
forward 50x	so	as	to
command	GRAVEL	FARM	with
its	fire	with	Rifle
~~canadiens~~	in	support	of this
platoon			
③ No 10	platoon	will move	so as
to	~~support~~ face	E	and also
cover	GRAVEL	FM.	

From
Place
Time

The above may be forwarded as now corrected. (Z)

Censor. Sig. of Addressor or person authorised to telegraph in his name.
* This line should be erased if not required.

"A" Form.
MESSAGES AND SIGNALS.

Army Form C. 2121.
(In pads of 100.)

No. of Message..........

Prefix....... Code........	Words.	Charge.	This message is on a/c of:	Recd. at........m.
Office of Origin and Service Instructions.	Sent			Date............
	At........m.		............Service.	From............
	To			
	By		(Sig. of "Franking Officer.")	By

TO { | | ② | | |

| Sender's Number | Day of Month | In reply to Number | AAA |

④ N° 11 platoon will move forward 100 yds into any position in that vicinity considered most suitable by O.C. HUMBLE

⑤ Two fresh platoons from the two Companies in Reserve will be brought up to make real and flank attack from North. They will advance from present position of N° 11 platoon, the one in support of the other and close behind. The advance will be made on to the line of road running

From Place Time: from ros of GRAVEL FM to huts in V1 Long where

The above may be forwarded as now corrected. (Z)

.... Censor. | Sig. of Addressor or person authorised to telegraph in his name.
* This line should be erased if not required.

"A" Form.
MESSAGES AND SIGNALS.

Army Form C. 2121.
(In pads of 100.)

The Right or inner flank should not be nearer to GRAVEL FM than N 8 a 0.4 (i.e 200 yds from enemy position)

At Zero 11pm N° 10 and 12 platoons will open fire with L.G's and rifle fire on to the enemy position for five mins allowing the attacking platoon to get as near GRAVEL FM as possible. At Zero plus 5 mins the enemy position will be assaulted with the bayonet one platoon being left as a garrison.

"A" Form
MESSAGES AND SIGNALS.

Army Form C.2121.
(In pads of 100.)

Prefix......Code......in	Words.	Charge.	This message is on a/c of:	Recd. at......m.
Office of Origin and Service Instructions.				Date......
	Sent		......Service.	
	At......m.			From......
	To......			
	By......		(Signature of "Franking Officer.")	By......

TO {

(4)

Sender's Number.   Day of Month.   In reply to Number.   **A A A**

(6) The post held by the enemy must be reconnoitred forthwith to see if the enemy is still in occupation. The attacking platoons will also send representatives to reconnoitre routes of advance, in particular the point at which the advance moves South ~~along~~ at V.8.a.0.4 towards GRAVEL FM.

7. <u>Artillery Support</u>

Artillery will open fire on SOS lines from V.8.c.8.6 to V.8.a.1.8 also 4.5 Hows at point 1.2.4 and 5: at Zero hour. Arty will slacken off at Zero plus 30 and die away at Z plus 45.

From HUSK
Place
Time 4.15 pm

H.C. Morgan Capt.

The above may be forwarded as now corrected. (Z)

1.   Attached to
                                      WAR DIARY
Headquarters   17ᵗʰ Sept 1917
   52 Inf Bde.

   In accordance with orders, 12th Bn
Manchester Regt raided the enemy trenches
WIT and WOOL at midnight on 16/17 Sept
1917, on a frontage of 250ˣ and to a depth
of 250ˣ approximately.

2. TROOPS EMPLOYED c'd their objectives
   9 officers 210 other ranks, with 1 officer and
20 other ranks Royal Engineers attached.
These were divided into 5 parties to tackle
objectives as follows:-

(a) WIT trench for 100ˣ North of   B Co. 2 offrs 50 OR
    its Jn with WOOL
(b) WIT trench for 150ˣ South of   A Co. 2 offrs 50 OR
    its Jn with WOOL
(c) WOOL (Communication) trench   } 1 offr 30 OR
    40ˣ north and of its junction with } C Coy
    its Southern arm   }
(d) NORTHERN ARM of WOOL   1 offr 30 OR
(e) SOUTHERN ARM of WOOL   D Co. 2 offr 50 OR
    The R.E. were divided among the parties.
    Major E.R. THOMPSON in the north of Lancs
    was detailed to command of the raiding party.

3. Short narrative of Events
   The preparation of the ground on which

2 War Diary

D.A.A
G.H.Q
3rd Echelon.

Herewith W. Diary for the month
of July forwarded in accordance with
G.R.O. 1598

Ma Jones
Lt Col
Commanding 8/4 R West Kent Rgt

12th Manchesters
vol: 4
Jan 1916

17th Div
52 Bde

WAR DIARY or INTELLIGENCE SUMMARY

(Erase heading not required.)

Army Form C. 2118

Instructions regarding War Diaries and Intelligence Summaries are contained in F.S. Regs., Part II. and the Staff Manual respectively. Title Pages will be prepared in manuscript.

Place	Date	Hour	Summary of Events and Information	Remarks and references to Appendices
	Jany 1st 1916		In Rest Camp at Dragon Huts Brandhoek	
	2nd	3 pm	Left Rest camp and proceeded to trenches at Hooge and relieved the 2nd Bn York Regt. Relief completed without incident	
	9 pm		Enemy shelled our front line trenches but were not very effective the damage done being easily repaired.	
	3rd		Quiet day	
	4th			
	5th		Some shelling by the enemy of our front line, which was ineffective the majority of the shells being premature	
	6th		Enemy snipers very active paying great attention to Bn H.Q. were relieved by the 8th Bn Royal West Kents of the 24th Division. Relief completed by 2.0 am of the 7th	
	7th	6.30 am	Battn spent the night of 6/7th in huts at Vlamertinghe Moved out of camp and proceeded to entrain at Poperinghe for Watou arriving 10.0 p.m. Companys in billets by 12.0 midnight	
	8th		Rattacu at Bell.	
	9th to 15th		Battalion over rested in Coy Drill and Foot Hardening	

Officer i/c A.G. Office
Base.

Herewith original copy of War
Diary for the month of February.

J.H.Hanson   Lieut Col
Commdg 12th Bn Manchester Regt

29-2-16

WAR DIARY
or
INTELLIGENCE SUMMARY

(Erase heading not required.)

Army Form C. 2118

Instructions regarding War Diaries and Intelligence Summaries are contained in F.S. Regs., Part II. and the Staff Manual respectively. Title Pages will be prepared in manuscript.

Place	Date	Hour	Summary of Events and Information	Remarks and references to Appendices
	Feb 4th 1/4th		Brigade Training in Poonch. Trenches. Battalion also trained in General Trench digging	
	5th	6.30 a.m	Battalion moved from Epuleagues and marched to Aigues, thence by rail to Godevaernevelde and proceeded by road to camp at Reninghelst vacated by 1st Bn Royal Scots Fusiliers	
	6th	2.30 pm	Battalion moved to trenches situated I.31.d.2.5. and relieved the 1st Bn Royal Scots Fusiliers. Relief completed by 10.30 p.m	
	7th		Quiet day. Work commenced at once rebuilding Parapets and dugouts. Also built new traverses to prevent an enfilading sweeping fire	
	8th		Enemy shelled Vormezeele from 3.0 pm to 3.45 pm destroying about 40 shells, but did little damage, otherwise quiet day. Continued work	
	9th		commenced yesterday. Enemy again shelled Vormezeele with things bangs from 4.0 to 4.30 pm Enemy machine gun active on the townghete. S'Elor Bn leaving entered the village.	
	10th		Enemy snipers very active. Enemy also dropped a few shells on our front line to which our Artillery replied effectually quieting them for a time	
	11th	10.30 pm	Enemy bombed our front line causing a few casualties	
	12th		Enemy threw a few grenades into our front line doing little damage and causing two casualties. Remainder of day quiet	
	12th		Enemy snipers very active during the day otherwise quiet.	

WAR DIARY
or
INTELLIGENCE SUMMARY

(Erase heading not required.)

Army Form C. 2118

Instructions regarding War Diaries and Intelligence Summaries are contained in F. S. Regs., Part II. and the Staff Manual respectively. Title Pages will be prepared in manuscript.

Place	Date	Hour	Summary of Events and Information	Remarks and references to Appendices
	13th		Our Artillery very active shelling enemy supports and trenches night increased in intensity, causing great damage. No reply by the enemy	
	14th		Artillery again active which developed into a bombardment by both sides. Enemy Reg by 1st Yorks Regt were enfiladed owing to the bombardment.	
	15th		Enemy Snipers less active owing to the close attention paid to them by our sniping squad. A Boy moved to Redoubt R.11 where they sniped Enemy trees owing to enemy objective	
	16th		Enemy dropped a few Whizzbangs into our ng us doing little damage.	
	17th		Quiet day Enemy snipers effectually silenced.	
	18th		Morning quiet. From 3.0 to 4.0 pm both our and the Enemy Artillery engaged in a duel. A shell fell into the arming place doing no damage.	
	19th	5.30 am 6. 3 pm	Enemy aeroplanes very active. Otherwise quiet day	
	20th	8.0 am 3.0 am 4.0 pm	Aeroplane bombs were dropped on Bnr H.Q. Enemy bombarded the camp and village of Voormezeele. Were relieved by the 1st Bn Yorks Regt. Relief completed by 10.30 pm.	
	21st		In Rest Camp situated M.C.3 (I Camp)	
	22nd	2.30 pm 10.30 pm	Left Camp and proceeded to trenches situated I.34.6.3 and relieved the 1st Bn Gordons. Relief completed.	
	23rd		Enemy dropped a few Whizzbangs in to our camp causing a few casualties. We suffered 3 casualties by our own shells dropping short.	

1875 Wt. W593/826 1,000,000 4/15 J.B.C. & A. A.D.S.S./Forms/C. 2118.

WAR DIARY
or
INTELLIGENCE SUMMARY

(Erase heading not required.)

Army Form C. 2118

Instructions regarding War Diaries and Intelligence Summaries are contained in F.S. Regs., Part II. and the Staff Manual respectively. Title Pages will be prepared in manuscript.

Place	Date	Hour	Summary of Events and Information	Remarks and references to Appendices
	24th		Morning quiet. During the afternoon our Artillery bombarded the enemy's lines effectively. There was no reply from the enemy.	
	25th		Morning again quiet. During the afternoon the enemy heavily bombarded our supports and the enemy's old, causing two casualties in Artillery.	
	26th		Continuously shelled the enemy's line. Enemy bombarded our supports and enemy heavily during the afternoon and again in the early evening causing 3 casualties. Our Artillery replied effectively practically destroying the enemy's new parapet.	
	27th		Morning quiet. During the afternoon our Artillery bombarded the enemy's line causing great damage. There was no reply by the enemy. Pot. of employed by night. C Coy relieved by the 9th Bn West Riding Regt.	
	28th		In Rest Camp attached M.S.a. C Coy remaining in support	
	29th		In Rest Camp. D Coy moved to the trenches at section J 34. 6 6 3 to relieve C Coy.	

Officer i/c A. G.'s Office
Base

Herewith original copy of
War Diary for the month of
March 1916

B.D.W. Kay Lt & adjt for Major
Commdg 12th Bn Manchester Regt

3-4-16

Army Form C. 2118

WAR DIARY
or
INTELLIGENCE SUMMARY
(Erase heading not required.)

Instructions regarding War Diaries and Intelligence Summaries are contained in F. S. Regs., Part II. and the Staff Manual respectively. Title Pages will be prepared in manuscript.

Place	Date	Hour	Summary of Events and Information	Remarks and references to Appendices
	March 1st 1916 2nd 5th		In Rest Camp at M 3 C.	
	6th	2.30 pm	Left camp and proceeded to trenches at Vermiyeele and relieved the 7th Bn Yorks Regt. Relief completed by 10.30 pm without incident	
	7th		Morning exceptionally quiet. During the afternoon our Battery dropped about 40 shells in enemy's front line who did not reply. Work was commenced repairing front line and communication trenches	
	8th		Morning again quiet. Work of repair continued.	
	9th		Quiet day. Men relieved by 7th Bn Yorks Regt. Relief completed by 8.30 pm. Bat" proceeded to J Camp at M 3 C.	
	10th		In Rest Camp	
	11th		Left Camp and proceeded to Rest Billets	
	13th 14th 15th		In Rest Billets	
	16th		Inspection of Batt" by Corps Commander.	
	17th 18th 19th		In Rest Billets	

WAR DIARY or INTELLIGENCE SUMMARY

Army Form C. 2118

(Erase heading not required.)

Instructions regarding War Diaries and Intelligence Summaries are contained in F.S. Regs., Part II. and the Staff Manual respectively. Title Pages will be prepared in manuscript.

Place	Date	Hour	Summary of Events and Information	Remarks and references to Appendices
	March 20 1916	6.30 am	Left Rest Billets and proceeded by road to La Crèche.	
	21st	6.30 am	Left LA CRECHE and proceeded to billets in ARMENTIERES arriving 10.30 a.m.	
	22nd		In Billets at ARMENTIERES. Batt" moved into the trenches at relief C 22 D and relieved the 12th Bn. Northumberland Fusiliers. Relief completed by 8.30 p.m.	
	23rd		Enemy machine guns very active at "stand to" and stand down sweeping the parapets. They also threw about 20 shells of small calibre into reserve billets at HOUPLINES.	
	24th		Enemy machine guns again active at same periods as yesterday. Otherwise quiet day.	
	25th		Enemy snipers showed great activity, they also directed air shells traversing the line of enemy French trenches.	
	26th		Enemy threw 12 French Mortars of the carriage variety into our supports, doing much damage to the trenches.	
	27th		Enemy machine guns again active at "stand to" and "stand down".	

Army Form C. 2118

WAR DIARY
or
INTELLIGENCE SUMMARY
(Erase heading not required.)

Instructions regarding War Diaries and Intelligence Summaries are contained in F. S. Regs., Part II. and the Staff Manual respectively. Title Pages will be prepared in manuscript.

Place	Date	Hour	Summary of Events and Information	Remarks and references to Appendices
	March 28th		Quiet day.	
	29th		Enemy threw 6 small shells in vicinity of Batt H.Q. doing no damage. Were relieved by 4 Br East Yorks. Relief completed by 10.0 p.m and proceeded to reserve billets at HOUPLINES.	
	30th 31st		In Reserve at HOUPLINES.	

1875 Wt. W593/826 1,000,000 4/15 J.B.C. & A. A.D.S.S./Forms/C. 2118.

12 Manchester
1 off 6 vol 7

XVII

WAR DIARY
or
INTELLIGENCE SUMMARY
Army Form C. 2118

(Erase heading not required.)

Instructions regarding War Diaries and Intelligence Summaries are contained in F.S. Regs., Part II. and the Staff Manual respectively. Title Pages will be prepared in manuscript.

Place	Date	Hour	Summary of Events and Information	Remarks and references to Appendices
	Apl/16 2/4/16	10am to 12.15pm	Billets were heavily shelled. Approximate number of shells 100 Kg h. Eroplane. Destroyed no billet	
	3rd 4th 5th		In reserve. Quiet days	
	6th	7.30pm	Left Reserve Billets and proceeded to trenches C 22. B and relieved 1st Bn East Yorks Regt. Relief completed 9.0pm	
	7th		Enemy dropped about 40 shells of different calibre into the support trenches to which our artillery replied vigorously.	
	8th		Enemy aeroplane great activity at periods sweeping the top of the parapets with M.G. fire.	
	9th		Quiet day	
	10th		Enemy again shelled support trenches doing no damage.	
	11th		Morning quiet. Considerable aeroplane activity during the afternoon. Enemy bombarded the front line and supports doing damage to the front parapets and dug-outs.	
	12th			
	13th		Enemy threw a few light shells probably 3½ inch into the front line, to which our Artillery replied vigorously effectively silencing their fire.	
	14th		Quiet day. Were relieved by 1st Bn East Yorks Regt, relief completed by 9.0pm.	

WAR DIARY or INTELLIGENCE SUMMARY

Army Form C. 2118

(Erase heading not required.)

Instructions regarding War Diaries and Intelligence Summaries are contained in F.S. Regs., Part II. and the Staff Manual respectively. Title Pages will be prepared in manuscript.

Place	Date	Hour	Summary of Events and Information	Remarks and references to Appendices
	April 22nd		In Divisional Reserve at Armentieres, and supplied working parties for front line trenches.	
	23rd		The Battalion proceeded to the trenches and relieved the 1/4th Bn. East Yorks Regt. Relief completed by 9.0 p.m.	
	24th	7.23am 9.3am	Enemy ordinarily bombarded Pont Ballot, Salient, Vancouver, the Orchard and the front line. Roughly about 300 shells were directed against the points mentioned and considerable damage was done to the trenches. 2nd Lieut. McKenzie L.C. was wounded by shell in the head. He has since joined the Battn on the 23rd inst.	
	25th	11.30am to 2.10pm	Throughout the day, the enemy maintained an intermittent bombardment of the area about EDMEADS FARM and the communication trenches. Many heavy shells were dropped into HOUPLINES, a very high proportion of these were blind.	
	26th		Following on his recent bombardment of our trenches the enemy attempted an attack on a small scale which failed completely.	
	27th		The enemy's artillery was inactive during the day, with the exception of a few shells scattered at various periods, but his machine guns displayed considerable activity during the night 26/27th.	

WAR DIARY or INTELLIGENCE SUMMARY

(Erase heading not required.)

Army Form C. 2118

Instructions regarding War Diaries and Intelligence Summaries are contained in F. S. Regs., Part II. and the Staff Manual respectively. Title Pages will be prepared in manuscript.

Place	Date	Hour	Summary of Events and Information	Remarks and references to Appendices
	April 28	6 am to 9 am	Enemy shelled EDMEADS FARM, the communication trenches, and the support trenches; they also shelled HOUPLINES	
	29		Enemy's Artillery was active during the day.	
	30		Opposite HOBBS FARM the enemy has completed a new trench – this trench cuts across the re-entrant in his old front line. Enemy Artillery was active during the day.	

12. Menin Gate
XVII
Vol g 52/17

WAR DIARY or INTELLIGENCE SUMMARY

(Erase heading not required.)

Place	Date	Hour	Summary of Events and Information	Remarks and references to Appendices
	May 1st 1916		A quiet day. The Battn was relieved by the 7th Bn EAST YORKS and marched back to billets in ARMENTIÈRES	
	2nd		Battalion rested	
	3rd		Hostile shelling of an area just SOUTH of NIEPPE. German aeroplanes, which were seen flying over our lines at about 5.0pm Several Shrapnel Shells burst over our Transport lines wounding 1 mule and 2 horses.	
	4th to 7th		Battalion in Divisional Reserve and found various working parties	
	8th		The Battalion proceeded to trenches and relieved the 7th Bn EAST YORKS. Relief completed at 10pm without incident.	
	9th		A quiet day. The enemy put about 12 light Shrapnel Shells into HOUPLINES between 5am and 6am.	
	10th	5am	Hostile Artillery opened on EDMEADS FARM and about 85. About 50 high explosive 6inch shells fell in this area. The farm was much damaged and a small breach made in our front line parapet.	
		9.15am	Eight light Shrapnel Shells were fired into HOUPLINES where our reserve lay, but did no damage. Our snipers accounted for two of the enemy during the day.	

WAR DIARY
or
INTELLIGENCE SUMMARY

(Erase heading not required.)

Army Form C. 2118

Place	Date	Hour	Summary of Events and Information	Remarks and references to Appendices
	May 11th		A Quiet day. An enemy working party was noticed by an observer at 4.0 am in rear of LES HALLOTS FARM. Two machine guns were turned on this party which consisted of about 20 men, with good results.	
		4.15pm	The enemy shot down one of our aeroplanes; it fell behind our lines. A party of one Officer and 20 men of the 2nd Bn. OTAGO REGT. NEW ZEALAND EXPED. FORCE reached HOUPLINES in the afternoon and were billeted with our reserve Company.	
	12th		During the morning, the enemy displayed considerable artillery activity in the neighbourhood of PONT BALLOT, the ORCHARD, HOUPLINES, and the Subsidiary Line. On our guns retaliating, the enemy stopped. The afternoon was very quiet. The party of the 2nd Otago Bn. inspected the trenches.	
	13th		Quiet day. The Officers of the 2nd Bn. OTAGO REGT. were taken round the trenches preparatory to taking over.	
	14th		Quiet day. The Battalion was relieved during the night 14/15th by the 2nd Bn. OTAGO REGT. N.Z. and proceeded into billets in ARMENTIERES.	
	15th		The Battalion left ARMENTIERES at 11.30 pm and marched to ESTAIRES. Dress full Marching Order.	

Army Form C. 2118

WAR DIARY
or
INTELLIGENCE SUMMARY
(Erase heading not required.)

Instructions regarding War Diaries and Intelligence Summaries are contained in F. S. Regs., Part II. and the Staff Manual respectively. Title Pages will be prepared in manuscript.

Place	Date	Hour	Summary of Events and Information	Remarks and references to Appendices
	May 16	11 a.m.	The Battalion reached ESTAIRES, and went into billets	
		1.30 p.m.	The Battalion left its billets at ESTAIRES and proceeded by route march to MORBEQUE arriving there at 7.0 p.m. The Battalion was billeted in farms near the town.	
	17th		The Battalion rested.	
	18th	7 a.m.	The Battalion left billets and proceeded by march route to WARDRECQUE arriving at 12.0 noon	
	19th	6.15 a.m.	The Battalion left billets and proceeded by march route to the training area ZUDAUSQUES arriving 12.0 noon	
	20th & 21st		Battalion Rested.	
	22nd		Battalion commenced training. Company and Extended Order Drill. Practice at the assault trenches. Marching by compass at night per Specialists training under Specialist Officers.	
	23rd		Training continued as per programme of May 22nd	
	24th		Battalion practiced on the Range; also practiced assault on trenches	

WAR DIARY
or
INTELLIGENCE SUMMARY

(Erase heading not required.)

Army Form C. 2118

Place	Date	Hour	Summary of Events and Information	Remarks and references to Appendices
	May 25th		Battalion practised in marching in Artillery Formation and assault on trenches	
	26th		Battalion trained in Company Drill in the morning. At night the Battalion marched out and on from a given point marched back by compass. A large percentage of the Battalion inoculated with anti-paratyphoid.	
	27th		Training till noon in Company Drill. Night march and advancing in Artillery Formation at night.	
	28th		Battalion rested (Sunday)	
	29th		Battalion exercised in Musketry during the morning and practised the attack during the afternoon.	
	30th		The Battalion was practised in the attack under Brigade arrangements	
	31st		The 52nd Infantry Brigade assembled in the Divisional Training Area at 10 a.m. and carried out an attack on an imaginary enemy entrenched on a ridge North of DIFQUES.	

WAR DIARY or INTELLIGENCE SUMMARY

Army Form C. 2118

XVI 12 Man clarlan
June Vol 9

(Erase heading not required.)

Place	Date	Hour	Summary of Events and Information	Remarks and references to Appendices
	June 1st 1916	9.15 am	The Battalion took part in a Divisional Route March	
	2nd		The day was devoted to training under Battalion arrangements	
	3rd		The Battalion took part in a Brigade Field Day.	
	4th		Sunday Church Parade.	
	5th		The Battalion took part in a Brigade Field Day.	
	6,7		The day was devoted to training under Battalion arrangements.	
	8th		The Battalion was practiced in the assault in trenches.	
	9th		Trained under Battalion arrangements. Major J Dixon left the Battalion to take command of the 10th B. Near Yokes. Major GSH Rutledge, 1st Duke of Wellington joined the Battalion as 2nd in command	
	10th		Trained under Battalion arrangements	
	11th and 12th		The Battalion left its billets at 11.0 pm and marched to St Omer where it entrained. Troop train left St Omer at 3.10 am and arrived at Amiens 12 noon. The Battalion then marched to Poulainville arriving there at 3.0 pm	
	13th		Trained under Battalion arrangements	
	14th		Twenty NCOs and men were sent to represent the Battalion at a Memorial Service to the late Lord Kitchener. The senior Officers of the	

WAR DIARY or INTELLIGENCE SUMMARY

Army Form C. 2118

(Erase heading not required.)

Place	Date	Hour	Summary of Events and Information	Remarks and references to Appendices
	July 15th		Battalion were present at the Service which was held at the 51st Brigade H.Q. near Allonville.	
	16th		B Company. The Battalion Bombers and a platoon of C Coy were inspected by the Brigadier General 52nd Bde during the morning.	
	17th		The Battalion went for a Route March in the afternoon	
	18th		Training under Battalion arrangements	
	19th		Sunday Church Parade. The Battalion practised Dump and Carrying Party under Brigade arrangements	
	20th		Training under Battalion arrangements. The C.O. and four senior Officers under Brigade arrangements visited the trenches at Fricourt	
	21st and 22nd		Training under Battalion arrangements	
	22nd		Two more Officers visited the trenches between Fricourt and Albert.	
	23rd		The Battalion was practised in sword fighting in the Bois de Mai near Allonville.	
	24th		The Battalion went for a 12 mile route march. Parties of Officers visited the trenches near Fricourt	

WAR DIARY
or
INTELLIGENCE SUMMARY

(Erase heading not required.)

Army Form C. 2118

Place	Date	Hour	Summary of Events and Information	Remarks and references to Appendices
	June 25th		The G.O.C. delivered a short address prior to the Battalion taking part in the pending operations.	
	26th		The Battalion together with the rest of the Brigade were practised in night marching (following a lamp).	
	27th		Transa under Battalion arrangements. The Battalion left its billets at Poulainville at 12 noon and marched to HEILLY, arriving there at 4.30 pm and went under canvas in the adjoining wood.	
	28th		Orders for the Battalion to move to Bois des Tailles were cancelled at HEILLY.	
	29th		The Battalion went for a route march in full marching order.	
	30th	7.30pm	The Battalion left its billets at HEILLY and proceeded by road to Bois des Tailles	

52nd Inf.Bde.
17th Div.

WAR DIARY

12th BATTN. THE MANCHESTER REGIMENT.

J U L Y

1 9 1 6

Army Form C. 2118
7/Manchesters
12 Manchester
Vol 10

WAR DIARY
or
INTELLIGENCE SUMMARY
(Erase heading not required.)

Instructions regarding War Diaries and Intelligence
Summaries are contained in F.S. Regs., Part II.
and the Staff Manual respectively. Title Pages
will be prepared in manuscript.

Place	Date	Hour	Summary of Events and Information	Remarks and references to Appendices
Hébuterne	1.7.16		At Bois des Tailles. Here the Battalion completed its equipment in accordance with table A.	77/M BM
	2.7.16		Battalion paraded at 5.0am and marched to Morlancourt arriving there at 8.0am.	
	3.7.16		Battalion standing to under ½ hours notice (in close billets) joined 8th & 9th M.H.O. pres. & 7.7. Bn. from 17th Division. Takes up the attack towards Railway Copse and Bottom Wood. 5 & 7 Brigade units ready to move at half an hours notice. Battalion sent reconnoitring parties forward over the German front line. Battalion left Morlancourt to relieve 21st Division line N. of Fricourt.	77/M BM
	4.7.16		Relief completed by 6.0am. At night 4/5 2nd Battn moved in support of attack by 10th Lancs. Fusiliers and 9th Northumberland Fus. on Quadrangle Trench. Objective reached and held by remaining Cos.	77/M BM
	5.7.16		Battalion moved back to Lozenge Wood during the morning. At night we supplied a working party to dig new trench on line x.22.a.3.x - x.22.c.2.central facing N.E. Major G.S.W. Russbridger in charge. Half company with Major D.J. Crowell and the whole of "C" Coy with Capt B. Chatteron. 2nd Lieut. W.J. Rathbone was wounded.	77/M BM
	6.7.16		Battalion remained in Lozenge Wood until 8.0pm when ordered to assemble in Hicourt Wood as Brigade Reserve and remained there until 1.30am when orders were received to relieve 9th Northumberland Fus. in Quadrangle trench and descend an Officer to Brigade H.Qrs. for Orders. Lieut N.J. Cranshaw was sent.	77/M BM
	7.7.16		Battalion arrived at Railway Copse at 6.30am and were distributed in trenches on ridge under ridge 800yds N of Copse whilst they rested under heavy fire and until zero hour. 7.25am Lieut. N.J. Cranshaw arrived with orders that we were to assault Quadrangle Support at 8.0am, the 9th Worthamerland Fus and 9th West Riding Regt having failed, there being no time to issue written orders the C.O. (Lieut Col. G.Harrison) and Adjutant (Cpt. B. DuVal) went up to Brigade to organise attack. Lieut Cranshaw at 7.50am from Bridge to go over 9 P.C.	77/M BM

WAR DIARY or INTELLIGENCE SUMMARY

Army Form C. 2118

Place	Date	Hour	Summary of Events and Information	Remarks and references to Appendices
			Northumberland Fus. in Quadrangle Trench. Organization D and B by leading C Coy support, A Coy Reserve, Batt. Bombers held by D.Q. About 10.0 a.m. news came of complete failure of attack under barrage and enfilade M.G. fire. At 2.30 p.m. the C.O. was ordered to go up and organise attack with all available troops in Quadrangle Trench and was wounded while on his way up. The Adjutant sent orders to O.C. 9th North'd. Fus. and advised 52nd Brigade. Battalion relieved by 51st Bde at 7.30 p.m. The following casualties occurred. Lieut. Col. S.J. Harrison CB.D.S.O. Wounded. Major G.S.W. Rusbridger Wounded. Major W.J. Bromell Wounded. Capt. H. Mc Kean killed. Capt. E.R. Thompson Wounded. Capt. J.B. Betts killed. Lieut. W. Pate wounded & missing. Lieut. W.J. Crawshall Wounded & Missing. 2nd Lt. E. Thorogood Wounded & missing B.K. 2nd Lt. F. Latimer killed. 2nd Lt. J. Adams Wounded. 2nd Lt. F.S. Greenwood killed. 2nd Lt. A.B. Young killed. 77/h B.W. 2nd Lt. C.F. Smith killed. and 539. O.R. 2nd Lt. F. Alderton killed.	
			Wright 7/8th Battn returned to Meaulte	
	8.7.16		Major P.W. Maguay joined & took over Command of Battalion.	
			Battn moved by march route to VILLE.	77/h B.W.
	9.7.16		A period of re-organization and refitting commenced.	77/h B.W.
	10.7.16		Battn entrained at Mericourt and proceed to AILLY-Sur-Somme to billets at OISSY.	77/h B.W.
	10/15.7.16		Reorganisation etc. A draft of 66 O.R. joined Battn on 14.7.16. Capt W.M. Rentor joined Battn from Base.	77/h B.W.
	15.7.16		Battn proceed by march route to LONG. 23 O.R. joined Battn today.	77/h B.W.

WAR DIARY
or
INTELLIGENCE SUMMARY

(Erase heading not required.)

Army Form C. 2118

12 Manchester Regt
52 Brigade 17 Divn

Place	Date	Hour	Summary of Events and Information	Remarks and references to Appendices
	16/8/7/16		Reorganisation, etc. 18th and 2nd Lts F.A. Pickles & F.B. Fairham joined Batt. 77/1/90V	
	19/7/16		A Draft of 172 O.R. joins Batt. today. 77/W/BDV	
	20/7/16		Lieut. A.J.C. Sington, 2nd Lt. W.L. Johnston, 2nd Lt. E.M. Leche, 2nd Lt. S.G. Turner and 100 O.R. joined Batt. today. 77.	
	21/7/16		Capt E.R. Thompson rejoined Batt. 77.	
	22/7/16		The Adjutant (Capt. B. DuVal) admitted to hospital. Lieut. F. Lowes takes over duties of Adjutant. 77.	
	23/7/16		Batt. move to Bivouac in valley about 2 miles S.W. of Albert 77.	
	23/31/7/16		Batt. form part of XV Corps Reserve and having to retained by the enemy remaining close to Bivouac 77.	

52nd Brigade..
17th Division.

1/12th BATTALION

MANCHESTER REGIMENT

AUGUST 1 9 1 6

Vol 11 52/17

WAR DIARY
12th Manchester Regt.
August 1916.

WAR DIARY
INTELLIGENCE SUMMARY

(Erase heading not required.)

12th MANCHESTER REGT.

Army Form C. 2118

Place	Date	Hour	Summary of Events and Information	Remarks and references to Appendices
	Aug 1916		The Battⁿ moved up into Brigade Support in old German Second Line, and occupied trenches LONGUEVAL - BAZENTIN-LE-PETIT, and relieved 16th Bn Royal Warwicks. Relief complete 7.30 p.m. During the night 1/2nd both our and enemy Artillery maintained a vigourous bombardment, between 1.0 am and 2.0 am enemy gas shells.	77 77
	2nd		Still in Brigade Support	
	3rd		Battⁿ received orders to attack enemy line between ORCHARD TRENCH in conjunction with 9th Bn Northumberland Fusiliers. Shortly before the Battⁿ left the trenches to launch the attack the enemy set up a barrage and seriously interfered with our preparations Order of Battle A and C Coy attack. D Coy in Support, and B Coy in Reserve The attack was launched at 12.50 am but failed.	77 77
	4th 4th	2.30 pm	Were relieved by 10th Bn Lancs Fusiliers, and moved into Brigade Reserve in MONTAUBAN ALLEY.	77
	5th		Brigade moved into Divisional Reserve. The Battⁿ occupied trenches near CARNOY.	77
	6th to 9th		In Divisional Reserve. Working parties provided for construction of C.T.'s	77

WAR DIARY or INTELLIGENCE SUMMARY

Army Form C. 2118

Place	Date	Hour	Summary of Events and Information	Remarks and references to Appendices
	Aug 10th		Batt. moved into MONTAUBAN ALLEY and relieved the 10th Bn Sherwood Foresters as left support Batt.	77.
	11/12		Batt. remain as left support Batt. 77. Batt. were relieved by 6th Bn Somerset Light Infantry and marched to bivouac 3 miles west of ALBERT. In Corps Reserve.	77.
	13/14th		In Corps Reserve.	77.
	15th		Left bivouac at 2.0 p.m. and entrained at MERICOURT at 7.30 p.m. for CANDAS arriving at 2.30 a.m. 16th inst. Here we were attached to 3rd Army	77.
	16th		Left CANDAS at 2.30 p.m. and proceeded by march route to MEZEROLLES arriving there at 5.30 p.m.	77.
	17th		Left MEZEROLLES at 6.0 a.m. and proceeded by march route to GROUCHES arriving there 12 noon.	77.
	18th to 20th		Batt. rested at GROUCHES	77.
	21st		Batt. left GROUCHES at 6.30 a.m. and proceeded by march route to SOUASTRE arriving there at 1.45 p.m. In Divisional Reserve.	77.
	22nd to 26th		In Divisional Reserve.	77.
	27th		Batt. left SOUASTRE and proceeded to trenches and relieved the	77.

Army Form C. 2118

WAR DIARY
INTELLIGENCE SUMMARY
(Erase heading not required.)

Instructions regarding War Diaries and Intelligence Summaries are contained in F. S. Regs., Part II. and the Staff Manual respectively. Title Pages will be prepared in manuscript.

Place	Date	Hour	Summary of Events and Information	Remarks and references to Appendices
	28th		9th Bn Duke of Wellingtons Regt. Relief completed by 4.30 p.m.	7.1
	29th		Quiet Day.	7.1
	30th		Quiet day	
			Quiet day. Batt" warned that gas was to be launched at 10.0 p.m; order cancelled later, wind not being favourable	7.1
	31st		Quiet day. Batt" warned that gas was to be launched at 10.0 p.m. postponed to 11.0 p.m. and then cancelled wind not being favourable	7.1
			Casualties for the month	
			Cap" N. M. Benton wounded (since died of wounds)	
			2nd Lieut W R.O. Moulton killed	
			" F.J. Bolton wounded	
			" A.H. Blythe missing	
			" R.M. West wounded	
			O.R. 169 killed, wounded, and missing	
			Reinforcements	
			2nd Lieut D.F. Hyne. joined Batt" 6.8.16	
			" C Byrne " 6.8.16	
			Captain T.H. Dixon " 26.8.16	
	Aug 4th		2nd Lieut D. Graham " 31.8.16	
			O.R. 28.	7.1

Vol 12

CONFIDENTIAL.

War Diary.
of.
12th Manchester Regiment.
From 1st September 1916 To. 30th September 1916.

VOLUME. XV.

WAR DIARY 12th Batt Manchester Regt

INTELLIGENCE SUMMARY

(Erase heading not required.)

Army Form C. 2118

Instructions regarding War Diaries and Intelligence Summaries are contained in F.S. Regs., Part II. and the Staff Manual respectively. Title Pages will be prepared in manuscript.

Place	Date	Hour	Summary of Events and Information	Remarks and references to Appendices
In the Field	Sept 1st		Enemy shelled our front line for half an hour with light Shrapnel doing little damage. Remainder of day quiet.	77.
	2nd		Quiet day. Much work done on general improvement of trenches.	77.
	3rd		Enemy shelled front line with 5.9 shells for about 3 hours dropping about 50 shells for about. Damage was not great; casualties 3.	77.
	4th		Enemy dropped several shells in the vicinity of Bn. H.Q. doing no damage. Otherwise quiet day.	77.
	5th		Batt. was relieved by 9th Bn Duke of Wellington's Regt. Relief complete by 6.0 p.m. without incident. Bn moved into Brigade Reserve. Two Coys and Bn Bombers to garrison FONQUEVILLERS and two Coys in CHATEAU DE LA HAIE.	77.
	6th 7th 8th 9th 10		In Brigade Reserve; various working parties provided.	77.
	11th		Bn was relieved by 9th Bn Highland Light Infantry. Relief completed by 10.0 p.m. without incident. Bn marched to huts in ST AMAND.	77.
			Bn left Billets and proceeded by march route to billets in WARLENCOURT.	77.

WAR DIARY
or
INTELLIGENCE SUMMARY
(Erase heading not required.)

Army Form C. 2118

Place	Date	Hour	Summary of Events and Information	Remarks and references to Appendices
In the Field	Sept 13th		Battn. received a draft of 6.O.R. joined Battn.	77.
	13th to 16th		Battn. commenced training. A draft of 11.O.R. joined Battn 2	77
	16th		A draft of 9.O.R. joined Battn.	
	17th to 20th		Battalion training at WARLENCOURT.	77
	21st		Battn. proceeded by route march to GROUCHES starting 10.0 a.m. arriving at 1.0 p.m. A draft of 7.O.R. joined Battn.	77
	22nd		Battalion proceeded by route march to FROHEN-LE-GRAND starting at 8.0 a.m arriving at 12 noon	77
	23rd		Battalion proceeded by route march to MAIZICOURT starting at 6.0 a.m arriving at 1.0 p.m. Lieut Col P.Mc.Shagney and Capt J.W.M. White proceeded on leave to England. Capt A.J. Hawthorne takes over duties of Commdg. Officer.	77
	24th		Battn. proceeded by route march to GAPENNES starting at 8.30 am arriving at midday.	77.

Army Form C. 2118

WAR DIARY
or
INTELLIGENCE SUMMARY

(Erase heading not required.)

Instructions regarding War Diaries and Intelligence Summaries are contained in F. S. Regs., Part II. and the Staff Manual respectively. Title Pages will be prepared in manuscript.

Place	Date	Hour	Summary of Events and Information	Remarks and references to Appendices
In the Field	Ypres 25"		Battn. raided.	
	26"		Battn. commenced intensive training	7.1.
	27"			7.1.
	28"			7.1.
	30"		Continued Training	

A. J. Mackenzie Capt.
Comdg. 125 March. Bn.

WAR DIARY
or
INTELLIGENCE SUMMARY
(Erase heading not required.)

Army Form C. 2118

Instructions regarding War Diaries and Intelligence Summaries are contained in F.S. Regs., Part II. and the Staff Manual respectively. Title Pages will be prepared in manuscript.

Place	Date	Hour	Summary of Events and Information	Remarks and references to Appendices
The Field	October 1	—	Battalion continued intensive training	af
	8		Battalion left Billets at GAPENNES and proceeded by march route to NEUILLY-LE-DIEN and ACQUET.	af
	9		Battalion proceeded by march route to FROHEN-LEGRAND.	af
	10th		Battalion proceeded by march route to HALLOY.	af
	11th		In Coy. Reserve at HALLOY.	af
	11th–18			af
	19th		Bn. proceeded by march route to billets at BOUQUEMAISON.	af
	21st		The Brigadier inspected the Battalion.	af
	22nd		The Battalion vacated billets at BOUQUEMAISON and proceeded by Motor Lorries to ALLONVILLE	af
	23rd		Proceeded by march route to Billets at CORBIE.	af
	27th		Proceeded by march route to Sand Pits Camp at MEAULTE.	af
	29th		Proceeded to camp 1 mile N of CARNOY.	af
	30th		Battalion left camp & proceeded to trenches about 1 mile W of LE TRANSLOY. Casualties: 2/Lt. E.M. TUKE.	af

Reinforcements during the month 2 off. C.E. DAY 15.10.16 Capt. W.H. BAKER 18.10.16 OR 10
Wastage in Officers during the month. 2 Lt. G. ALLCOTT Lieut. A.H. WILLIAMSON, Capt. F.M.M. WHITE.
2 Lt. E.M. TUKE,

A.J. Woodrunes Col. in Comd. Col.
Comdg. 12th Bn. Manchester Regiment.
31.10.16

1875 Wt. W593/826 1,000,000 4/15 J.B.C. & A. A.D.S.S./Forms/C. 2118.

Vol/4

CONFIDENTIAL.

WAR DIARY OF 12TH MANCHESTER REGT.

FROM 1ST NOVEMBER TO 30TH NOVEMBER

1916.

VOLUME IX.

WAR DIARY or INTELLIGENCE SUMMARY

Army Form C. 2118

Place	Date	Hour	Summary of Events and Information	Remarks and references to Appendices
In the Field	Nov 1/1916		Enemy shelled our front line periodically during the day, causing much damage. They also paid close attention to the support trenches and communication trench, wrecking the latter. Battalion was relieved by the 9th Bn Northumberland Fusiliers. Relief completed by 3.30 a.m. 2nd inst. Battalion proceeded into Divisional Reserve at D Camp situated near TRONES WOOD	7.7
	2nd & 3rd		In Divisional Reserve.	7.7
	4th	2.30 pm	Battalion proceeded to trenches and relieved 9th Bn Northumberland Fusiliers. Relief completed by 11.30 p.m. Two prisoners gave themselves up in our line about midnight.	7.7
	5th		Enemy shelled Battn H.Q intermittently during the day; no damage done. Weather conditions very bad. Trenches being in places waist deep in mud and water. One prisoner taken behind our lines.	7.7
	6th			7.7
	7th		Battalion was relieved by the 9th Bn Northumberland Fusiliers and 1 Coy 10th Bn Sherwood Foresters. Relief completed by 12.30 p.m. Battalion proceeded to H Camp situated near CARNOY.	7.7
	8th & 9th		Battalion rested at H Camp.	7.7
	10th		Battalion moved into the trenches and relieved the 9th Bn Northumberland Fusiliers. Relief completed by 9.30 a.m.	7.7

WAR DIARY or INTELLIGENCE SUMMARY

Army Form C. 2118

Place	Date	Hour	Summary of Events and Information	Remarks and references to Appendices
In the Field	Nov 11th		Enemy Artillery active during the day on our front doing little damage. At night the enemy showed some activity with Machine Gun fire which was ineffective.	7.7
	12th		Three Platoons of the 2nd Bn Scots Guards relieved A Coy in front line trenches and two Coys of 2nd Bn Scots Guards relieved C and B Coys in support trenches. C Coy 12th Bn Manchester Regt relieved B Coy 12th Bn Manchester Regt in front line trenches. After relief A, B and D Coys proceeded to Camp F situated near MONTAUBAN.	7.7
	13th		Quiet day. One Coy 4th Bn Grenadier Guards relieved C Coy in front line trenches. Enemy Artillery very active during relief but few casualties occurred. C Coy and Batt: H.Q. withdrew to F Camp. A, B and D Coys proceeded to H Camp.	7.7
	14th		C Coy and Batt: H.Q. joined remainder of Batt: at H Camp	7.7
	15th		Battalion left H Camp and proceeded by March Route to MEAULTE arriving at 2.0 p.m.	7.7
	16th		Battalion left MEAULTE and entrained at EDGEHILL Station for HANGEST arriving at 3.0 p.m. and proceeded by motor bus to the training area SAISSEVAL.	7.7
	17.18 19th		Battalion rested at SAISSEVAL	7.7
	20th		Battalion commenced training	7.7
	21st 22nd 23rd		Battalion continued training	7.7

Army Form C. 2118

WAR DIARY
or
INTELLIGENCE SUMMARY

(Erase heading not required.)

Instructions regarding War Diaries and Intelligence Summaries are contained in F. S. Regs., Part II. and the Staff Manual respectively. Title Pages will be prepared in manuscript.

Place	Date	Hour	Summary of Events and Information	Remarks and references to Appendices
	Nov 29th 1916		Battalion was inspected by G.O.C. Division	7.7
	30th		Battalion entering a training under Battalion arrangements.	7.7
			Reinforcements	
	20th		1 draft of 45 O.R. joined Battalion	
	21st		" " " 60 " " "	7.7
	22nd		" " " 26 " " "	
	29th		" " " 9 " " "	

30-11-16

S. M. Hupay. Lieut Col
Commdg 12th Bn Manchester Regiment

CONFIDENTIAL.

WAR DIARY

OF

12TH. MANCHESTER REGT.

FROM 1ST. DECEMBER. TO. 31ST. DECEMBER 1916.

VOLUMN ~~XVIII~~

WAR DIARY or INTELLIGENCE SUMMARY

Army Form C. 2118

Place	Date	Hour	Summary of Events and Information	Remarks and references to Appendices
In the Field	Dec 1st to 11th		Battalion continued training at SAISSEVAL.	
	12th		Battalion proceeded by route march to HANGEST, and entrained to EDGEHILL, thence by route march to MEAULTE.	
	13th to 21st		Battalion in Corps Reserve at MEAULTE, and were employed renovating the billets in the village.	
	22nd		Battalion proceeded into Divl. Reserve at CARNOY.	
	23rd		Battalion proceeded into Brigade Reserve at GUILLEMONT.	
	24th		In Brigade Reserve at GUILLEMONT.	
	25th		Battalion moved into trenches situated T5b central to T5a central and relieved 9th Bn Duke of Wellington Regt. Ref. MAR.57.C.S.W. Relief complete without incident by 10.0 p.m.	
	26th		Own Artillery bombarded enemy's position from 1.30 p.m. to 4.0 p.m. doing great damage. Enemy replied by setting up a barrage at 2.15 p.m. which dwindled to desultory fire. 18 prisoners were brought in during the early morning by an Officer of EAST YORKS, and we provided an escort to conduct them to the back area. Casualties 4 killed 1 wounded.	
	27th		Quiet day. Battalion was relieved by 10th Bn. Sherwood Foresters. Relief complete by 10.5 p.m. Battalion moved to rest camp CARNOY.	
	28th & 29th		Battalion rested at CARNOY.	
	30th		Battalion moved into Bde Reserve at GUILLEMONT.	

Army Form C. 2118

WAR DIARY
or
INTELLIGENCE SUMMARY
(Erase heading not required.)

Instructions regarding War Diaries and Intelligence Summaries are contained in F. S. Regs., Part II. and the Staff Manual respectively. Title Pages will be prepared in manuscript.

Place	Date	Hour	Summary of Events and Information	Remarks and references to Appendices
3	Dec 3,2		Battalion moved into trenches situated at T5.b Central to T5.a Central. Ref. Map 57 O.S.W. and relieved 9th Bn Duke of Wellingtons Regt. Reinforcements during month: 2nd Lieut M Liggett joined Battalion 18.12.16 " " H B James " " 18.12.16 " " R Kelly " " 22.12.16 " " A V Michaelis " " 22.12.16 Lieut W A Loran " " 23.12.16 " " B M Barnes " " 23.12.16 2nd Lieut L n t Ireland " " 30.12.16 A draft of 12 O.R " " 2.12.16 " " " 137 O.R " " 10.12.16 " " " 9 O.R " " 16.12.16	

Lieut for
O.C. 12th Bn Manchester Regiment

Army Form C. 2118.

Wharncliffe Vol 16

WAR DIARY
or
INTELLIGENCE SUMMARY.
(Erase heading not required.)

Instructions regarding War Diaries and Intelligence Summaries are contained in F. S. Regs., Part II. and the Staff Manual respectively. Title pages will be prepared in manuscript.

Place	Date	Hour	Summary of Events and Information	Remarks and references to Appendices
In the field	Aug 1917 1st		Quiet day	
	2nd		Battalion relieved by 7th Bn. East Yorks. Relief completed by 11.0 pm.	
	3rd 4th		In Rest Camp at CARNOY	
	5th		Battalion moved into Brigade Reserve at Guillemont	
	6th		In Brigade Reserve at Guillemont. Battalion employed on general French Fatigue.	
	7th		Battalion moved into trenches vacated from U.I.D Central to T6 b 5.15. and relieved 9th Bn. West Riding Regt. Battalion Hd Qrs situated T12 a 3.9.	
	8th		Two Platoons of Battalion relieved by 10th Bn. Lancs. Fus. Bn. Hd Qrs moved to T10. a. 7. 7.	
	9th		Battalion relieved by 10th Bn. Sherwood Foresters and proceeded to Rest Camp at CARNOY.	
	10th 11th		In Rest Camp at CARNOY.	
	12th		Battalion proceeded by route march to MEAULTE arriving at 1.30 pm	
	13th		Battalion proceeded by route march to FRANVILLERS arriving at 2.30 pm	
	14th 23rd		Battalion training at FRANVILLERS.	
	24th		Battalion proceeded by route march to MEAULTE and billeted in Huts	
	25th & 26th		Battalion in Cd at MEAULTE	

Army Form C. 2118.

WAR DIARY
or
INTELLIGENCE SUMMARY.
(Erase heading not required.)

Instructions regarding War Diaries and Intelligence Summaries are contained in F. S. Regs., Part II. and the Staff Manual respectively. Title pages will be prepared in manuscript.

Place	Date	Hour	Summary of Events and Information	Remarks and references to Appendices
In the Field	Jany 27th 1917		Battalion proceeded by route march to BRONFAY arriving there at 5.10 pm	N.B.
	28th		Battalion in Divisional Reserve at BRONFAY.	
	29th		Battalion moved into Brigade Reserve at COMBLES.	
	30th		In Brigade Reserve at COMBLES.	
	31st		Reinforcements	
			2nd Lieut L.L. Boardman joined Bn. 2.1.17.	
			— " E. Huggins " " 2.1.17.	
			— " R.F. Henry " " 2.1.17.	
			— " D. Stuart " " 9.1.17.	
			Lieut J.H. Williamson " " 9.1.17.	
			Capt C.S. Ridge " " 17.1.17.	
			Lieut J.F. Bromley " " 18.1.17.	
			1 draft of 20 O.R. " " 6.1.19	
1-2-17				

R. Bor. H. Lieut & for Captain
Commdg 12" Bn Manchester Regiment.

Vol 17

Confidential

War Diary

of

12th Bn The Manchester Regt.

for

February 1917

Army Form C. 2118.

WAR DIARY
or
INTELLIGENCE SUMMARY.
(Erase heading not required.)

Place	Date	Hour	Summary of Events and Information	Remarks and references to Appendices
In the Field	July 1st 1917		Battalion relieved 7th Bn Yorks in left subsection SAILLYSEL SECTOR. Relief completed by 10.0 p.m.	7.1.
	2nd		Our Artillery bombarded enemy trenches with good effect. Otherwise quiet day.	7.1.
	3rd		Battalion relieved by 10th Bn West Yorks. Relief complete by 9.0 p.m. Casualties 2nd Lieut R.V. Richards and 3 O.R.	7.1.
	4th		Battalion in Brigade Reserve in COMBLES. Battalion found working parties. Casualty 1 O.R.	7.1.
	5th		Battalion relieved 10th Bn West Yorks in trenches. Relief completed by 10.0 p.m.	7.1.
	6th		Our Artillery bombarded enemy trenches causing much damage. Casualties 1 O.R.	7.1.
	7th		Battalion H.Q. B and C Coys were relieved by 7th Bn Yorks Regt. A and D Coys remain in Sector under orders of O.C. 7th Bn Yorks Regt. Two Coys 10th West Yorks in COMBLES come under our orders. Casualties 4 O.R.	7.1.
	8th	7.30 am	7th Bn Yorks Regt. attack and capture 300 yards of enemy trench opposite the subsector. A Coy provide carrying parties to captured trench. B Coy garrison strong points. Casualties Capt H.F.D. Dixon, 2nd Lieut S. Speakman, 2nd Lieut R.F. Delmer, 51 O.R.	
		11.0 am	C Coy move up from COMBLES and come under orders of 7th Bn Yorks Reg	
		4.0 pm	B Coy move up from COMBLES and come under orders of 7th Bn Yorks Regt.	7.1.

Army Form C. 2118.

WAR DIARY
or
INTELLIGENCE SUMMARY.
(Erase heading not required.)

Place	Date	Hour	Summary of Events and Information	Remarks and references to Appendices
In the Field	Sept 1916 9.7.		Coys relieved in trenches by 10th Bn. West Yorks Regt.; and return to COMBLES. Casualties 11. O.R.	7.7.
	10th		Battalion rested at COMBLES.	7.7.
	11"		Battalion taken over line from 10th Bn. West Yorks Regt. Relief completion by 11.0 pm. B and C Coys under command of Capt. R.J. Moorhouse occupy new frontline. Casualties 2nd Lieut. L.N.C. Iveland killed. 3. O.R.	
	12"		Quiet day. Casualties 3. O.R.	7.7.
	13"		Our Artillery bombarded enemy positions effectively, and enemy retaliated strongly. New front line heavily bombarded by both artilleries. Battalion relieved by 7th Bn. Yorks Regt. Relief completed 12.0 midnight. Battalion withdrew to Brigade Reserve in COMBLES. Casualties 2 killed R Jaure. 14 O.R.	7.7.
	14"		D Coy move up to the trenches and attached to 10 Bn. West Yorks.	7.7.
	15"		In the evening the Battalion withdrew to Divisional Reserve at BRONFAY. Casualties 1. O.R.	7.7.
	16" and 17"		In Divisional Reserve at BRONFAY.	7.7.
	18"		Battalion proceeded by march route to billets am MÉAULTE arriving there at 2.0 pm.	7.7.
	19"		Battalion proceeded by march route to billets in HEILLY arriving there at 2.30 pm.	7.7.

Army Form C. 2118.

WAR DIARY
or
INTELLIGENCE SUMMARY.
(Erase heading not required.)

Place	Date	Hour	Summary of Events and Information	Remarks and references to Appendices
	Feby 20 to 28		Training at MEILLY.	77.
			Reinforcements	
			2nd Lieut R James joined Battn 6.2.17	
			2" " F.P Bee " " 6.2.17	
			2" Lieut R M Neal " " 13.2.17	
			Lieut D J Osborn " " 20.2.17	
			2" Lieut G H Doughty " " 20.2.17	
			2" Lieut C P R Lumby " " 20.2.17	
			2" Lieut H W Vachor " " 20.2.17	
			Europes 20 O-R " " 6.2.17	
			10 " " " 20.2.17	
			41 " " " 24.2.17	
				77.

A.J. Morhouse Major
Commandg 12th Manchester Regiment

vol 18

WAR DIARY.

OF.

12ᵗʰ MANCHESTER REGT.

FROM 1ST MARCH 1917.

TO 31ST MARCH 1917

VOLUME XXI

CONFIDENTIAL

Army Form C. 2118.

WAR DIARY
or
INTELLIGENCE SUMMARY.
(Erase heading not required.)

Place	Date	Hour	Summary of Events and Information	Remarks and references to Appendices
In the Field	March 10th		Battalion training at Puchevillers.	7.7.
	11th		Battalion proceeded by route march to Beauval.	7.7.
	12th		Battalion proceeded by route march to Bonnière.	7.7.
	13th		Battalion proceeded by route march Bn.H.Q. & Coys. D Boys to Vacqueriette and	7.7.
	14th		A and B coy to Wail.	7.7.
	15th to 21st		Battalion training at Vacqueriette and Wail.	7.7
	22nd		Battalion proceeded by route march to Villers l'Hôpital.	7.7
	23rd		Battalion proceeded by route march to Sus St Leger.	7.7
	24th to 31st		Battalion training at Sus St Leger.	
			Reinforcements	
			2nd Lieut N.N. Vaoker joined Battalion 27.2.17. & draft of 12 O.R. joined Battalion 3.3.17	7.
			" G.H. Dougty " 27.2.17. " 10 " " 5.3.17	
			" B.O.R. Lumby " 27.2.17. " 32 " " 16.3.17	
			" E.18 Johnson " 11.3.17. " 65 " " 18.3.17	
			Lieut E.L. Campbell " 18.3.17. " 93 " " 21.3.17	
			2nd Lieut C.L. Baldwin " 21.3.17. " 26 " " 24.3.17	
			" J.B. Conway " 21.3.17. " 11 " " 24.3.17	
			" F.F. Taylor " 21.3.17.	
			" E.C. Hislop " 24.3.17	
			" H. Holt " 26.3.17	

P.M. Mapray, Lt Col.
Comdg. 12th Bt Manchester Regt.

Vol 19

1917

CONFIDENTIAL

WAR DIARY

OF

2nd MANCHESTER REGT.

FROM 1ST APRIL — 30th APRIL.

VOLUME XXII

WAR DIARY or INTELLIGENCE SUMMARY

Army Form C. 2118

Place	Date	Hour	Summary of Events and Information	Remarks and references to Appendices
In the Field	1917 April			
	5		Battalion Training at SUS ST LEGER	
	6		Battalion proceeded by march route to BERLENCOURT arriving at 12-0 noon.	
	7		Battalion rested at BERLENCOURT	
	8		Battalion proceeded by march route to BEAUFORT arriving 11-30 a.m.	
			Battalion proceeded by march route to SIMENCOURT, as an Advance Guard with 1 section 93rd Field Coy. Royal Engineers and one section Machine Gun Coy attached to 52nd Brigade Front.	
	9		Battalion left SIMENCOURT at 5 p.m. and proceeded by march route to ARRAS arriving there at 8-0 p.m. and billeted there	
	10		In Divisional Reserve at ARRAS.	
	11		Battalion proceeded into trenches situated from H.34.a.9.4. to H.28.d.9.3. into Divisional Support. Map Sheet 51 B.N.W.	
	12		In Divisional Support. Casualties 9 O.R.	
	13		In Divisional Support. Battalion again heavily shelled, causing the following casualties; Lieut. Col. P.M. Magrory, C.O.; Capt. J. Lowen, Adjt; 2nd Lieut. W.B. Jothleton and Lieut J.A. Gregory R.A.M.C. attached to the Battalion, also 13 O.R.	
	14		Capt. (A.) Morhouse assumed Command of the Battalion and Lieut. A.J.G. Sington took up duties of Adjutant. Enemy threw over the shells intermittently during the day. Battalion moved into Brigade Reserve in trenches situated at H.28.a.4.4 to H.28.a.4.9 Ref. Map Sheet 51 B.N.W. Battalion employed in constructing trenches on ORANGE HILL. Casualties 12 O.R.	
	15		Battalion in Brigade Reserve. Two boundaries employed on ORANGE HILL defences and carrying parties for rations to 9th Northumberland Fusiliers at night. Casualties 2 O.R.	
	16		Battalion in Brigade Reserve. Battalion again provided a party for carrying rations to 9th Northumberland Fusiliers, also continued work on ORANGE HILL defences. Casualties 16 O.R.	

WAR DIARY
or
INTELLIGENCE SUMMARY
(Erase heading not required.)

Army Form C. 2118

Instructions regarding War Diaries and Intelligence Summaries are contained in F.S. Regs., Part II. and the Staff Manual respectively. Title Pages will be prepared in manuscript.

Place	Date 1917	Hour	Summary of Events and Information	Remarks and references to Appendices
In the Field	April 18		The Battalion relieved the 9th Bn. Northumberland Fusiliers in trenches situated O1.6.4.4. to H3.6.a.3.2. north of MONCHY WOOD. Casualties 4 O.R.	
			Battalion was relieved by 4th Bn. Border Regt and proceeded to billets in ARRAS. Casualties 9 O.R.	
	19(&)20)		In Divisional Reserve at ARRAS.	
	23		Battalion moved at 4.0 a.m. to Railway TRIANGLE situated H19 Central. At 9.30 p.m. Battalion moved to Divisional Support to same position as held on the 14th and 15th inst. Casualty 1 O.R.	
	24		Battalion moved forward to front line at 1.0 p.m. and relieved the 9th Bn. Northumberland Fusiliers occupying line North of MONCHY Station Wood with right and left flanks resting on roads East and West of Wood. Casualties 1 Off. 20 O.R.	
	25		At 3.30 a.m. Battalion made a surprise attack on RIFLE trench on a three Company front (One Company in support). RIFLE trench runs parallel to the position held by this Battalion and 300 to 400 yards from it and between B1 and HARNESS Lanes (see sketch). 9th Battalion West Riding Regt co-operation on right. At 3.34 a.m. enemy discovered movements and opened fire with his Machine Guns and enemy barrage started. The objective was gained about 3.45 a.m. except on right where two platoons of 3 prisoners (one of whom stated he belonged to the 121st Infantry Regt) the 3rd Division (Germans) were believed to be opposed to us. One Machine Gun was captured also some valuable documents etc. "C" Coy (in support) then withdrew from RIFLE trench to original front line (according to instructions) half an hour after the objective was gained and where a Coy. of 10th Bn. East Yorks had taken up their position in support in the meantime.	

WAR DIARY
or
INTELLIGENCE SUMMARY
(Erase heading not required.)

Place	Date	Hour	Summary of Events and Information	Remarks and references to Appendices
In the Field	1918 April 25		The two platoons on right remained in County Hollersalley till all ammunition was exhausted and afterlies had lost their Officers and all N.C.Os. and 5% of their strength. These two platoons then withdrew to the support line at dusk on night of 25/26th. Two platoons of C. Coy. then went up at dusk and started to dig a strong point to connect the line up where the two Platoons had been held up, and to guard our right flank which was in the air as 3rd. Division did not co-operate in the attack. 4th Coy. 1st. West Riding attacked on left which except one Company on their right. This Company was driven out again by enemy during course of 25th. Our barrage prevented enemy attacking our position in reply to our S.O.S. signals. Consequently both our flanks were in the air and enemy in large numbers on each flank on further side of both BIT and HARNESS Lane. Casualties about 120 O.R.	4 O[?]
	26		On night of 25/26th. Battalion was relieved by 4th Bn. Norfolk Regt. and strong point which we had begun on right was handed over. Bn. Battalion then moved to ARRAS arriving about 5.30 a.m. and at 10-30 a.m. entrained for SAULTY and thence by march route to SUS ST LEGER in XVIII Corps Area. Casualty 1 O.R. The Brigadier and Divisional General both complimented the Battalion personally	
	27/28/29/30		In rest billets in SUS ST LEGER Reinforcements 34 O.R. joined Battalion 29.4.14 59 O.R. joined Battalion 30.4.14	

BIT LANE
RIFLE TRENCH
B'n H.Q.
MONCHY WOOD
HARNESS LANE
N

Vol 20

WAR DIARY
of the
12d(s) Bn MANCHESTER REGIMENT

From 1/5/17 to 31/5/17

Vol XXIII

CONFIDENTIAL

Army Form C. 2118

WAR DIARY
or
INTELLIGENCE SUMMARY
(Erase heading not required.)

Instructions regarding War Diaries and Intelligence Summaries are contained in F.S. Regs., Part II. and the Staff Manual respectively. Title Pages will be prepared in manuscript.

Place	Date 1917	Hour	Summary of Events and Information	Remarks and references to Appendices
In the Field	May 1		Lieut. A.J. to Lingten appointed Adjutant with effect from 14-4-14. Bn. moved off from SUS ST LEGER at 9 a.m. and enclosed outside village for LARESSET where Bn. bivouaced in huttments at TALAVEIRA Camp.	apx
	2		Bn. marched at 1.50 p.m. for camp at G14A (Ry. map 51 B.N.W.) off ST NICHOLAS - ST LAURENT BLANGY road. Bn. Supt. remained at LARESSET. Major E.G.S. TRUELL assumed command of Bn. and granted rank of Lieut. Col.	apx apx apx
	3		From midnight 2/3rd Bn. under XVII Corps	apx
			B echelon formed at G14A. Bn. moved at 5-30 A.M. to Ry. butting from H.Y.D.8.8 to H.I.D.4.0. XVII Corps attacked line WEED-WHY-WEA trenches and BIACHE-GAVRELLE road from its junction with WEAK trench to junction with bank at I2A5.8 (ref. 51 B.N.W.)	apx aps apx apx apx apx
Hands			5 2nd. Inf. Bde in Divisional Reserve under orders of 9th Division.	
and			Bn. at Ry butting in Divisional Reserve.	apx
			Bn. at Ry butting in Divisional Reserve. Battle burying party supplied by day and Digging party by night for R.E. (200 men) Casualty 1st May, 1 O.R.	apx
	8		Bn. at Ry. butting in Divisional Reserve.	apx
	9		Bn. moved up to front line 8.30 p.m. relieving S. AFRICAN Composite Bn. (composed 1st and 4th Regts) and took over left situation with B and A Coys. in front line S of GAVRELLE, I.B.5.1 to C.25.C.80.15 and with Bn. Hq. and D and C Bldgs. in Bn. Reserve in GREEN LINE, HELFORD trench (H.l.c.15.40 to H.l.c.3.9) Ref. PLOUVAIN 1:10000 and 51 B.N.W.	apx
	10		Two Coys. in GREEN line moved up to support line, relieving 1 Coy. of 9th Bn. W. Riding	apx

WAR DIARY
or
INTELLIGENCE SUMMARY

(Erase heading not required.)

Army Form C. 2118

Instructions regarding War Diaries and Intelligence Summaries are contained in F.S. Regs., Part II. and the Staff Manual respectively. Title Pages will be prepared in manuscript.

Place	Date	Hour	Summary of Events and Information	Remarks and references to Appendices
Lichenfield	May 10 1915		Regt D Coy. occupying CORK trench and B Coy CIDER and S half CORK (late CIVIC) trenches (Ref. GAVRELLE trench map and PLOUVAIN 1/10000) Bn. Hqs. as before. Officers Patrol sent out. Casualty 1 O.R	afr
	11		Bn. relieved by 9th Northumberland Fusiliers and moved into Brigade Support with 3 Coys in GREEN line at HELFORD trench and A Coy in Bn. Reserve in BROWN line, (HQA). Bn. Hqs. withdrew to gun pits at H+D.5.4. (Ref. 51 BNW) Casualties 4 O.R. A draft of 40 OR joined Bn.	afr afr afr afr
	12		10th Lancs. Fusiliers and 9th Northumberland Fusiliers attacked CHARLIE and CUTHBERT trenches at 6 A.M. Attack unsuccessful. Bn. relieved 10th Lancs. Fusiliers in Right Subsector with B and D Coys. in front line from 14B1.4 to CURSE inclusive. C Coy in support at CAVE and CUBA and A Coy in Bn. Reserve in GREEN line at HUSSAR trench. Dividing line from Bn on left being CALEDONIAN. Bn. Hqs. in HUSSAR trench. Heavy shelling of Communication trench (CHILI) during relief. Front trench bombarded all night. Casualties 25 O.R	afr afr afr afr afr
	13		Front trench bombarded intermittently during day. Trenches worked in at night. Aeroplane having reported CHARLIE and CUTHBERT unoccupied, patrol sent from B Coy who reported same occupied. Attack on right at night during which trenches bombarded (9 pm to 11 pm) and also intermittently by day and night. Casualties 2nd Lieut A.E. Conway, Wounded and 5 O.R.	afr

WAR DIARY or INTELLIGENCE SUMMARY

Army Form C. 2118

Place	Date	Hour	Summary of Events and Information	Remarks and references to Appendices
In the Field	May 14 1917		Intermittent shelling during day. Inter-company relief. A Coy relieved B Coy and C Coy relieved D Coy. B Coy taking the position of A Coy in GREEN line. Owing to Howitzer bombarding enemy front line next day at 10.0 AM, D Coy was ordered to withdraw from support (trench formerly held by C Coy) to GREEN line at night. A Coy patrol sent out on night reported little enemy movement, but hostile Very lights 50yds in front of enemy trenches. Patrol bring in a wounded Pte of the Lanc. Fusiliers. Casualties 10 O.R.	do
	15		1 Officer and 3 O.R. Lancs. Fusiliers walked into our front line (held by A Coy) in early morning - reported a few wounded men of Lancs. Fusiliers still out. Stretcher-bearers consequently sent out at dark. A Coy and C Coy both withdrew by 10.0 AM from front line to CAVE and CUBA for our Howitzer bombardment. Front line held only by all Bn Lewis guns. Howitzer finished bombardment by 2 PM and A Coy and C Coy resumed their original positions in front line. CUTHBERT and CHARLIE reported empty by aeroplane Patrols ordered At 8.15 P.M. Coys. reported first 50 enemy entering their trenches and then much movement, enemy digging forward and others without equipment moving back. 4th Lincolnshire Regt relieved Bn. who moved back to Brigade Reserve in BLACK line at G.12.B (R) 51 B.N.W. (OBERMEYER trench and shelters) Casualties 4 O.R.	do do do do do do do
	16		Just as Relief completed, Bn. clear of trenches about 3.30 A.M. enemy put down barrage and attacked from chemical works at ROEUX-GAVRELLE Road. Bn. arrived at BLACK line and at 9.0 A.M. orders to move forthwith to Ry. Cutting (H.9.D and H.1.D) in place of 9th Northumberland Fusiliers, enemy having pierced front of line near CURLY trench and taken chemical works	do do do

WAR DIARY or INTELLIGENCE SUMMARY

Army Form C. 2118

(Erase heading not required.)

Place	Date 1916	Hour	Summary of Events and Information	Remarks and references to Appendices
In the field	May 10		Arrived Ry. cutting 10.30 A.M. Bn. in Brigade Reserve at Ry. cutting.	
	14		Bn. in Brigade Reserve at Ry. cutting.	
	18 to 20		Bn. moved into Brigade Support and relieved 9th West Riding Regt. Same positions occupied as on 11th May. B. Coy. in BROWN line.	
	21		2 Lewis parties 80 O.R. and digging party 90 O.R. ordered for work in PIONEER trench from CURSE to CUBA under R.E.	
	22		Bn. in Brigade Support. Working parties same as previous day. Casualties 14 O.R.	
	23		Bn. in Brigade Support. Bn. Hqs. shelled about 3.30 P.M. and 1 signaller killed. Relieved 9th Northumberland Fusiliers in left subsector. Bn. Hqs. in GREEN line (HELFORD trench) 4 Coys. (less 2 platoons B Coy. in support at CORK late CIVIC) in front line, from C25 C9 1 to CURSE inclusive 1.D.4.3 (Ref PLOUVAIN map 1/10000) Front line shelled intermittently. Party 90 O.R. ordered for work on PIONEER trench and dug out at CUBA. Patrols sent out. One patrol of A. Coy. (1 N.C.O. and 4 men) does not return. Casualties 4 O.R.	
	24		1 man of lost patrol returned 10.0 A.M. slightly wounded. Reported remainder staying out all day to get further information. Working parties as previous night. Remainder of Patrol came in at dark and reported CHARLIE occupied by enemy both by day and night. Enemy shell front line on right about 11 A.M. to 1.0 P.M. with 5.9 shells. Casualties 2 in front. 1 Lyne wounded.	
	25		Front line wired. Enemy sniping CONRAD. Digging party as before. 21 O.R.	

WAR DIARY or INTELLIGENCE SUMMARY

Army Form C. 2118

Place	Date	Hour	Summary of Events and Information	Remarks and references to Appendices
In the Field	May 1917 27		Hostile T.M.B. troublesome at 10.0 P.M. Retaliation obtained. Brigade frontage turned into 1 Bn. frontage. CURSE trench handed over at night to 4th Lincoln Regt and 30 men of C. Coy. moved into CONRAD. Boundaries now from N as before and I/C 8.4 - H6C 3.2 (Ref. PLOUVAIN 1/10000) Capt. J. Thompson and 2nd Lieut. Abstall join Bn. from Depot as reinforcements. Casualties 2 O.R.	
	27		Raid on right by Staffordshire Regt at 12.53 A.M. into CURLY, CASH and CHAPLIN N. of CASH. Hostile T.M.B. active and shelled by 18 pounders. Relieved by 9th W. Riding Regt. Casualties 4 O.R.	
	28		Bn. moved to Brigade Reserve in same position as formerly in Ry. cutting after relief arriving 3.30 A.M. Ry. cutting shelled as Bn. arrived. Casualty 1 O.R.	
	29		Bn. in Brigade Reserve in Ry. cutting. Quiet. Occasional enemy shelling. Bn. relieved at 4.30 P.M. by 2nd Bn. Northumberland Fusiliers of 103rd Infantry Brigade and moved to Camp at ST NICHOLAS.	
	30		Bn. left Camp at 12.30 P.M. and entrained to SAULTY for Rest Area at 3.0 P.M. from ARRAS goods station. Bn. marched after detraining to billets at COULLEMONT.	
	31		Brigade Depot march from LARESSET and rejoined Bn. at COULLEMONT. Bn. transferred from XVII to XVIII Corps.	

Army Form C. 2118

WAR DIARY
or
INTELLIGENCE SUMMARY
(Erase heading not required.)

Place	Date	Hour	Summary of Events and Information	Remarks and references to Appendices
In the Field	May 31 1915		Reinforcements. Capt. C.J. Thompson 2nd Lieut. A.C. Staite and 2nd Lieut. W.S. McGowan and 105 O.R. join Bn. from Corps Depot.	An
	1.6.14.			

E.G.S. Truell. Lieut. Col.
Commdg. 12th Bn. Manchester Regt.

Vol 21

CONFIDENTIAL

WAR DIARY
of
12th Bn Manchester Regt

From 1/6/17 to 30/6/17

VOL XXII

WAR DIARY
or
INTELLIGENCE SUMMARY.

Army Form C. 2118.

(Erase heading not required.)

Place	Date 1917	Hour	Summary of Events and Information	Remarks and references to Appendices
	JUNE 15 to 16		Battn. Training at COULLEMONT. Training area taken over by XVII Corps from night of 6/4.	
	4 to 14		Battn. Training at COULLEMONT. Capt. J. Thompson proceeded to CALAIS as Instructor to Reinforcement School. Personnel for boys.	
	18		Shot returned to SAVY.	
	18/19		Battn. Training at COULLEMONT.	
	20		Battn. Entrained at COULLEMONT for forward area and detrained at ROND POINT, ARRAS. From this point Battn. marched to camp at ST NICHOLAS at G.14.A.9.4. (Ref map 51B NW 1/20000). 1st line transport marched from rest area to ST NICHOLAS camp. Battn. came under orders of XVII Corps. Casualties nil.	
	21		Bde. report formed at G.10.D.2.2. Between 8 pm & midnight behind at ST NICHOLAS camp G.10.D.2.2. the Battn. moving forward into Bde. support and relieving 21st Battn. Northumberland Fusiliers night of 21/22. Battn. occupied — LEMON, LUCID and HERON trenches in FAMPOUX–GAVRELLE line H.10.D.4.1 to H.11.A.6.1 approx. Battn. Hqrs in sunken road H.11.A.6.1 (Ref map 51B NW 1/20000) casualties nil.	
	22		B and D Coys carried wiring material to front line Batts. SCULL and SCORN respectively. A and C Coys deepened CLYDE C.T. from its junction with CUBA at I.4.D. (Ref PLOUVAIN map 1/10000) under R.E. at night. Casualties nil.	
	23		B Coy carried to SCORN in front line at night. C, D and A Coys dug and wired ness eye trench in night under R.E. in front of HALO trench H.M.A.9.9 to H.11.C.9.6 approx (Ref map 51B NW) Casualties 2 O.R. wounded.	
	24		A and C Coys dug and wired trench in front of HALO at night under R.E. wire night. 2 O.R. 115 men employed. Casualties nil.	

WAR DIARY or INTELLIGENCE SUMMARY

Army Form C. 2118.

Place	Date 1917	Hour	Summary of Events and Information	Remarks and references to Appendices
	JUNE 25		Trench improved. Casualties nil.	
	26		Major A.J. Moorhouse (in command of Battn) and 1 O.R. wounded by a shell in the morning when on way to visit HQrs of Household Battn. Major G.F. Jones, D.S.O. assumed command. Battn. moves into front line at 10.0 P.M. relieving Household Battn. and 9th Battn. West Riding Regt. on night 26/27. Position occupied :- "D" Coy (and 2 sections "A" Coy attached) and "B" Coy in front line from Ry (inclusive) COCKBURN, CAMBRIAN and COD trenches to junction of CASH (I.14.A Beutral to I.14.D 95.90) with advance post of "A" Coy 2 sections and 1 Lewis Gun (under O.C. "D" Coy) at COAL trench across Ry (I.14.A.95.90 to I.14.A.65.90). "A" Coy (less 2 sections and 1 platoon at quarry (I.13 A.2.3) and 1 platoon in CRUSH (H.18.D.3.2 to H.18.D.1.6) - Battn. HQrs at H.18.D.1.6. Ref (I.13.B.central) "C" Coy in Reserve with 1 platoon at quarry (I.13 A.2.3) and 1 platoon in CINEMA (I.13.B.central). PLOUVAIN map 1/10000.	
	27.		Boys were found on a 2 platoon basis for the town up the line. During night 26/27 CASH and CURLY LANE trenches were heavily shelled from 12.0 midnight to 10.0 A.M. About 1.15 A.M. immediately after front line boy had relieved their opposite number, about 20 enemy rushed advance post in COAL Trench from the rear and threw a few bombs. 2 O.R. were wounded and the N.C.O. i/c post is believed to have been wounded and taken prisoner of war. The enemy were seen disappearing, dragging 3 of their number who were evidently casualties, and fire was opened on them. The post was immediately reorganised. Intermittent shelling during day by both sides. Trenches (which were very bad) were cleared and front line deepened. Hostile Aircraft active. Hostile Trench Mortars active night 27/28 vicinity of Rly Cutting. Casualties 2 O.R. wounded by bombs, 1 O.R. missing (believed prisoner of war).	
	28.		Defensive line CURLY LANE and CUPID trenches wired and T Heads dug. Our Aircraft active. At 8.45 P.M. hostile Trench Mortars laid a barrage behind CURLY LANE Trench. Hostile Trench	

WAR DIARY
or
INTELLIGENCE SUMMARY

Army Form C. 2118.

(Erase heading not required.)

Place	Date 1916	Hour	Summary of Events and Information	Remarks and references to Appendices
	JUNE 28		Mortars threw over a few gas shells in early morning. M.G. fire at 4.30 A.M. Intermittent shelling by both sides during day. Hostile sniping more active. Our Artillery active. Casualties 1 O.R. accidentally wounded, 4 O.R. gassed by gas shells, but remained at duty.	
	29		CUPID trench and defensive line wired and improved. Intermittent shelling during day. A shell fell by Batt. H.Qrs. killing 5 and wounding 3 O.R. during afternoon. Hostile Aeroplanes active. At 6.0 P.M. to 6.15 P.M. some of our shells (4.5" or 6") fell short on left front. Our Artillery active during night. Lieut. Col. B.G.R. Sewell reported Batn. from Line and resumed command. Casualties 4 O.R. killed, 5 O.R. wounded and 1 O.R. wounded and remaining at duty (all by shell fire).	
	30		Our Artillery fired short on right flank at 4.15 A.M. — Work on CURLY LANE and defensive line continued. Major J.W. Bullock (Lt. Dorsets) joined the Batn. as 2nd in command. Major Jones returned with the Lancs Fusiliers. Intercompany relief. "A" relieved "B" Coy. and "C" relieved "D" Coy. Intermittent shelling during day. Left flank, neighbourhood of CURLY LANE heavily bombarded by hostile Heavy Trench Mortars. Casualties 4 O.R. killed, 2 O.R. wounded (all by shell fire).	

WAR DIARY or INTELLIGENCE SUMMARY

Army Form C. 2118.

12 Manchester

Place	Date 1917	Hour	Summary of Events and Information	Remarks and references to Appendices
In the Field	July 1st		Our artillery active. Intermittent shelling by enemy. Hostile aircraft active, several stars flying over our lines. Relieved by 9th Bn West Riding Regt. and moved on night 1st/2nd to position held by Bn on 21st June on GAVRELLE Switch, where the Bn was in Brigade Support. Casualties:- 1 O.R. killed and 2 O.R. wounded.	B.
	2nd		Bn in Brigade support at GAVRELLE Switch. Working and carrying parties amounting to 13 Officers and 150 O.R. provided at night.	B.
	3rd		Bn in Brigade Support. Bombardment heard on our right front and enemy fired several shells at our trenches and in vicinity of Bn. H.Qrs. at about 2-a.m. About ½ an hour later gas alarm heard from direction of front line on right which proved to be only on account of gas shells. Working parties provided at night amounting to 20 Officers and 158 O.R. Capt O. PECKHARD resumed duty at Echelon B. from DIVISIONAL DEPOT Bn SAVY after absence on sick leave in England. Casualties:- LIEUT. W.S. MACGOWAN wounded by machine gun bullet whilst with working party, also 1 O.R. wounded.	B.
	4th		Bn in Bde Support. About 6-30 p.m. enemy shelled our lines and Bn H.Qr. 8-30 p.m. and received 9th Bn West Riding Regt. Bn moved from GAVRELLE Switch (left subsector) taking over same positions as occupied on June 36th with "C" Coy on right and "A" Coy on left in front line, "B" Coy in support and "D" Coy in reserve. 9th Bn West Riding Regt. took over position in GAVRELLE Switch vacated by Bn. Casualties:- NIL.	B.
	5th		Intermittent shelling, 400 yards of wire erected in front of front line trench.	B.

WAR DIARY
or
INTELLIGENCE SUMMARY.
(Erase heading not required.)

Army Form C. 2118.

Place	Date	Hour	Summary of Events and Information	Remarks and references to Appendices
In the Field	5th (contd)		Patrol discovered enemy working party. One of our Lewis guns opened fire on hostile party and dispersed same. Capt. O.P.ECKHARD joined Bn. in the front line, working with the Transport bringing up Bns. rations. Transport shelled (while doing above) near the QUARRY at about 10-30 PM to 11-0 PM. Casualties:- 2 O.R. Killed and 3 O.R. wounded and 1 horse and 1 mule killed.	B
	6th		Occasional shelling on night of 5/6th. Dispositions of Bn. altered, "C" Coy on right, "B" Coy in centre and "A" Coy on left all holding the front line and each finding their own support. "D" Coy and Bn. HQ as before. Wire in front of front line completed, about 400 yards more of wire being put up. Patrol again reported enemy working party seen closing. Enemy party was fired on by us. Casualties - 1 O.R. wounded.	B
	7th		Relief. Occasional shelling. Relieved by 7th Bn. Yorkshire Regt. and moved into Div. reserve at ST. NICHOLAS Camp night 7/8th. Casualties.- 3 O.R. wounded.	B
	8th		At ST. NICHOLAS Camp in Divisional reserve. Deficiencies in fighting equipment made good.	B
	9th		At ST. NICHOLAS Camp in Divisional reserve. Training carried out.	B
	10th		Training in Divisional reserve at ST. NICHOLAS Camp. 175 men provided as working party for burying cable near FAMPOUX.	B
	11th & 12th		Training at ST. NICHOLAS Camp. In Divisional reserve.	B B

Army Form C. 2118.

WAR DIARY
or
INTELLIGENCE SUMMARY.
(Erase heading not required.)

Instructions regarding War Diaries and Intelligence Summaries are contained in F.S. Regs, Part II. and the Staff Manual respectively. Title pages will be prepared in manuscript.

Place	Date	Hour	Summary of Events and Information	Remarks and references to Appendices
In the Field	13th		Training at ST NICHOLAS Camp in Divisional reserve. Lieut Col. E.G.S. TRUELL evacuated sick. Major T.W. BULLOCK took over Command of the Bn. 3 officers reinforcements:- 2nd Lieuts M.E. BARLOW, T.W. BRADLEY, S.COULTER, and 23 O.R. joined Bn. from DIV. DEPOT BN.	
	14th		Training at ST NICHOLAS Camp in Divisional reserve. Capt R.V.L.DALLAS (9th Bn. Northumberland Fusiliers) joined Bn and posted as 2nd in Command.	
	15th		Bn in ST NICHOLAS Camp in Divisional reserve. Brigade Church Parade at 10-30 P.M. Bn moved from ST NICHOLAS Camp at 8-45 P.M. into left Bde support relieving 7th Bn Border Regt. Bn. Qrs and A and C. Coys taking up position in BLACK line (OBEYMEYER trench) G 12.B and D and B Coys in HURRUM and HELFORD trenches, H 6 C 0.2 to H 6 A 4.1) in GAYRELLE switch, reference map 51.B.N.W. Edition 6A.	
	16th		In Bde support. B and D Coys (in GAYRELLE Switch) employed on working parties at night. N.B. During month of JUNE and JULY leave reopened and Officers and men were sent off on an average of about 15 per week.	
	17th		In Bde support. Trenches improved. Working parties produced at night, amounting to 2 officers 160 O.R. (30 from A Coy in BLACK line for digging and remainder from B and D Coys in GAYRELLE switch for carrying).	
	18th		In Bde support. The following reinforcements joined Brigade depot-	

WAR DIARY
INTELLIGENCE SUMMARY.
(Erase heading not required.)

Army Form C. 2118.

Instructions regarding War Diaries and Intelligence Summaries are contained in F.S. Regs., Part II. and the Staff Manual respectively. Title pages will be prepared in manuscript.

Place	Date	Hour	Summary of Events and Information	Remarks and references to Appendices
In the Field	18.		From Corps Depot for the Bn:- 2nd Lieuts. K.P. Cook, M. Rennie S. Jackson, and W.W. Wilshire and 13 O.R. Coys back at BLANGY. Working parties provided at night amounting to 1 Officer and 170 O.R. for carrying (30 O.R. from C Coy in BLACK line and remainder from 2 Coys in GAVRELLE switch.	B /
	19.		Bn in Bde support. Bn ordered to relieve 9th Bn West Riding Regt in front line. Relief cancelled owing to operation being carried out on left by NAVAL Division also because enemy reported massing for attack in front of GAVRELLE which latter appeared unfounded as NAVAL Division' operation was carried out early following morning on front of GAVRELLE. "B" and "D" Coys in GAVRELLE switch depend extension of GAVRELLE switch, N/ HELFORD trench (NAVAL trench) Casualties: - 1 O.R. Wounded.	B /
	20.		Bn in Bde support. Bn relieved 9th Bn West Riding Regt on left subsector at night. Bn H.Qrs and 'A' and 'C' Coys moved from BLACK line at 8.45 P.M. Dispositions occupied by Bn after relief: - Front line - CONRAD and COLIN trenches from 11.B 10.75 to 11.D 60.35 held by "C" Coy on right and "A" Coy on left. In support "D" Coy on right and "B" Coy on left. CORT. Bn. H.Qrs on HELFORD French in GAVRELLE switch. (Ref map PLOUVAIN 1/10,000 July 1917) 2nd Lieut A.C. STAITE sent sick to hospital. Minor operation with patrols by the 9th Bn Northumberland Fusiliers on Bn's right at 10.30 P.M. Enemy retaliated with 4.2's and 5.9s along our front line for 15 to 20 minutes. Patrols reconnoitred our wire cut in front and reported same in very bad condition.	B /

WAR DIARY
INTELLIGENCE SUMMARY.

Army Form C. 2118.

Place	Date	Hour	Summary of Events and Information	Remarks and references to Appendices
In the Field	21st		Trenches improved. C.S.M. MILLS of "A" Co. went out 4 p.m. during daylight and reconnoitred our wire. Wire tricked in front of front and support trenches at night.	JB
	22nd		Work on trenches continued. Considerable aerial activity in the morning, several enemy machines flying over our trenches some of whom fired lights. One enemy machine brought down by our planes and fell E. of GAVRELLE. Enemy trench mortars active between 6.0 A.M. and 8.0 A.M. Occasional shelling during morning by both sides. Patrols at night located hostile machine gun and also enemy wiring party of about 50 strong. This party was dispersed by our Lewis Guns and rifle grenades. Our artillery and machine guns bombarded enemy tracks behind his trenches from 11-0 P.M. to 11-57 P.M. Wiring our trenches continued at night. Casualties:- 1 O.R. Killed, 2 O.R. Wounded (1 of whom remained at duty) all by French mortar fire. 2nd Lieut W.W. WISHLADE joined Bn from Bde Depot and was posted to B Co.	JB
	23rd		Aerial activity during morning, several enemy machines flying low over our trenches. They were engaged by machine guns and anti-aircraft guns. Work and wiring continued. Bodies found at parts of about 60 of the enemy covering in front of W17. This party was surprised by our Lewis Guns and Stokes Mortars. 2nd Lieut WEST in charge of a patrol found WISH trench 11D (Ref map 1/10000 PLOUVAIN) unoccupied by enemy. 5 dead Germans were	JB

WAR DIARY
INTELLIGENCE SUMMARY

Army Form C. 2118.

Place	Date	Hour	Summary of Events and Information	Remarks and references to Appendices
In the field	23rd (Cont) 24th		on the trench. 1 man sent sick to hospital. Aeroplanes again active during the morning. Several enemy machines flew over our lines, one flying low over "A" Co'ys trench. Little shelling during day. A few gas shells fired by enemy about midnight. Work and wiring continued as previously. 2nd Lieut S.T. JACKSON joins Bn from Base Depot and was posted to "A" Coy. Patrols reported large enemy party repairing wire in front of W.17. Enemy wiring party dispersed by our Lewis Guns and Stokes mortars. Another enemy wiring party heard behind W.17 and also his transport at WHIP cross roads at 1-1.15 A.M. 24/25th. Enemy seen coming out in two's and three's and occupying shell holes at night in front of his wires where he pulls up very lights. Work continued. 2nd Lieuts R. JENNISON, C. NEY and D.F. HYNE joined Bn at Base Depot from 17th DIV. DEPOT BN.	J.B.
	25th		Quiet during morning. Communication trenches shelled intermittently during afternoon. Relieved at night by 9th Bn. West Riding Regt. on left subsector (CALEDONIAN subsector) Bn moved into H.Q. Bn support at GAVRELLE switch occupying trench between junction with CHILI and CIVIL. Bn H.Qs remained in same position. 4 casualties from shell fire about noon. Relief carried out without casualties. Capt. A.J.C. SINGTON and 6 O.R. left line to attend Court-Martial at Base Depot on 26th. Casualties - 5 O.R. Wounded.	J.B.
	26th		Bn working during day in GAVRELLE switch improving trenches, shelters and laying duck-boards. Enemy artillery normal during day. Enemy aerial activity nil evening over our lines. Working parties at night of 1 Officer and 150 O.R.	J.B.

WAR DIARY or INTELLIGENCE SUMMARY.

Army Form C. 2118.

(Erase heading not required.)

Instructions regarding War Diaries and Intelligence Summaries are contained in F. S. Regs., Part II. and the Staff Manual respectively. Title pages will be prepared in manuscript.

Place	Date	Hour	Summary of Events and Information	Remarks and references to Appendices
In the Field	26th (cont'd)		in addition to small parties working on extensions to Bn. H.Qrs and HOOD Trench. Our artillery and machine guns active in evening. Letter of Commendation received from G.O.C. Division on 'A' and 'C' Coy's patrols under L/Cpl Borley and Sgt Barter.	B/
	27th		Bn. still in same position. Work continued during day. Observation good, aerial activity on both sides. Lieut A.J.C. SINGTON went on leave to England. Working parties at night. 2 Officers and 60 O.R. wiring new supportline between CIVIL and CALEDONIAN. Carrying parties 1 Officer and 85 O.R. Joined from Brigade Depot:- 2nd/Lieuts R. TENNISON to 'B' Coy and G. NEY to 'D' Coy and 18 O.R.	B/
	28th		Bn occupied in clearing of trenches. Relieved 17th Bn West Riding Regt. at in front line of left subsector. Bn H.Qrs situated in CIVIL Trench.	B/
	29th		Bn H.Qrs was shelled during the day with H.E. Enemy aerial activity less than usual owing to bad weather conditions. Bn furnished working parties of 2 Officers and 130 O.R. for wiring and completing new support line. Reinforcements of 17th Divisional Depot Bn:- 4 O.R. casualties. - 1 O.R. Wounded (remaining at duty)	B/
	30th		Trenches in bad condition owing to wet weather. Active Bn front line. Enemy trench mortars active Bn front line. Our artillery replied effectively silencing them. 'A' and 'C' Coys completed wiring at night. 1 casualty. - 1 O.R. Wounded (remaining at duty).	B/

A.5834 Wt. W.4973/M687 750,000 8/16 D, D. & L. Ltd. Forms/C.2118/13

Army Form C. 2118.

WAR DIARY
or
INTELLIGENCE SUMMARY.
(Erase heading not required.)

Instructions regarding War Diaries and Intelligence Summaries are contained in F. S. Regs., Part II. and the Staff Manual respectively. Title pages will be prepared in manuscript.

Place	Date	Hour	Summary of Events and Information	Remarks and references to Appendices
In the Field	31st		Weather dull rendering observation difficult. Work of clearing trenches and draining continued all day. Relieved by 7th Bn Yorkshire Regt and proceeded into Divisional Reserve at ST NICHOLAS Camp. Casualties:- 1 O.R. wounded.	B/1

J W Rollson
Lieut. Col.
Commanding 12th Bn Manchester Regt.

Vol 23

4/53

War Diary
of
12th Manchester Regt
for Month of
AUGUST 1917

Army Form C. 2118.

WAR DIARY
~~INTELLIGENCE SUMMARY~~
(Erase heading not required.)

Instructions regarding War Diaries and Intelligence Summaries are contained in F. S. Regs., Part II. and the Staff Manual respectively. Title pages will be prepared in manuscript.

Place	Date	Hour	Summary of Events and Information	Remarks and references to Appendices
In the Field	1917 August 1		Battalion in Divisional Reserve at ST. NICHOLAS. 3 Officers and 61 O.R. joined Bn. from Brigade Depot. Bn. supplied Brigade Guard.	
	2		Men resting and cleaning up despite dirty weather. In Div. Reserve. Bn. occupied in cleaning up. 2nd Lieuts. B.J. Snow and J.O.R joined Bn.	
	3		In Div. Reserve. Bn. reorganised in fighting equipment. Bn. commenced training.	
	4 & 5		Bn. continued training in Div. Reserve. A Bn. Mess Dinner at Officers Club, ARRAS. 24 Officers present.	
	6		Bn. moved from ST NICHOLAS at night and relieved 10th Shurwood Foresters in front line CHEMICAL WORKS Sector. 3 Coys. front line and supports, CROFT TRENCH D. Coy. A. Coys. Support Coy. 'B' in CRETE. Very wet during relief. Enemy very quiet during relief. but sent over a few trench Mortars from HAUSA Wood about 4-0AM.	
	9		2nd Lts. HARROP, WINDER, GRAHAM and JACOB joined Bn. from Brigade Depot and posted to B D A & C Coys. respectively. Capt. E.R. THOMPSON also joined and took over 'A' Coy. Capt. CAMPBELL moved to D Coy. Work - Improving trenches in front line. "C" Coy. at 4.30 P.M. Enemy trenches were blown in and 29 prisoners taken. We had out 10 patrols during 24 hours. D. Coy. sent out 3 daylight patrols. 2nd Lieut. E.R. LAWTON got up to enemy during day. Casualties 3 O.R. wounded.	
	10		2nd Lieut. F. HUDSON 4th Border Regt attached to Bn. Work on trench system	

Army Form C. 2118.

WAR DIARY
of
INTELLIGENCE SUMMARY
(Erase heading not required.)

Instructions regarding War Diaries and Intelligence Summaries are contained in F. S. Regs., Part II. and the Staff Manual respectively. Title pages will be prepared in manuscript.

Place	Date	Hour	Summary of Events and Information	Remarks and references to Appendices
In the Field	1917 August 10		As usual. 2nd Lt. E.R. Lawton killed whilst on daylight patrol near enemy line. Body brought in. Enemy activity quiet. We had 5 shouts out. B.Coy found 2 dead Germans in COAL trench. Much enemy movement seen in front of HAUSA WOOD. Casualties, 1 Officer 2nd Lt. E.R.Lawton and 1 o.R. killed, 2 o.R. wounded.	At
	11		2nd Lt. E.R. Lawton buried at night in FAMPOUX Cemetery by Rev. T.H. CLEWORTH. Bn. relieved at night by 9th West Riding and moved into Bde. Reserve. 2 Coy "A" and "C" GAVRELLE Switch. - 2 Coy. 9th W.R. Coy RAILWAY CUTTING. Enemy shelled vicinity of and Rly. Bridge with a few heavies. Enemy patrol of 6 men were repulsed by our Right boy. about 10.40 p.m.	At
	12		Bn. in Bde. Reserve. Coys. resting and cleaning up. Working parties of 50 o.R. by day and 3 Officers and 100 o.R. by night. Adjutant joined Bn.	At
	13		Bn.in Bde. Reserve Rly. Cutting. Light training carried out. About 4 shells fell in Cutting about 6.30 a.m. 2nd Lt. H. BUCKLEY joined from Depôt and attached to Bn. Casualty 1 oR. accidentally injured (sprained ankle) whilst on duty.	At
	14		Bn. in Bde. Reserve. Light training. Raid practised. General B'N.G. commanding XVII Corps, General WHEATLEY R.A. and the Brigadier General attending. Casualty 1 oR. wounded	At
	15		Bn. in Bde. Reserve. Light training. Raid practised. 2nd Lt. Buckley and 10 o.R. reinforcements join Bn. Depôt for the Bn. Relieve 9th Bn. West Riding Regt. (less 1 Coy.) in Right Subsector of CHEMICAL WORKS sector. "D" Coy on right, "B" Coy centre, "A" Coy left and "C" Coy in Reserve. 2nd Lt. N.A. SMITH joins both Depôt and is posted to Bn.	At

Army Form C. 2118.

WAR DIARY
or
INTELLIGENCE SUMMARY.
(Erase heading not required.)

Instructions regarding War Diaries and Intelligence Summaries are contained in F.S. Regs., Part II. and the Staff Manual respectively. Title pages will be prepared in manuscript.

Place	Date	Hour	Summary of Events and Information	Remarks and references to Appendices
In the Field	1914 August 15th contd.		6 enemy machines flew over our lines at 7.30 P.M.	
	16		Quiet. Hostile T.M's. active from Rly. Cutting at night. Also our Artillery and T.M.S. 500ˣ of wire erected in front of support line. El daylight posted sent out by our cond. listening posts by night. Bgs. dep. wired as Bigade cable to personnel Mine sent to join the Bn. Much enemy movements seen in Rly. Cutting at Inf. a 6.5 (Ref. 1/10000 PLOUVAIN map) Observers Kruzel Rev. Brualles 1 O.R. Killed + O.R. wounded.	
	17		Snipers post established in Rly. Cutting. Snipers reported having hit 5 of the enemy and that 2 German officers were also observed in the Rly. Cutting. Wiring of support line continued.	
	18		CRETE trench and Bn. Hd. Qrs. heavily shelled by 5.9's. About 400 shells fired during day, presumably by a Railway gun. Wiring of support-line continued. 1 casualty for Killed, 2 wounded.	
	19		New O.P. found by the shelters in the CHEMICAL works commanding full view of the front. Our left shelled by hostile T.M.S. Wire erected at night. Brualles 1 O.R. Killed, 1 O.R. wounded. Working observed 100ˣ white tape observed at 6.0 A.M. parallel to our wire in no mans land.	
	20		Patrols sent out by relieving unit. Relieved (less "C" Coy) by 9th West Riding Regt. and Bn. in Res. (Reserves as follows:- A and B Coy in GAVRELLE switch (PUDDING trench) and Bn. Hd. Qrs. and D Coy in Rly. Cutting. "C" Coy remained in CORDITE trench for work under R.E. in CORFU Communication trench (Ref. PLOUVAIN map) Day quiet during relief.	
	21		Bn. in Brigade Reserve. Carrying party 85 o.r. provided at night from GAVRELLE switch. Snipers and Lewis Gunners started course of training in Rly. Cutting 1 wounded, 1 o.r. wounded.	

Army Form C. 2118.

WAR DIARY
INTELLIGENCE SUMMARY.
(Erase heading not required.)

Instructions regarding War Diaries and Intelligence Summaries are contained in F. S. Regs., Part II. and the Staff Manual respectively. Title pages will be prepared in manuscript.

Place	Date	Hour	Summary of Events and Information	Remarks and references to Appendices
In the Field	1917 August 22		Bn. in Brigade Reserve. "D" Coy. went into GAVRELLE Switch with "A" and "B" Coys. Bn. Hd. Qrs. and men under specialist training remain in Bly. Bertin.	
	23		Bn. in Brigade Reserve. An advanced Bn. Hd. Qrs. established in GAVRELLE Switch.	
	24		Bn. in Brigade Reserve. Relieved by 4th Yorkshire Regt. and Bn. moved into Divisional Reserve at GRIMSBY Camp, ST NICHOLAS. "A", "B" and "D" Coys. afterwards detailed to dig CORFU communication trench at night. After completion of work it was engaged by lorries to camp. A shell struck one of our lorries during the relief wounding two buglers, mortally wounding the driver and wounding 1 O.R. besides 3 O.R. wounded.	
	25 to 31		Bn. in Divisional Reserve. Training carried out and Range constructed during the week. 2nd Lt. N.A. SMITH and A/R.S.M. PRIEST, R.W., joined Bn. 27th Aug.	

M. Winter Capt. ad
12. March Rgt.

Army Form C. 2118.

WAR DIARY
or
INTELLIGENCE SUMMARY.
(Erase heading not required.)

Instructions regarding War Diaries and Intelligence Summaries are contained in F. S. Regs., Part II. and the Staff Manual respectively. Title pages will be prepared in manuscript.

Place	Date 1917 Sept.	Hour	Summary of Events and Information	Remarks and references to Appendices
In the Field	1		Bn. in Divisional Reserve - ST NICHOLAS Camp. Bn. relieved 4th Bn. Sherwood Foresters in left subsector of GREENLAND HILL Sector (CONRAD and COLIN trenches) I.1 Band D (Ref. PLOUVAIN map 1/10,000) and moved off from ST NICHOLAS Camp at 4.30 p.m. Dispositions:- Front line 'A' Coy right, 'B' Coy centre and 'C' Coy left. Each finding own supports in CORK trench. Reserve "D" Coy. Bn. Hd. Qrs. @ CIVIL Communication trench. N.B. Whilst the Bn. had been in Divisional Reserve a Regimental WET and DRY canteen was started.	
	2		Work on improvement of trenches and strong points. Quiet. Casualties 2 OR. wounded.	
	3		Work on improvement of trenches and strong points. Quiet.	
	4		Stores and ammunition carried into strong points. Hostile aeroplane flew low over our lines about 1.0 p.m. and fired on. Quiet. Relieved during afternoon by 9th Bn. West Riding Regt. and Bn. moved via Communication trenches and CAM valley to Ry. Cutting at H.4.D. (Ref. map 51 B NW) which it reached in Brigade Reserve.	
	5		In Brigade Reserve. Raid practised. 15 O.R. reinforcements joined Bn. from Div. Depot Bn.	
	6		In Brigade Reserve. Major R.V.L. DALLAS acting 2nd in Command of the Bn. accidentally injured through his horse falling down, causing him to strike the ground with his head. Major E.R. THOMPSON took over the duties of 2nd in Command of Bn. (Lieut. Sir Charles Sergeason Birt Commander and G.O.C. 14th Artillery attended the practise during afternoon at 2.30 p.m. Raid practised. Third Army commander (General BYNG) XVII Corps and Divisional Commander present during practise Raid in the afternoon. 2nd. Lieut. R. JENNISON accidentally injured whilst riding his horse. 1 Casualty. 2nd. Lieut. H.R. COOK killed.	
	7			
	8		Move up at 3.0 p.m. into GAVRELLE Switch in Brigade Reserve to left subsector of GREENLAND HILL Sector (CONRAD and COLIN trenches). Bn. raid junction of WIT and WOOL trenches opposite front line trenches (CONRAD and COLIN trenches) S. of	

A8734. Wt. W.4973/M687 750,000 8/16 D.D.&L.Ltd. Forms/C.2118/13.

WAR DIARY
INTELLIGENCE SUMMARY

Army Form C. 2118.

2/W. Manchester

Place	Date	Hour	Summary of Events and Information	Remarks and references to Appendices
In the Field	Sept 1914 (cont) 8		GAVRELLE at 10-0 P.M. Our barrage provided by artillery. Major E.R. THOMPSON 96 rank and 8 officers (2/W. Bays) and 2/Lt. O.R. took part in raid and all 8 detachment 1 Officer and 15. O.R. of 93rd Field Coy. R.E. for destroying dugouts, M.G.s, and hostile Trench Mortars) – Total Major E.R. THOMPSON 99 officers and 245 O.R. Raid had to last 25 minutes at most and object was to harden, kill and obtain identification – Recall signal – golden rain rocket – at ZERO + 25 minutes. Extent 100 yds. of WIT on either side of junction WIT and WOOL trenches and WOOL to just E. of North and South arms of WOOL trench. 1. 2. A + 3 + 5. (Ref. PLOUVAIN map 1/10,000) (See also attached orders and map attached to operation orders under 1st Sept.) Bn. Hd. Qrs. in CORK support. (Advanced Hd. Qrs. at junction CONRAD and COLIN. Raid only partially successful, the raiding parties reaching WIT successfully but failing to pierce WOOL the desired distance and our right flank shot at direction Prisoners captured - 3 of the 31st Infantry Regt., 238th Div. showing no enemy change of front on our front. Our barrage was very good and enemy wire cut. Only 3 hostile M.G.s were troublesome. Enemy artillery retaliated about 10.1 till 11.8 P.M. on CORK, CURSE and CIVIL and CALEDONIAN communication trenches. Capt. T.H. DIXON rejoined Bn. at Echelon B from Hospital. Our casualties Capt. J.T. BROMLEY (96/A Coy) wounded and missing, O.R. 4 killed, 4 missing (including believed killed and 1 wounded and missing) and 20 wounded.	
	9.		In left Brigade Reserve (GAVRELLE Switch). Quiet. O.R. 100 provided during evening and night on working parties.	
	10.		In left Brigade Reserve. Quiet. Off. 1, O.R. 220 detailed for working parties at night. 2nd Lieut. R. STODDART joined Bn. from Base Bn.	
	11		In left Brigade Support. Quiet. Off. 4, O.R. 260 detailed for working parties at night.	
	12.		In Brigade Support. The Bn. having asked permission to interrupt the raid a second time, plans were carried on with. Relieved 9th Bn. West Riding Regt. in left subsector during afternoon.	

Army Form C. 2118.

WAR DIARY
or
INTELLIGENCE SUMMARY.
(Erase heading not required.)

Instructions regarding War Diaries and Intelligence Summaries are contained in F.S. Regs., Part II. and the Staff Manual respectively. Title pages will be prepared in manuscript.

1st Manchester

Place	Date	Hour	Summary of Events and Information	Remarks and references to Appendices
In the field	Sept. 12 1914 (contd)		Dispositions:- Front line. 'A' Coy right, 'B' Coy centre, 'C' Coy left. Reserve D Coy. Quiet. Work on improving trenches. Japs in enemy wire fired on by L.Gs. and M.Gs. during night. Brigade reported bodies enemy seen moving in wire about 4.30 P.M.	
	13.		In left subsector 11.38 A.M. one of our aeroplanes belonging to 43rd Squadron R.F.C. hit by enemy Anti-Aircraft shell and fell by our support line near CHIPS Alley in the open. Bodies of the Pilot and Observer (2nd Lieut. F. MARSHALL-LEWIS and Capt. S. RICKARDS respectively) were brought in by 2nd Lieut. F. HUDSON (attached) and taken to the rear for burial. Hostile aircraft active and much enemy movements just before dusk, which together with reported movement of preceding night pointed to probability of enemy relief in progress. Brigade artillery were informed of movement and fired on places directed about 8.O.P.M. Enemy artillery quiet.	
	14.		Work on improvement of line continued. Japs in enemy wire fired on by our L.Gs. and M.Gs. Coils of wire to repair gap made for the raid on 10th observed on 12th and 13th on enemy's parapet. Quiet. Relieved by 9th Bn. West Riding Regt during morning. (8.0 A.M. to 10.O.A.M.). Bn moved into left Brigade Support in GAVRELLE switch where dinners were taken. During afternoon parties for raid and Bn. Hd. Qrs. started moving from GAVRELLE switch to Ry Cutting gap before. Remainder of Bn. including Intelligence Officer (who was to supervise laying tape for marking jumping off point for raid on 16th) stayed at GAVRELLE switch. Raid practised near Ry cutting at dusk. Work carried on by parties in GAVRELLE switch.	
	15.		In Brigade Support as above. Quiet. Raid practised in morning (when Coys and Bn Hd Qrs moved up) and at night. Rations were sent up to all units at night for consumption 16th and 17th (no limbers being allowed to go towards front line trenches night 16th). In Brigade Support as above. Church Parade during morning. Parties in Ry cutting and	
	16.		to GAVRELLE Switch between 2.0 and 3.0 P.M.	

Army Form C. 2118.

WAR DIARY
OF
INTELLIGENCE SUMMARY.
(Erase heading not required.)

Instructions regarding War Diaries and Intelligence Summaries are contained in F. S. Regs., Part II. and the Staff Manual respectively. Title pages will be prepared in manuscript.

Place	Date 1916	Hour	Summary of Events and Information	Remarks and references to Appendices
In the Field	Sept. 17		The raid was carried out at 12.0 midnight 16/17th after attached orders, and was a complete success (see attached copy of report on raid). 2 M.Gs. captured, 6 dugouts and 2 saps blown up and 4 prisoners captured (1 of 2nd Supenburg (Regt)). Information obtained from prisoners that Capt. J.T. BROMLEY was captured (slightly wounded) might 8th/9th; and also 2. O.R. Five of our dead men were also seen in no mans land thus accounting for all the missing men in the previous raids on 8/9/16. Quiet during morning after raid over. Airplane flew low over our lines about 2.40 P.M. During afternoon enemy bombarded communication trenches N.E. of our position. Congratulatory wires and letter received from C. in C. at G.H.Q, Army Corps, Div. and Brigade Commanders (copies attached). Relieved after dark by the 10th Bn. West Yorks. and moved to GRIMSBY Camp. ST. NICHOLAS.. Divisional Reserve. Casualties on raid: Major E.R. THOMPSON and 2nd Lieut. M. RAESIDE wounded and remaining at duty. Capt. O. PECKHARD wounded. O.R. 6 Killed, 24 wounded (including those remaining at duty).	
	18.		In Divisional Reserve. Baths allotted to Bn. and men cleaned up and deficiencies made up for.	
	19.		Bn. inspected by G.O.C. 14th Division at 10.0 a.m. and congratulated. C.S.M. MILLS, J. granted D.C.M. No parade after the General's inspection.	
	20.		In Divisional Reserve. Training carried out. Major G.T. WILKES of the 4th Bn. East Surrey Regt. was posted to and took over duties of 2nd in Command of Bn.	
	21.		In Divisional Reserve. Training carried out.	
	22.		Bn. moved off from ST. NICHOLAS Camp at 10.40 a.m. for HAUTEVILLE near AVESNES LE COMTE in the XVII Corps Rest Area. Bn. arrived at billets in HAUTEVILLE by 4.40 P.M.	

Army Form C. 2118.

WAR DIARY
INTELLIGENCE SUMMARY
(Erase heading not required.)

12th Manchesters

Place	Date 1917	Hour	Summary of Events and Information	Remarks and references to Appendices
Hauteville	Sept. 23		In Rest billets HAUTEVILLE. Church Parade held. Bn. rested and cleaned up etc. 2nd Lieut. F. HUDSON (attached) 4th Border Regt. was transferred and posted to Bn. Lieut. L.L. BOARDMAN sick to Hospital.	
	24		In Rest billets HAUTEVILLE. Training. A draft of 4 Officers and 125 O.R. from the 1st. D.L.O.Y. and another of 59 O.R. from Manchester Regt. joined Bn. The title of the Bn. from this date ceases to be the 12th Bn. Manchester Regt. and has been changed to 12th (D.L.O.Y.) Bn. Manchester Regt.	
	25		In Rest billets at HAUTEVILLE. Training. A draft from Div. Depot Bn. of 63 O.R. belonging to the Manchester Regt. joined Bn. At 4.0 P.M. all three drafts that arrived dr'd 24th were inspected and addressed by G.O.C. 52nd. Brigade.	
	26.		Bn. marched from rest billets at HAUTEVILLE started out at 4.0 A.M. to BREVILLERS to commence training.	
	27.		In billets at BREVILLERS. Training.	
	28.		In billets at BREVILLERS. Draft of 220 O.R. (3 Manchester Regt. and 19 D.L.O.Y.) joined Bn.	
	29		In billets at BREVILLERS. Training and baths.	
	30		In billets at BREVILLERS. Church Parade held.	

Remarks. Following joined Bn. D.L.O. Yeomanry :- Maj. N.E.R. Regt. Capts. T/S PIRRAT, J. Grenwell, 2/Lt. H. JAMIESON, H. DENNIS, WATERS, M. GRAY HILL. 2/Lts E. MARSH Hopton & 2 S.G.M. men & 10 men from Bn DCM [...] [...] Lieut. Col. Commanding 12th (D.L.O.Y.) Bn. Manchester Regt.

WAR DIARY
17/9/17

SECRET   Copy No. 2

Ref Maps.   12TH MANCHESTER REGT. OPERATION ORDER No.3.
17th Div Map   **
E.1, No.5, part 1
1/2,500,
(revised) and   14th September 1917.
GREENLAND HILL
1/10,000

INTENTION   12th Bn. Manchester Regt will furnish a party
1.   which will raid the enemy trenches opposite I.1/2, I.1/3
                on the night of 16/17th Sept. 1917. Zero hour will be
                notified later.
                                                          99.22
OBJECTIVE   WIT TRENCH from I.2.C.1.7. to I.1.B.   and
2.   WOOL TRENCH as far Eastwards as I.2.A.48.15. including
                two trenches which branch off from WOOL and are called
                respectively the NORTHERN ARM and the SOUTHERN ARM. as far South
                as I 2.C.6.9.

OBJECT OF   (a) To kill and to secure identifications.
RAID.   (b) Destruction of M.G's, T.M's, and dugouts in WIT.
3.   (c) Destruction of M.G's T.M's and Dugouts in WOOL and
                    its Arms.

DETAIL   (a) O.C.Raid Major E.R.Thompson.
4.   (b) For attack on WIT :-
                    A.Coy 2 Offrs. 50 O.R., attached 2 sappers R.E.
                    B.Coy.2 Offrs. 50 O.R., attached 2 sappers R.E.
                (c) For attack on WOOL and its Northern Arm :-
                    WOOL C.Coy(1 Offr. 30 O.R. attached 2 sappers R.E.
                    N.Arm.   (1 Offr. 30 O.R. attd. 1.offr.6.sappers R.E.
                (d) For attack on Southern Arm :-
                    D.Coy. 2 offrs. 50 O.R. attached 3 sappers R.E.

                Total.   9.offrs. 210 O.R. Attd. 1 offr. 15 O.R. R.E.

DRESS.   Drill Order (Belt, Bayonet and Scabbard and
5.   Rifle) with steel helmets and Box respirators.
                    Officers will wear two white bands on each arm
                and will carry a revolver and 12 rounds.
                    Other leaders will wear one white band on each
                arm.
                    All ranks will wear a white bow with dangling
                ends on each shoulder strap.
                    Searchers will wear a broad white band on right
                arm and will carry a sandbag in which to carry away
                documents etc.
                    Each searcher will carry a pocket torch, so also
                will all officers and as many other leaders as can be
                provided with them.
                    It must be a particular point of honour with all
                ranks that they carry with them no papers or letters
                that can afford any information to the enemy in the
                event of their falling into his hands. All such
                articles and any others will be left behind in safe
                keeping under Company Arrangements. O.C. Companies will
                render a certificate by 5.pm on 16th inst that all ranks
                of the raining party have surrendered all maps, letters,
                documents etc. likely to be of use to the enemy.

(2).

AMMUNITION.
6.

30 rounds per man viz - 9 in the magazine, 1 in the chamber and & chargers in the Right jacket pocket.

All ranks will carry one Mills No.23 bomb in the Left Jacket pocket.

Lewis Gunners will carry one drum each in addition to their other weapons.

Bombers and Rifle Bombers will carry 8 Mills No.23 each and Bombing sections will each carry 6 buckets.

PLAN OF ACTION
7.

artillery
A standing/barrage will be put down at zero as follows:-

(a) WIT
(b) WIBBLE
(c) WOOL between WIT and WIBBLE.
(d) NORTHERN ARM.
(e) SOUTHERN ARM.

At zero plus 1 the barrage will lift off WIT to the line of the Northern Arm.

At zero plus 4 - lift to the line of the Southern Arm.

At zero plus 6 - lift to the line of WIBBLE.

The barrage on WOOL conforming to these lifts

Other artillery co-operation and action by T.M's and Stokes batteries and M.G'Coys. have been arranged.

The Raiding party will be in position in No Man's Land close to the British wire at Zero minus 5 minutes ready to advance.

Formation - Two lines of sections; the first in extended order at 2 paces interval, the second in lines of sections in file.

The first line will move forward at zero and rush WIT establishing bombing stops in the trench and Lewis gun stops above ground on both flanks.

One L.G. will be pushed forward into No Man's Land on each flank, midway between I.1/3, I.1/2 and WIT TRENCH at zero hour and will remain there as a flank guard during the operations.

The second line, consisting of parties detailed to raid WOOL and the two arms, will follow the first line at a distance of 20 paces, cross over WIT, deploy immediately after crossing WIT and proceed to their objectives.

WOOL party will raid along both banks of the trench as far as I.2.A.48.15. with a bombing party inside, and will establish a stop as soon as possible at I.2.A.48.15, unless the Southern Arm party has got there first, and put out the stop.

The Northern and Southern Arm parties will go direct to their objectives above ground moving parallel to WOOL. The Southern Arm party will put a bombing stop in WOOL at I.2.A.48.15 unless the WOOL party gets there first, and also establish a Stop in the Southern Arm at I.2.A.6.9.

INSTRUCTIONS FOR R.E. PERSONNEL.
8.

The R.E. personnel attached will destroy T.M's, T.M.emplacements, deep dugouts, and chains preventing the removal of M.G's. or destroy the M.G's. themselves in their emplacements.

(3)

SEARCHERS
9.

One man will be detailed in each section to act as searcher, and will be allocated in the first instance to a particular dugout in his objective. His role will be rapidly to search through the pockets of any enemy killed for papers, pay books etc., to search dugouts for documents and to secure shoulder straps for identification purposes.

They will each wear a broad white band on the Right Arm, will carry a sandbag slung by a strap and sling across the shoulder and also a pocket torch, and a sharp knife for cutting off Shoulder straps. If a searcher should become a casualty another man must immediately replace him securing the bag.

TIMEKEEPERS.
10.

Officers or N.C.O's commanding a party must have a timekeeper, whose important duty it will be to keep his Commander posted as to the passing of the time and who will act as his observer. He will keep special lookout for, and notify immediately the recall signal. If he becomes a casualty another man must at once take his place.

REPORTING PROGRESS.
11.

On reaching the objectives, and at other times if there is anything of vital importance to report, O.C Companies will notify the O.C.Raid by runner.

WITHDRAWAL.
12.

BLUE Rockets will be fired from Advanced Battn. H.Q. and from the position of O.C. Raid at zero plus 25 minutes as a recall signal.

The raiding parties will not withdraw before zero plus 25 minutes and will return in the order:- Southern Arm party - WOOL party - Northern Arm party - WIT party. The Wit party will remain in possession of enemy trench until all other parties have passed through and have been given time nearly to reach our lines.

Prisoners taken from WIT and N. Arm will be sent at once to Battalion Headquarters and handed over to an escort of the West Riding Regt. Prisoners taken in the S.Arm will be brought back when the raiding parties return.

In the event of any enemy M.G's being captured or any other bulky article they will be sent to the nearest Company Headquarters in the line.

Machine guns Must be brought out of the enemy line if possible, at any rate into No. Mans Land, when at the worst there will be a chance of salvaging them later on.

On return to our trenches parties will proceed forthwith to the reassembly points in the GAVRELLE SWITCH, where reports will be taken under Battalion arrangements. Company Commanders will as far as possible get preliminary reports from their parties and report to Advanced Battalion Headquarters on their way back to the reassembly point.

FIRST AID POST.
13.

A First Aid Post will be established at I.1.C.52.35.

REPORTS.

Advanced Battalion Headquarters will be at I.1.A.50.45. from zero minus one hour to zero plus one hour. Headquarters of O.C.Raid will be at I.1.D.75.95. during the same period.

Copy No.1 to Office
    2 to War Diary.
    3 to Bde H.Q.
    4 to O.C.Raid.
    5 to O.C.A.Coy.
    No.6 to O.C.B.Coy.
    7 to O.C.C.Coy
    8 to O.C.D.Coy.
    9 to R.E.Officer Attd.
    10 to spare.

(Sd)T.W.BULLOCK, Lt.Col.,
Commanding 12th Bn. Manchester Regt.

WAR DIARY
17/9/17

SECRET.

COPY No. 9

WAR DIARY
8/9/17

12th Manchester Regt Operation Order
No. 1 is cancelled and the following substituted:-

OPERATION ORDER No.1.

Ref .maps
17th Div Map
E.1.No.5. part 1
1/2,500. dated
29/8/17. and
GREENLAND HILL 1/10,000

7th September 1917.

INTENTION
1.
12th Bn. Manchester Regt will furnish a party which will raid the enemy trenches opposite I.1/2 - I.1/3 on the night of 8/9th Sept. 1917. Zero hour will be notified in due course.

OBJECTIVE
2.
WIT TRENCH from I.2.C.18.80 to I.1.B.99.22. and WOOL TRENCH as far Eastwards as I.2.A.43.15 including two trenches which branch off from WOOL and are called respectively the NORTHERN ARM and the SOUTHERN ARM.

OBJECT OF RAID.
3.
(a) To kill and to secure identifications.
(b) Destruction of M.G's T.M's and dugouts in WIT
(c) Destruction of M.G's. T.M.'s and Dugouts in WOOL and its Arms.

DETAIL.
4.
(a) O.C. Raid Major E.R. Thompson.
(b) For attack on WIT:
A. Coy 2 officers 50 O.R. attached 2 sappers R.E.
B. Coy 2 officers 50 O.R. " 2 sappers R.E.
(c) For attack on WOOL and its Northern Arm

WOOL) C .Coy. (1 Offr. 40 O.R. attached 1 Offr.
N.Arm.) 6 sappers R.E.
(1 offr. 30 O.R. attached 2 sappers R.E.
(d) For attack on Southern Arm
D.Coy 2 offrs 50 O.R. attached 3 sappers R.E.

TOTAL. 9 offrs. 220 O.R. Attd. 1 offr. 15 O.R
R.E.

DRESS.
5.
Drill Order (Belt and bayonet and scabbard and rifle) with steel helmets and box respirators.
Officers will wear two white bands on each arm and will carry revolver and 12 rounds
Other leaders will wear one white band on each arm.
All ranks will wear a white bow with dangling ends on each shoulder strap.
Searchers will wear a broad white band on right arm and will carry a sandbag in which to carry away documents etc.
Each searcher will carry a pocket torch, so also will all officers and as many other leaders as can be provided with them.
It must be a particular point of honour with all ranks that they carry with them no papers or letters that can afford any information to the enemy in the event of their falling into his hands. All such articles and any others will be left behind in safe keeping under company arrangements. O.C. Companies will render a certificate by 5.pm on 8th inst that all ranks of the raiding party have surrendered all maps letters, documents etc. likely to be of use to the enemy

AMMUNITION. 6.	30 rounds per man viz - 9 in the magazine, 1 in the chamber and 4 chargers in the right jacket pocket.
All ranks will carry one Mills No. 23 Bomb in Left jacket pocket.
Lewis Gunners will carry one drum each in addition to their other weapons.
Bombers and Rifle bombers will carry 8 Mills No.23. each.
PLAN OF ACTION. 7.	Artillery barrages will be put down at zero as follows:-

    (a) WIT.   )
    (b) WIBBLE.   ) STANDING
    (c) WOOL between WIT and WIBBLE.)
    (d) NORTHERN ARM.   ) BARRAGE.
    (e) SOUTHERN ARM.   )

    (f) NO MAN'S LAND advancing   ) CREEPING
        through WIT as far as WIBBLE) BARRAGE.

When the creeper leaves WIT a flanking barrage will be put down on each flank of the objective. at Zero
    Other Artillery co-operation and action by T.M's. and Stokes Batteries and M.G' Coys. have been arranged.
    The raiding party will be in position in No Man's Land close to British wire at Zero minus 5 minutes ready to advance.
    Formations - Two lines of sections; the first in extended order at 2 paces interval, the second in column.
    The first line will move forward at zero and get as close to the creeping barrage as possible the creeper will lift on to WIT at zero plus 2 mins. and the raiding party will move up towards WIT as far as possible. All barrage on WIT will lift at zero plus 3 minutes and the first line will then penetrate the enemy wire and rush WIT establishing bombing stops in the trench and Lewis Gun stops above ground on both flanks.

    The second line, consisting of parties detailed to raid WOOL and the two Arms will follow the first line at a distance of 20 paces, cross over WIT and proceed to their objectives.
    WOOL party will raid along both banks of the trench as far as I.2.A.43.15. with a bombing party inside, and will establish a stop as soon as possible at I.2.A.43.15. unless the Southern Arm party has got there first, and put out the stop.
    The Northern Arm and Southern Arm parties will go direct to their objectives above ground moving parallel to WOOL and each pushing out a small covering party Eastward of their objectives. The Southern Arm party will put a bombing stop in WOOL at I.2.A.43.15 unless the WOOl party gets there first.

INSTRUCTIONS FOR R.E. PERSONNEL. 8.	The R.E. Personnel attached will destroy T.M's, T.M.emplacements, Deep dugouts, and chains preventing the removal of M.G's. or destroy the M.G's themselves in their emplacements.
SEARCHERS 9.	One man will be detailed in each section to act as searcher. His role will be rapidly to search through the pockets of any enemy killed for papers pay books etc; to search dugouts for documents and to secure shoulder straps for identification purposes.

(3).

He will wear a broad white band on the Right Arm, will carry a sandbag slung by a strap and sling across the shoulder and also a pocket torch, and a sharp knife for cutting off shoulder straps. If he should become a casualty another man must immediately replace him securing the bag.

TIMEKEEPERS 10.

Each Commander either Officer or N.C.O. must have a timekeeper whose important duty it will be to keep his commander posted as to the passing of time and who will act as his observer. He will keep special lookout for, and notify immediately the recall signal. If he becomes a casualty another man must at once take his place.

Reporting Progress. 11.

On reaching the objectives and at other times if there is anything of vital importance to report O.C. Companies will notify O.C. Raid by runner.

WITHD-RAWAL 12.

The raiding parties will withdraw as soon as they have completed their tasks, in the order Southern Arm party, WOOL party, Northern Arm party, WIT party. The WIT party will remain in possession of enemy trench until all other parties have passed through and have nearly reached our lines.

Golden Rain Rockets will be fired from Advanced Battalion Headquarters and from position of O.C. Raid at Zero plus 25 minutes as a recall signal. On this parties will return to our lines in succession from the East if they have not already done so.

Prisoners will be brought at once to Battalion Headquarters and handed over to an escort of the 9th West Riding Regt.

In the event of any enemy M.G's being captured or any other bulky article they will be sent to the nearest Company Headquarters in the Line.

Machine Guns MUST be brought out of the enemy line if possible at any rate into No. Man's Land when at the worse there will be a chance of salvaging then later on.

On return to our trenches parties will proceed forthwith to their Company quarters in the GAVRELLE SWITCH where reports will be taken under battalion arrangements. Company Commanders will as far as possible get preliminary reports from their parties and notify O.C. Raid on return to our trenches.

FIRST AID POST. 13.

A First Aid Post will be established at I.1.C.50.45.

REPORTS. 14.

Advanced Battalion Headquarters will be at I.1.C.8.8. from zero minus one hour to zero plus one hour. Headquarters of O.C.Raid will be at I.1.D.75.95. during the same period.

Copy No 1 to Office.
    2 to Bde H.Q.
    3 to O.C. Raid.
    4 to O.C.A.Coy.
    5 to O.C.B.Coy.
    6 to O.C. C.Coy.
    7 to O.C.D.Coy.
    8 to R E. officer Attached.

(Sd) T.W.BULLOCK, Lt. Col.,
Commanding 12th Bn. Manchester Regt.

WAR DIARY
8/9/17

Third Army No. G.12/114.
XVII Corps No. G.25/10.

III Corps.
IV Corps.
VI Corps.
VII Corps.
XVII Corps.
4th Cavalry Division.
G.O.C., R.A.
3rd Bde., R.F.C.
O.C. Spec. Co's R.E.
Third Army Infantry School.
Third Army Musketry Camp.

Copy to 2nd Command
then Regtl file

"The Army Commander has the greatest pleasure in communicating the following message received from the Commander-in-Chief, and wishes to add his sincere congratulations to those who have prepared and carried out these successful enterprises."

"The Commander-in-Chief congratulates you and your troops on the repeated successes gained in your local operations which shew excellent spirit and skill. These successes help appreciably in the general plan."

For orders
RSC
20-9-17

(Sgd) Louis Vaughan.
Major General.
General Staff, Third Army.

13th September 1917.

2.

17th Division.
G. 557

50th Inf. Bde.
51st Inf. Bde.
52nd Inf. Bde.
C.R.A.
C.R.E.
A.D.M.S.
Signals.

H.Q.
52ND INFANTRY BDE.
529
3728

17th September 1917.

"For communication to the troops under your command".

P B O'Connor
Major G.S.
17th Div d on.

Copy to :-
'Q'
17th Div. Dep. Bn.

"C" Form (Original).   Army Form C. 2123.
(In books of 50's in duplicate.)
MESSAGES AND SIGNALS. No. of Message..........

Prefix.... Code.... Words....	Received From..........	Sent, or sent out At........m.	Office Stamp.
£ s. d.			
Charges to collect	By..........	To..........	
Service Instructions. *fullerphone*		By..........	

Handed in at **WB19**   Office 5.30 m.   Received 5.40 m.

TO **UD10**

| Sender's Number | Day of Month | In reply to Number | AAA |
| BM19 | 17/9 | | |

ROUND wire begins following message received from corps commander aaa many congratulations to you all for successful raids last night by ROSE and RENOWN aaa they deserve great credit for their enterprise and dash

FROM PLACE & TIME **UB19 5.30 PM**

File
Reg Hole

(1086) Wt.W16552/M1615 250,000 Pads. 21/3/17. J.R.&C. E/685 Forms/C2122/6.

"B" Form. Army Form C2122 (In pads of 150)

MESSAGES AND SIGNALS. No. of Message......

Prefix SM Code ID m.	Received At 9.27 p.m.	Sent At ......m.	Office Stamp
Office of Origin and Service Instructions. UB19	Words 29 From UB19 By Carlton	At ......m. To ...... By	UD10 17/9/17

TO	UD10		

Sender's Number. BM34	Day of Month. 17	In reply to Number.	AAA
Barbed	wire	begins	aaa
following	from	army	commander
aaa			
Please	congratulate	RENOWN	and
ROSE	on	their	successful
raids	last	night	aaa
Ends.			

From	UB19	
Place		
Time	9.20 p.m.	

* This line should be erased if not required.

(2)

the raid forming up was an intricate and laborious task, carried out under intermittent rifle and m/gun fire. It was successfully accomplished by zero minus 90 minutes, after several hours work on previous evenings. Upon the correctness of the taping of the forming up ground depended the successful direction of the attack.

Troops were in position on the tapes and ready to start, at ZERO minus 7 minutes.

At ZERO barrage opened on WIT and other places, and the first line advanced, at a stepping out pace quickening to a rush as WIT was neared. There was not much opposition. One light machine gun was captured, with its gunners, near junction of WIT and WOOL. A Coy bombing stop worked to its South according to orders and succeeded in capturing a light machine gun from a beaten emplacement about I 2 C 1.7. This was a most fortunate capture, for the machine gunners were firing about in the neighbourhood, and would have decimated the raiders on their return if this gun had not been secured, a minute or two before withdrawal.

The second line — D Coy on the right and B Coy on the left — followed the first line at a short distance. Owing to smoke and dust, the electric light signal

(3)

arranged to be shewn from the junction of WIT and WOOL by special men in the first line was not seen by the centre party of the second line, whose role it was to explore WOOL. This party struck WIT some 30ˣ too much to the North. ~~The Commander~~ Capt. HYNE crossed over WIT with this party and bearing half right got into WOOL east of the junction a little bit later than might have been and worked Eastward until the objective was reached. No opposition was met. If this party had been able to hit the junction of WIT & WOOL direct they might have been in time to head off and kill or capture some 20 enemy whom another party saw running Eastwards along WOOL.

The Northern Arm party crossed WIT extended at once from single file to 2 paces extension and moved to the attack of North Arm. Wire interfered. One section therefore filed into WOOL and out again behind the wire, the other hunted for and found a gap. The whole reached Northern Arm just after the barrage on it lifted. No opposition. No trench mortar emplacements or TMs found. Four large dugouts found and one machine gun (light) which was brought away ~~but of~~ which there is now no trace. The enemy refused to come up from his dugouts so they were destroyed.

(4)

The Southern Arm party reached its objective without difficulty just after the barrage on it lifted. The left section of the party opened rifle fire on a party of 20 Germans running eastwards in WOOD between Northern & Southern Arms.

No TMS or emplacements were found in Southern Arm. No opposition. Enemy would not leave his dug outs of which one was found with two shafts and several glorified cubby-holes. Remains of one destroyed m/gun were found, and the condenser tube brought back. Presumably the m/g had been smashed by our gun fire. Enemy fired up shafts and made destruction difficult. It was P bombed and the top of the shafts blown in.

At Zero plus 25 minutes the recall signal was fired from our own places and the raiding party returned without incident.

4. Losses inflicted on enemy.

Four prisoners actually reached our lines. Three more are known to have started under escort for our lines, but were killed en route. One escaped in NO MANS LAND, his escort being wounded by m/g fire.

Apart from men supposed to have been

(5)

entombed and bombed in dug outs. 30 enemy are reported to have been killed by various individuals of 12th Manchester Rgt and two by the Sjt R.E. attached. From close inquiry I am satisfied that their statements are worthy of credence.

In Southern part of WIT a shaft was found with enemy in it who would not come out. It was bombed, and some Very lights were fired from the shaft. R.E. blew in the shaft with guncotton several steps down.

In Northern Arm the R.E. officer blew up one M.G. emplacement. The R.E. Sjt and others blew 4 shafts thoroughly. One was blown with twelve slabs of G/C placed 7 steps down. Four enemy were seen at the bottom of one shaft. They would not come up and were bombed. A dozen were estimated to be at the bottom of another shaft. A long passage on a level with the trench was found and set on fire with P Bombs. One dead German was in it.

In Southern Arm the R.E. blew up one shaft effectually, and P bombed the other and set it on fire. The O.C. Coy states there were 20 to 30 enemy in the dug out. None came up. Instead they opened fire up the shaft. There was much shouting and screaming when Mills Bombs were thrown down. The P bombs seem to have put an

(6)

to that. The R.E. party works at this front are said not to have had sufficient explosives, probably this casualties.

Summarizing losses inflicted on enemy and damage done —

(a) Killed, if the news claims are admitted about 30. Fifteen dead were actually seen.

(b) Entombed in ? Bombed dug-outs — 8 dug-outs at say six each 48 (conservative estimate.)

(c) Prisoners 4.

(d) Two machine guns actually brought in, and part of a smashed up third.

(e) Eight shafts known to have been blown in or set on fire, and one M.G. emplacement. This is apart from damage by gunfire.

5. Our casualties.

Our casualties occurred mostly in No MAN'S LAND. from shell or trench mortar fire.

Officers   1 wounded (sh, hd.)
              2 wounded and remaining at duty
Other ranks   5 killed
              1 Died of wounds
              23 Wounded
              4 wounded remaining at duty

(7)

6. General remarks

Our barrage was perfect.

WIT trench has steps cut in the parados at intervals of about 30 yards.

Northern and Southern arms are fire-stepped and are about 7 feet deep.

Three T.M's were observed firing from rear of WIBBLE by O.C. Coy in Southern Arm.

An officer got to WIBBLE at its junction with WOOL and found no sign of infantry there. He heard four m/g firing from WIBBLE. He did not remain there long. He was inside the barrage zone he says. Capt HYNE accompanied by S/L COX R.E.

A trench has been traced with tape for digging prolonging Northern Arm to the South.

The enemy Very lights assisted our attack.

7. Two lessons stand out from this operation — That our barrage has no terrors for those who have once been under it — and that there is difficulty in getting prisoners.

[signature]
O.C. 12 Manchester Regt.

(8)

8. I cannot close without reference to the co-operation of other units.

I feel that the work done by 2Lt THOMAS RE and the detachment from 93rd Fd Coy RE was done well and as thoroughly as circumstances permitted.

The assistance given by O.C. 9 (D of W) West Riding Regt has been invaluable. He has helped in every possible way. A party of his Bn under Capt HUNTRESS prepared lanes in our wire for the raiders to pass through, an arduous and dangerous task involving many hours work. If it had not been properly done the success of the raid would have been jeopardized.

Of the action of the R.A., T.M. and Stokes Batteries and the M.G. Companies, I speak with great respect. They are beyond praise.

Jno Rutland
Lt Col
Comdg 12 Manchester Regt

17/9/17

P.F.

XVII Corps No. G.'5/11.

The following memo. received by 17C.
17th. Division. Div is published for information

The following remarks, made by the Army Commander on your two raids of the night Sept. 16/17th., are forwarded for communication to the troops :-

"Two most successful and enterprising operations. The loss to the enemy is great in casualty and greater in moral. The conduct of all who took part is most commendable."

(sd) J.R.C.CHARLES,

H.Q., XVII Corps.
22nd. September, 1917.

Brigadier-General,
General Staff.

- 2 -

17th. Division.

G. 747

23rd. Septr., 1917.

51st. Inf. Bde.
52nd. Inf. Bde.
C. R. A.
C. R. E.

H.Q.
52ND INFANTRY BDE.
52 G
3780

Forwarded for communication to the troops concerned.

Major G.S.,
17th. Division.

Manch Regt

Passed to you

24/9/17

COPY.

17th. Division.

On the occasion of the Division leaving the XVII Corps, I wish to express to all ranks, my appreciation of the fine soldierly spirit which has been conspicuous in the Division during the last few months while serving on this front.

Its activity in patrolling, its keenness in Raids have both been admirable. But most conspicuous of all has been the splendid spirit shown in the work done in consolidating the line. In spite of weakness in numbers and the absence of the Pioneer Bn., the work done has been remarkable; showing not only excellent organisation on the part of the Staff, but also energy and zeal on the part of Regimental Officers and men. All ranks may be proud of their record in this respect, R.A. and R.E. as well as Infantry.

I wish goodbye, and good luck to all in the Division, with every confidence that they will fully maintain the reputation they have gained wherever their duty may call them.

(Sgd) CHARLES FERGUSON,
Lieutenant-General.,
Commanding, XVII Corps.

24-9-17.

17th. Division.
G.807.
25th. September 1917.

- 2 -

To all Units 17th. Division.

Forwarded for communication to all ranks.

Lieut.- Col.,
G.S., 17th. Division.

Lancashire Fusiliers.
West Riding Regt.
Royal West Kent Regt.
Manchester Regt.
Machine Gun Company.
Trench Mortar Battery.
93rd F.Coy. R.E.
D.T.M.O.

      The Brigadier General Commanding 52nd Infantry Brigade wishes to congratulate most heartily ALL RANKS of the 12th Manchester Regt and the Detachment 93rd F.Coy. R.E. on the success of their raid last night. The whole operation from start to finish ran in the very best military style, and reflects the greatest credit on the battalion and this detachment R.E.

      The work of the Divisional (Medium) Trench Mortar Battery and of the 52nd Light Trench Mortar Battery has been of the greatest benefit and assistance to this undertaking, for, by their whole hearted zeal and co-operation during the past fortnight in cutting the enemy's wire, etc what might have proved a formidable obstacle unconsciously seemed to disappear.

      The ~~batteries~~ barrage put down by the Batteries of the Divisional Artillery (who have been thanked in a separate letter) and also by the 52nd Machine Gun Company proved of inestimable benefit in making this operation a success.

      Battalions when in the Front Line System have also contributed in no small measure towards achieving these results by their continuous and efficient use of patrols and Lewis Gun detachments at night.

      In conclusion the Brigadier takes this opportunity of drawing attention to the manner in which by close co-operation between various Arms and Units , such excellent results have been achieved. He feels sure, too, that this will serve as an example and an incentive to the Brigade in carrying out whatever work it may be called upon to perform in the future.

17/9/17.

                    Captain,
                  a/Brigade Major,
                52nd Infantry Brigade.

WAR DIARY / INTELLIGENCE SUMMARY

Army Form C. 2118.

57/17/2 Manch C 25

Place	Date	Hour	Summary of Events and Information	Remarks and references to Appendices
In the Field	Oct 1917 3		12 K (D.C.O) Bn marches in. Bn. in billets at BREVILLERS. Training.	ref
	4		Bn. in billets at BREVILLERS. Training and firing on LUCHEUX Range.	at
			Bn. in billets at BREVILLERS. Training during morning. During afternoon resting preparatory to move. On night 4/5th inst. Bn. marched to MONDICOURT and entrained for PROVEN, BELGIUM at 1.32 a.m. 5th.	at
	5		Bn. arrived at PROVEN and marched to PERA Camp E.16.B.0.5. (Sheet 21 Belgium) Under XIV Corps, Fifth Army.	
	6/7		Bn. training at PERA Camp.	at
	8		Bn. training at PERA Camp. Reformed for Corps Depot moved to BOLLEZEELE.	at
	9		Bn. training at PERA Camp.	
	10		Bn. entrained at 2.0 p.m. at PROVEN, detraining at INTERNATIONAL CORNER A9A 1.5. for staying camps and occupied DRAGON II Camp A10C. (Ref. map 28. 1/40,000 BELGIUM and FRANCE. Bn. in Divisional Reserve under Tactical command 29th. Div. until commencement of Divisional front passed to G.O.C. 14th Division. Transport move to new camp by road.	at
	11.		Bn. training at DRAGON II Camp. In Divisional Reserve.	
	12.		Bn. at DRAGON II Camp. In Divisional Reserve. Attack resumed by XIV Corps (Guards 14th and 4th Divisions). Bn. moved at 2.30 p.m. to WHITE MILL Camp at ELVERDINGHE A.H.D. (Sheet 28. 1/40,000 BELGIUM and FRANCE). Bn. Depot formed and remained at DRAGON Camp. Casualty 1 O.R. wounded.	at
	13.		Bn. in Divisional Reserve, ELVERDINGHE.	at
	14.		Bn. in Divisional Reserve, ELVERDINGHE. Hostile aeroplanes bomb vicinity of camp, 1.30 p.m. Dix front line V.8.C.2.4. to V.1.C.2.8.	
	15.		Bn. in Divisional Reserve, ELVERDINGHE.	at

Army Form C. 2118.

WAR DIARY
of
INTELLIGENCE SUMMARY.
(Erase heading not required.)

Instructions regarding War Diaries and Intelligence Summaries are contained in F.S. Regs., Part II. and the Staff Manual respectively. Title pages will be prepared in manuscript.

Place	Date 1914	Hour	Summary of Events and Information	Remarks and references to Appendices
In the field	Oct. 10		Bn. in Divisional Reserve, ELVERDINGHE. Bn. marched to PARROY Camp B.I.b.9.5 (Ref. Sheet 28. 1/40,000) Division relieved by 3rd Division night 10/11th. Bn. remains for Pioneer work under orders C.E. XIV Corps. 6 casualties, 2 O.R. wounded.	
	14.		Bn. at PARROY Camp. Commenced work in forward area (near LANGEMARCK). During day in two reliefs of two Coys. each. Parties sent to R.E. & Field Ambulance whilst Division was in line rejoined Bn. 1 casualties, 3. O.R. wounded.	
	18.		Bn. at PARROY Camp. Work continued under XIV Corps. 11 Hostile Gotha aeroplanes and fighting planes as escorts, bombed vicinity of camp about 1-30 p.m. but driven off by Anti. Aircraft guns. Casualties 1, O.R. wounded.	
	19/20		Work under C.E. continued. Hostile aircraft active evening and early morning. Casualties (19th inst.) 3, O.R. killed, 6, O.R. wounded.	
	21		No working parties required by C.E. Hostile aircraft active evening and early morning.	
	22/23		Working parties under C.E. continued. Hostile aircraft active evening and early morning.	
			Brigade Depot personnel rejoined Bn. 23rd.	
	24.		Working parties under C.E. Hostile planes appeared at 1-0 a.m. but dispersed by A.A. guns.	
	25.		Working parties under C.E. Hostile aircraft active at night.	
	26.		Working parties under C.E. Bn. moved from PARROY Camp at 5-0 p.m. and entrained at BOESINGHE for INTERNATIONAL CORNER and proceeded to W. Camp AY.D.4.1 for night. Casualties 5, O.R. killed, 16. O.R. wounded (including 1, O.R. remaining at duty)	
	27.		Bn. moved from W. Camp to PROVEN Station at 6-0 a.m. and entrained for AUDRUICQ and proceeded from thence to billets at LUCHES. 2/Lt. BODDINGTON and 2nd Lt. HOLDRIDGE of D.L.O.Y. joined Bn.	
	28.		Bn. in billets at LUCHES. 60/70 Depot personnel and draft of 26, O.R. joined Bn. also 1 officer (un-informed)	
	29/31		Bn. training at LUCHES.	

T. Butler
Lieut. Col.
Commanding, 12th (S. of) R. Manchester Regt.

(2/Lt AH DIXON)

52/17
Vol 26

War Diary

of

12th (D.L.O.Y) Bn. Manchester Regt.

From 1st November 1917. To 30th November 1917.

(Volume XXIX)

Army Form C. 2118.

WAR DIARY
or
INTELLIGENCE SUMMARY.
(Erase heading not required.)

Place	Date 1914	Hour	Summary of Events and Information	Remarks and references to Appendices
In the Field	Nov. 3		Bn. in rest billets at LOUCHES. Training in attack practice. Reinforcements 24 O.R. arrived. Lieut. H. BUCKLEY M.C. rejoined from Hospital and took over duties of Intelligence Officer. No. 2 and Lieut. E. WINDER sent to Hospital same day.	
	4		In billets at LOUCHES.	
	5		In billets at LOUCHES. Brigade attack practice.	
	6		Bn. left LOUCHES at 5.4.30 a.m. and marched to AUDRUICQ, where entrained for ELVERDINGHE and marched to WOLFE Camp.	
	7		Bn. marched from WOLFE Camp ELVERDINGHE to RESERVE lines at HUDDLESTONE Camp. Working Parties, O.R. for R.E. HUDDLESTONE Camp at J.4.15.40. Scheldt B at B.23.b.	
	8		At HUDDLESTONE Camp.	
	9		Bn. moved from HUDDLESTONE Camp at 1.50 p.m. and relieved 6th Bn. Northumberland Fusiliers in front line from TURENIE Crossing VI.d.2.5. to GRAVEL Farm at WATERVLIETBEEK Stream. Front line, C Coy right, B Coy left. Sup. Coys A Coy (at TAUBE Farm). D Coy in Reserve at C.19 METRE HILL. Bn. H.Q. U.12a.2.0 in field (500 yds. N. of SCHAAP-BALIE 1/10000) Artillery active. Some casualties on relief. Heavy shelling. Killed by enemy at vicinity TRANQUILLE Farm about 11.30 a.m. A shell wounded all Coy M.O. and the Boy Officers. Colonel T. 1 Officer, 2nd. Lieut. S. JACKSON and 8 O.R. killed. 3 officers, 2nd. Lieut. J. THOMPSON, 2nd. Lieut. E.J. SUTER and 2nd. Lieut. A.H. DIXON, and 23 O.R. wounded; 1 officer, 2nd. Lieut. C.H. SNELL and 16 O.R. missing	
	10		Shortly after midnight 9th/10th a heavy barrage was put down by enemy in vicinity of GRAVEL Farm and No.9 Platoon, C Coy, holding GRAVEL Farm was attacked by the enemy and wiped out and the Farm captured. No. 12 Platoon came to extended order 3443 SW of CHATTERTON, C Coy was out-flanked to its Capt who led position. Our artillery active. Many aerial fighting. During the day increased by enemy, specially 5.45 a.m. when different Verylights thrown up by enemy. Germans he opened with all his guns. 20 hostile aeroplanes flew low and high. At 10 a.m. about 3 O.P. in which dropping two yellow lights, from which enemy shelled heavily. At night two Platoons were taken from A and D Coys (B near to GRAVEL Farm. Every man was also taken from D Coy to stiffen the line of C Coy, as with all C Coy Men we could not to send enemy to this withdrawal get it and not having stopped the advance and weakened. The Coy was to be to the one and last push was not Zone the attack which the Bn. 2/Platoon attacked from Col. Anck. J. came to DO midway R. The village was to guard.	

WAR DIARY or INTELLIGENCE SUMMARY

Army Form C. 2118.

(Erase heading not required.)

Place	Date 1917	Hour	Summary of Events and Information	Remarks and references to Appendices
In the Field	Nov 10 cont.		a barrage. At 11.0 p.m. orders C.O., 2/Lt, Col. T.W. BULLOCK was unfortunately displacing of the men for the attack. The barrage by a private gunner but the men were not ready. An attack was made to establish shortly after without a barrage but the enemy's M.G. opened over and owing to Artillery not opened as they attempt was abandoned. D. Coys. Platoon was left with 2 Coy. as a reinforcement (casualties) and reported attached. Casualties:- 1. O.R. killed, 23, O.R. wounded, 2. O.R. missing	
	11.		Hostile aircraft very active and firing with machine guns at small parties of our men. Henry Hostile artillery shelled frequently during day. Our artillery also. En. moved during the morning with support in new positions with A. Coy. in line of Support PURS S.V.T & 0.3. TAUBE FARM, SENEGAL FARM, STRING HOUSES. D Coy at MILLERS HOUSES in support and 2 Coys. B and C Coys. 9'd West (Ridge) under present command of 12 m R gunner. In hostile artillery active. Reported at J.13.a.6.2.5 and 19 METRE HILL. B and C. Coys were in Bn. Reserve at EAGLE Trench, SCHREIBOOM. Fm H.Q. at SOUVENIR HOUSE J/13.3.16 Casualties 4. O.R. wounded.	
	12.		Enemy sent a large number of garrelles over with machine gun in EAGLE trench from 3.0am to 4.0 p.m. during the morning hostile aircraft very active flying high & and very thick (absolutely). Several heavy casualty Rifle grenades near SOUVENIR HOUSE. Shelter B moved during day. At 7.0 p.m. Several heavy ones fell near SOUVENIR HOUSE and vicinity.	
		at 3.20.a.4.3.	Enemy opened with heavy bombardment at 3.0am and also dealt a very large number of the shell near EAGLE trench. Hostile aircraft active during today. All aiming above of our aircraft. We have 2 airwomen. Monday dropped by them and had been at dusk spread on by nicely waterline great. Pm. Relieved by 1/4 as orders Bn during of 55 in H.Q. Bn. B reddy B.m. moved to near BOESINGHE station which hostile and also give armed forces to the following. Casualties 3. O.R. wounded.	
	14.		Bn. entrained at BOESINGHE Station by train leaving 5.0 a.m. 7/4 INTERNATIONAL bornership, where Bn. marched to DRAGON Camp. Arr't. B.& B. (Ref. map 28 N.W.) Several dep of between hulls developed upon arrival and Camps owing to appalling condition of all waterlogged ground in the lines.	
15/16.		at DRAGON Camp	
	17. 18.		Bn. training at DRAGON Camp. Bn. (w/XIX Corps) Transferred to 2nd. Army.	
	19.		At DRAGON Camp. Church Parades. B Coy. sent forward during of Division Fatigue E.K. CANAL at C.13.d.3.3 /4/6 Permanent Bwn. Parking inside CRA. 1/4 Division on thuroughly spit. Training at DRAGON Camp. Pts. (400 B.B.m) arrived at 2.0 p.m. and Brigade Lighten at SOULT Camp, J23 a.1.1,	
	20.		Relieving 4'm Bn. Leicester Regt. Transport Arrived at R.M.H. Farm remained at B.20. a. 4.3.	
	21.		at SOULT Camp. Training at SOULT Camp.	
			At SOULT Camp. Working party 50, m. for Tunnel line.	

Army Form C. 2118.

WAR DIARY
of
INTELLIGENCE SUMMARY.

(Erase heading not required.)

Instructions regarding War Diaries and Intelligence Summaries are contained in F. S. Regs., Part II. and the Staff Manual respectively. Title pages will be prepared in manuscript.

Place	Date 1917	Hour	Summary of Events and Information	Remarks and references to Appendices
In the Field	Aug 22		At SOUT Camp. Working party 100 on aug. from 4/9 am to 3.0 p.m. at Brigade Cooks from STRAY Farm. C.3.4.3.7.	
	23.		At SOUT Camp. Also 50 m. for transport lines and 40 m. for Area Commandant SOUT Camp.	
			At SOUT Camp. Day made up of 100 on area fatigue, 5.6.39 and to CANDLE Street. C.7.8.2.3. Reg. map. 28 N.W. consisted of 30.6.17 afternoon working party at SCHREIBOOM area until relief by Signals. Working party 49 pm used to transport lines.	
	24.		At SOUT Camp. Working party 150 on work for west at CLAW and CANDLE Streets. C.3.4.3 plan 3.0 am till 3.0 p.m.	
			B. Coy working hard tonnes. Rn. Brigade relieved 10th Brigade and Bn. moved into Brigade Reserve at HUDDLESTONE Camp.	
	25.		D. Coy working hard tonnes. Rn.	
	26.		C.Y.a. 15.40 at 3.30 pm.	
			At Camp (above at HUDDLESTONE Camp.	
	27.		At HUDDLESTONE Camp. Working party (about 12 officers). 300 on. for work from CADDIE Bench near Camp.	
	28.		At HUDDLESTONE Camp. Rn. relieved 9th Bn. West Riding Regt. in Front Line.	
			Flank ring A, B and C Coys. D Coy in SOUVENIR HOUSE W.B.C. 3.6 (Ramji's) SCHAAFBALIE (10,000) 24/1050 Belt V.14.9.0. C. Coy AT MITRE HILL. Bn. M.Q. at GRAVEL FARM at N.28.0.9.0. Relief complete 9.15 pm. Two casualties during relief.	
			Bn. engaged in normal trench routine. During night 28/29 (Lieut.) Trulla received gunshot wounds in knee and back. He was evacuated to G.B.C.S. Lieut. J. Birchall wounded 3/0.	
	29.		Weather 24 hours very quiet. Only two messages during day	
			(4.30 pm, and 5 pm.) One from 2nd Army L.G. fired from all (guns not registered) in barrage from above 2.30 pm + about 3.30 pm. Much activity on	
			enemy lines. Work on (post made to 3 holes at one to bath from ½ coy. A (with relief from B and C) for estimating ½ coy of all, so and so night relief Capt. R. Burns (O.B. Lewis g) left in representative of Capt. Broke left wounded and M. G. Burns (B) and	
			the (ambulance) was sent up. About 6 an Capt. Banks Lt. Rag. Capt. Bhoure Capt. 2nd Bn. (and D) were sent out. All through day our went accounted 24 I.G.M.G. replied (for the enemy heavily (with activity)) before 5 am.	
	30.		During night 29/30 was very active. Many 'duds' noticed during night relief by 9th Bn. West Yorks. Relief commenced	
Aug 30.			11 p.m. All our normal trench activity was kept up. Relief completed about 4.40 am (sundown). Moved to YPRES -	
			STADEN railway. Our withdrawal was without incident. All units in area very quiet. During relief night 1st Army LG, 4 and 5.9. Band C were all quiet. The working on	
			Stencil was continued on tunnel of Kanary, ring 4 and 5.9. Band C Coys. carried out the work of removing from the Divisional Dump about half a million long rounds and about 500 yards	
			of barbed wire. During the afternoon, when the Cdg. was away and Rn.	
			Bn. was temporarily commanded by Major MO. R.B. (Capt.) landed at I. Tough Dives Qrs. at Enemy OP.	
			VANDYCK Farm. BELL Farm and BERNADOTTE Farm. Returned outpost observing the Enemy OP. in	
			Galloway, C.M. Amended hypoid a OLGA HOUSES.	

J.G. King Hay [signature] C.C. commanding 12th Bn. D.L.O.Y West Yorkshire Regt.

Army Form C. 2118.

WAR DIARY
of
INTELLIGENCE SUMMARY.
(Erase heading not required.)

Instructions regarding War Diaries and Intelligence Summaries are contained in F.S. Regs., Part II. and the Staff Manual respectively. Title pages will be prepared in manuscript.

Place	Date 1916	Hour	Summary of Events and Information	Remarks and references to Appendices
In the field	Dec 1		Hostile artillery quiet except for intermittent shelling of 19 METRE HILL especially between 6.0 a.m. and 8 a.m. Our artillery normal. Some hostile aircraft flew low over our lines. Bn. returned during evening by W.D. Light.	
	2.		Regt and moved to BOESINGHE where hot meal was provided prior to entraining. Cavalry 'B' Sqn. arrived. Bn. entrained at BOESINGHE by train leaving 3.30 a.m. for INTERNATIONAL CORNER from where Bn. marched to DRAGON Camp (Divisional Reserve) arriving 5.0 a.m. Bn. rested and cleaned up.	M
	3.		In Divisional Reserve - DRAGON Camp.	BM
	4.		At DRAGON camp. Training. Re-equipping carried out.	BM
	5.		Bn. moved from Divisional Reserve (LANGEMARCK III area) to PETWORTH Camp, X 25 d 2 y, near PROVEN, (PROOSDY area) Ref. map. 19 S.E. Brigade marched as one unit and Bn. passed Bde starting point INTERNATIONAL CORNER (Ref. map, sheet 28 N.W. Ed. 6A) at 9.30 a.m., leaving DRAGON camp at 9.10 a.m. Transport moved under Bde T.O. separately. Dinners were taken on arrival at new camp.	M
	6.		At PETWORTH Camp. Training - Bde Route march.	BM
	7.		1 Limber and Officers chargers proceeded at 8.30 a.m. by road to billets at LOCHES under Transport Officer. Bn. moved by train at 3.8 p.m. from PROVEN for AUDRUICQ, arriving billets at 9.0 p.m.	BM
	8.		At PETWORTH Camp. Bn. moved by route march to billets at LOCHES. Brokers, Mess Cart, Officers chargers &c. left with Bn. the following. Bn. to LOCHES in 9.0 p.m. train from PROVEN.	
	9.10.		Training at LOCHES.	
	11.		Training at LOCHES. Division held under 12 hrs notice to move.	BM
	12.		Bn. marched to billets at HOULLE (LA PLACE) leaving LOCHES at 9.0 a.m. Capt. D.F. HYNE and 12 O.R. reinforcements joined Bn.	BM
	13.		Training at HOULLE. Division ordered to move at 12 hrs notice. 'B' Coy sent forward to ARQUES station as entraining boy to Brigade.	BM
	14.		Bn. left HOULLE at 10.30 p.m. for ARQUES Station near St OMER for entraining.	M
	15.		Bn. and transport entrained at ARQUES Station by 3.24 a.m. train, arriving MIRAMONT 11.30 a.m. and marched to HENAM SOUTH Camp 300 yards W. of ACHIET-LE-PETIT no bird. Dummy area.	M
	16.		At HENAM SOUTH Camp, Division in 5th. Army Reserve ready to move at 2 hrs notice if required.	M

Army Form C. 2118.

Instructions regarding War Diaries and Intelligence
Summaries are contained in F. S. Regs., Part II.
and the Staff Manual respectively. Title pages
will be prepared in manuscript.

WAR DIARY
or
INTELLIGENCE SUMMARY.
(Erase heading not required.)

Place	Date	Hour	Summary of Events and Information	Remarks and references to Appendices
In the field	1917 Feb. (contd)			
	14-20		Bn. moved by route march at 12.5 p.m. to ROCQUIGNY. Training at ROCQUIGNY Camp.	M
	21.		At ROCQUIGNY Camp. Bn. with 4 Coys. Watercarts and L.G. Limbers marched to old British front line trenches at Q3a and Q3c at 1.45 p.m. relieving 10th Sherwood Foresters & became support to 59th Division on V Corps front (Ref. map 57° 1/40,000)	M
	22.		Q.M. Stores and Transport moved from ROCQUIGNY Camp to BERTINCOURT. Bn. moved at 3.45 p.m. and relieved 5th Leicester Regt (174th Inf. Bde.) in right Bde. support in HINDENBURG support line. 50th FLESQUIERES "B" Coy in front and "C", "A" and "D" Coys in rear. Relief completed 6.0 p.m. No casualties during relief. But my planes more active than for previous week owing to mist having cleared and bright moonlight. Third frost.	M
	23.		Situation quiet. Normal shelling of FLESQUIERES and neighbourhood. Working parties 15 OR detached to 93rd Field Coy R.E. and 49 OR working in 8hr shifts with 258th Tunnelling Coy on dug-outs in HINDENBURG support line. Coys engaged taking German wire and transferring it to our side of trench also renewing fire-step and similar improvements.	M
	24.		2.45 a.m. to 5.0 a.m. orbit heavy gas-shell bombardment by enemy all along our line and behind, and H.E. Barrage during the same time. This was neutralised effectively by our artillery. Bn. stands to in (But Confederation) this whole time. Working parties as on 23rd. Casualty 1 OR wounded (shell gas)	M P.S.
	25.		During night 24/25 enemy hostile shelling enemy's shells were particularly in the morning. Snowfell in the evening. Working with 3 OR under 258 Tunng Coy. Reinforcements 1 offr 9 OR. Relieving Regt. in right sector of the field line 25/24th. Casualty 1, OR wounded (effects of gas-shell bombardment 24th)	M
	26.		1 in sup. No hostile aeroplanes active. 2nd Lieut. R. STODDARD appointed T.O. in succession to 2nd Lieut. R. STODDARD appointed I.C. Relief cancelled and warning received for Brigade to be relieved by 55th Brigade night 24/28th. Casualties 2 OR wounded by shell fire.	M
	27.		Situation quiet. Bn. relieved by 6th Bn. Dorset Regt and proceeded to billets at BERTINCOURT P.963.5.	M M

A5834 Wt.W4973/M657 750,000 8/16 D.D.&L Ltd Form/C.2113/13

Army Form C. 2118.

WAR DIARY
INTELLIGENCE SUMMARY.
(Erase heading not required.)

Place	Date 1914	Hour	Summary of Events and Information	Remarks and references to Appendices
In the field	29		At BERTINCOURT. Bn. rested and cleaned up. Training at BERTINCOURT. Orders received to relieve 4/5 Bn. Lincoln Regt in the line, night 30/31/08.	AM M
	30		Bn. left BERTINCOURT at 1.0 p.m. and relieved 4/5 Bn. Lincoln Regt in left sector of Brigade front line K.15.a.9.3. with 2 Coys (B and D) in front and 2 Coys (A and C) in support. Relief delayed through difficulty in getting L.G. ammn forward from dump. Relief complete 11.55 p.m. Casualties nil.	M
	31		Enemy shelled HAVRINCOURT at 12.30 a.m. with Gas shells and Bn. stood to. Situation quiet. Casualties nil.	M

Malcolm Lieut. for
O.C. 12th (D.L.O.Y.) Bn. Manchester Regt.

Special Operation orders No. 1

10. N. 17

1. Humble will counter-attack the post lost at GRAVEL FARM last night, at midnight tonight.

2. OC C Coy will dispose his platoons as under

No. 12 move forward 50 yards, so as to cover GRAVEL FARM. Two Lewis guns from D Coy with teams will be attached to this party.

No 10 platoon will be faced East to cover GRAVEL FARM. Two Lewis guns will be attached to this platoon

No 11 will move forward N.E. 100 yards.

These movements to be completed by 11.30 p.m.

along the line of the road and assault GRAVEL FARM from the north by bayonet.

5. At 2 a.m. an artillery barrage will come down on the standing barrage line just west of VAN DYK Farm with special barrage on certain enemy strong points.

6. The C.O. will himself place the assaulting platoons of D & A Coys in position at V7694. A Coy platoon will parade on the duckboard at 10 p.m. where the C.O. will await it just south of Thulie ~~p.m.~~ D Coy platoon will arrive at the same place at 10 p.m.

7. After capture A Coy platoon will hold the GRAVEL FARM

The role of these 10 & 12 platoons will be to make a feint attack by fire on GRAVEL FARM at Zero and to continue for ~~ten~~ five minutes.

3. A platoon of 25 to 30 men from D Coy, and a platoon of 25 to 30 men from A Coy at TAUBE FARM will form an assaulting party which will move to V7 b 9.4 and form up in two lines of platoons facing South with the right flank resting on the road. D Coy platoon will lead and A Coy platoon will be 10 paces in rear.

4. At zero midnight both platoons will advance ~~along the~~ by the right

and OC C Coy will send forward a lewis gun with drums and ammn available to assist A Coy platoon.

8. 2Lt Hudson will go with D Coy platoon. If an officer of A is available he will go. The senior to command.

9. Reports to Adv Bn HQ on the duckboards when it crosses the WATERSLEITBEEK at V7d 6.9.

Ted Mullens
Lt Col
Cmdg Hawkins

issued 8.40

"H156" ~~go with~~ "W. Diary"
received 6.50 p.m.

In accordance with BM 3 of 10th inst. & I made arrangements as described in ~~a~~ special Operation Order No.1. attached.

The officer who brought me the Brigade Order stated I had the choice of hour for the raid. I chose 12 midnight, and he telephoned this in code from my HdQrs, at 7.30 p.m. Copy attached.

All ~~the~~ orders were carried into effect ~~ ~~ according to my calculations, and the assaulting party reached the WATERSLEITBEEK ~~ ~~ by myself at 10.59, (at V.7 c 5.9)

The stream had increased since I crossed it at 5 p.m. ~~ ~~ 10th from a ditch crossed by duckboards to a strongish stream some 20 to 30 yards wide.

In crossing it we were waist deep, and some deeper still.

At 11 p.m. an artillery barrage came down on VAN DYCK FARM, we at that moment being actually crossing the stream.

This entirely upset the plan and rendered the assaulting party liable to decimation by enemy rifle fire from GRAVEL FARM only 250x away. I noticed however that all the enemy Verey lights were damp and did not flare, consequently our proximity was not discovered.

I decided in view of this to try a rush GRAVEL FARM from the West. Sjt Chatterton of C Coy who knew the ground offered to pilot the men of the platoon selected ie the

leading platoon in a suitable position
for their attack. I consequently ordered
them to do so while I went to the
other platoon to explain the situation
and get it out of the way as I did not
want to many here.

~~Then~~ 11.10 to 11.25 ~~~~ one gun
I think a how was firing short and
dropping ~~rounds~~ very near us such
I noticed at least six shots.

By the time these arrangements were
complete it was ~~11.25~~ and
at about 11.20 the enemy had found some
verey lights that would burn and
his M/gun, one only, opened bursts
of fire towards us.

I intended to lead the platoon
forward myself as there was no

officers with it. The distance to be covered in the advance, about 130 yards the stiff mud of which the going consisted, the fact that the enemy had at least got his very lights to hand, and would be able to detect us long before we could push decided me in abandoning the enterprise.

The last man crossed the WATERSMEET BEEK at 11.50.

If the barrage had come down at 12 midnight, I think the operation would have been entirely successful. The men were cheery and in good fighting tone. The assaulting party could not have missed its way for it had only to go North-East, and the North Star was visible throughout.

There were no officers casualties.

I know so far of one man killed and two wounded all by the short bursts I understand.

11 bk Nov 4.7
J W Rutherford
Col HUMBLE

103

Confidential.

War Diary
of
12th (D.L.O.Y) Bn. Manchester Regt.

From 1st December 1917. To 31st December 1917.

(Volume xxx)

12 Manchester
Vol 28

Army Form C. 2118.

Instructions regarding War Diaries and Intelligence Summaries are contained in F. S. Regs., Part II. and the Staff Manual respectively. Title pages will be prepared in manuscript.

WAR DIARY
or
INTELLIGENCE SUMMARY.
(Erase heading not required.)

Bn M/chester

Place	Date	Hour	Summary of Events and Information	Remarks and references to Appendices
In the Field	Jan 1st		Bn in left sector of Brigade front K15 d.9.3 with two Coys (B and D) in front and 2 Coys (A and C) in support. At night B and D Coys were relieved by A and C Coys.	
	2nd		Four parts of the Brigade on our left driven in by the enemy. Our left Coy caught a good part of the barrage. Bn closed to. Counter attacks delivered by the Brigade on our left failed with news that the bombing stop in HINDENBURG SUPPORT line immediately on our left flank was very much closer than previously.	
	3rd		Situation very quiet. Lieut S.E. Turner (attached to Bde HQ) wounded.	
	4th		Situation very quiet. Night 4/5th Bn relieved by 9th W. Rid. Regt and took up position in immediate support. Relief was completed by a simultaneous re-adjustment of the Brigade and Divisional fronts. Right Bn of Brigade (10th Lan Fus) took over our right Coy front (C Coy). 9th W. Riding Regt relieved our left front Coy with one Coy, both support Coys with one other Coy, and unit remaining two Coys took over a portion of front of Brigade on the left. Gradually 1 O.R. killed in relieving Bombing Stop. Working parties carrying R.E materials to front line. Situation quiet.	
	5,6,7th 8, 9th			
	9		Bn relieved 9th W. Riding Regt on left sector of Bde front. Dispositions:- B Coy Right front. A Coy Centre D Coy Left. C Coy support. Bombers of B Coy were attached to D Coy to assist in holding Bombing Stop. Owing to thaw Bn went up in Gum Boots	
	10"		Unusual enemy movement reported by Bn Observers. Large numbers of	

Army Form C. 2118.

WAR DIARY
or
INTELLIGENCE SUMMARY.
(Erase heading not required.)

Instructions regarding War Diaries and Intelligence Summaries are contained in F. S. Regs., Part II. and the Staff Manual respectively. Title pages will be prepared in manuscript.

Place	Date	Hour	Summary of Events and Information	Remarks and references to Appendices
In the Field			men seen approaching our front, both fully armed and also carrying R.E. material. Special vigilance ordered. 8.30 pm special barrage by artillery over Brigade front. Enemy sent up S.O.S. and replied with heavy T.M. and Field Artillery bombardment of our front line, causing D Coy several casualties. Barrage lasted an hour. Casualties: 1 Officer (Lieut: P BODDINGTON) wounded. 1 O.R. killed. 6 O.R. wounded, including 1 remaining at duty.	
	11th		At 6.17 a.m a heavy barrage was opened by all calibres of our artillery on sections of enemy front where movement had been observed. Barrage ended 6.30 a.m. No enemy reply. At night C Coy relieved D Coy, bombers of B Coy remaining at Bombing Stop. Casualties 2 O.R. wounded.	
	12th		Situation quiet. Thaw continued. Trenches everywhere knee deep of water. At night, enemy shelled back areas with Gas shells. Bn not affected. B Coy changed places with A Coy.	
	13th		At 10 a.m one man of 9th Grenadier Reg'. 3rd Guards Division surrendered to Right Post of Centre Coy. Information valuable. Night 13/14 Bn relieved by 4th & Yorks Reg' and moved to SLAG HEAP J.34.c.9.1 in Divisional Reserve at immediate tactical disposal of G.O.C. Rifle Brigade. Relief complete 11.0 pm.	
	14th/15th		Working parts (whole Bn) supplied each day to C.E. V Corps, digging and wiring in the neighbourhood of K.32.a. (Corps line of defence) 1 O.R. accidentally wounded whilst on working party.	
	16th		Bn bath and re-equip.	
	17th		Bn find working parties under C.E. V Corps and in neighbourhood of camp under Y.8. Field Coy R.E.	

WAR DIARY
or
INTELLIGENCE SUMMARY

Army Form C. 2118.

Place	Date	Hour	Summary of Events and Information	Remarks and references to Appendices
In the Field	Jany 1917 19th		Same as for 14th inst: Bn found working parties as above for improvement of camp. Portion of Bn at camps J.3 & D moved to SLAG HEAP at J.35.D. and became Brigade Reserve at In Brigade Reserve.	
	20th 21st 22nd		Coys work during day making revetions of bashes wire. Working parties provided at night. 1 Officer and 50 O.R. for laying wire carrying duckboards for duckboard track to front line. 1 Officer and 50 O.R. carrying wire and sandbags to Right Front Bn. In Brigade Reserve.	
	23rd		Bn moved at 4.30 p.m. to relieve 9th Bn in Rifles Regt (Right Bn of Bde Sector) in the front line from approximately K.10 (HUGHES TRENCH). Dispositions:— Front Line D Coy right, C Coy left, Support A Coy Right, B Coy Left. Bn. H.Q. K.9.C.35.15. (Ref map DEMICOURT Special Sheet, Part of S.4.C. S.I.E. 1/10,000). Relief complete 8.0 p.m. Work carried out on improving trenches and small party of 20 men under R.E. employed wiring and barricading canal crossing at K.9 & 3.4. All quiet. Lieut. Col. E.G.S. Thrush proceeded to transport lines preparatory to going to going on leave to England on 24th inst. Major G.F. Wilkes M.C. assumed command of Bn. Patrol reconnoitred empty trenches NUGENT & ARTILLERY.	
	24th		Quiet. Work improving trenches & C.Ts as above. Rations now sent up by train. Patrols sent out. Casualties Nil.	
	25th		Quiet. Considerable aerial activity. Hostile aeroplanes flying over Bn	

WAR DIARY or INTELLIGENCE SUMMARY

Army Form C. 2118.

Place	Date	Hour	Summary of Events and Information	Remarks and references to Appendices
			area, especially between 12.0 noon and 8.0 p.m but dispersed by Anti-aircraft guns and our aircraft. Work improving trenches continued. B Coy in support relieved C Coy in front line; A Coy relieving D Coy and B Coy relieving C Coy. B Coy take over NUGENT trench west of Canal from K9 B 20.90 to K9 A 93.85. In new front line. Left Platoon D Coy took over position occupied by Right Platoon, C Coy in front line; remainder of D Coy moving into support position vacated by A Coy. One Platoon of C Coy remained in old front line at K9.b. 15.90. and the remainder of C Coy moved back to 1/10,000 vacated by B Boy and Platoon in old B Coy occupied NUGENT Trench with 2 Platoons and one Platoon in old front line west of Canal DU NORD and one at CROSS POST. K9a 95.90 [Reg Map MOEUVRES 1/20,000 and DEMICOURT 1/10,000]. Patrols sent out to reconnoitre. SCOTT, STRONG, & ALLEN from K9 L 81.95. to K10 A.4.6. well view to obtaining information for a raid. by 9th Bn West Riding Regt. Valuable information gained. Work improving trenches and NUGENT Trench carried out. Casualties nil.	Cr
	26.		Quiet. Visibility bad. Ration train cancelled. Rations continued to be sent by Reg. Transport. Patrol sent out to K9 a. 7.8. supposed enemy post near STONE POST. Our Patrol congratulates Sgt Frain to N.26.676. (A Coy) the native leader on his report. Work improving trenches and continuing NUGENT Trench to Canal carried out. Casualties 1. O.R. killed by M.G. or rifle bullet	Van

A 5834 Wt.W4973/1637 750,000 8/16 D.D.&L.Ltd Forms/C.2118/13.

Army Form C. 2118.

WAR DIARY
or
INTELLIGENCE SUMMARY.
(Erase heading not required.)

Instructions regarding War Diaries and Intelligence Summaries are contained in F. S. Regs., Part II. and the Staff Manual respectively. Title pages will be prepared in manuscript.

Place	Date	Hour	Summary of Events and Information	Remarks and references to Appendices
In the Field	Jany 27		Quiet. Misty. Bn relieved by 9th Bn W. Riding Regt and moved to area between K 14 and K 15 in Brigade Support. Bn HQ situated on road at K 13 d 45.30. Relief complete 7.0 pm. 2nd Lieut F. Taylor rejoined Bn from England. Casualties Nil.	
	28th		Quiet. Working parties amounting to 4 Officers 200 OR. provided for the Right Front Bn area. Digging in CAREY Trench and conveying material by night. Sapping with small shafts also carried out by day and night in CAREY French. Casualties Nil.	
	29th		Work continued as above. Casualties. 2. OR. accidentally wounded whilst cleaning up trench by old enemy detonator. Of these 1 remained at duty.	
	30th		Quiet. Working parties as above. 55 OR. reinforcements arrived at Transport Lines to join Bn. average age 19. Physique good. Casualties Nil.	
	31st		Quiet. Misty weather. Bn relieved by 7th Bn East Yorkshire Regt in the evening and marched to Ry siding into SLAG HEAP at J 34 D where Bn entrained for PHIPPS Camp from thence Bn proceeded to SAUNDERS Camp in Divisional Reserve at O.5.A afternoon. Bn should have entrained at HERMIES but orders were changed and Bn entrained as above owing to Bosch shelling at HERMIES Railway tem gas shelled. Casualties Nil.	

31-1-18.

B. M. Winter Maj
Commdg 12 (0427) Bn Manchester Regiment

WO 29

War Diary

of

12th (D.L.O.Y) Bn. Manchester Regt.

From 1st February 1918.   To 28th February 1918.

Volume XXXII.

Army Form C. 2118.

WAR DIARY
or
INTELLIGENCE SUMMARY.

17th (D.L.O.Y.) Manchester Regt.

February 1917

(Erase heading not required.)

Place	Date	Hour	Summary of Events and Information	Remarks and references to Appendices
St Nicholas	1916 1. Feb.		Personal Reserve at SAUNDERS Camp. Batt. Baths and clean up. Large leave allotment granted. Recruiting for month (over 100 vacancies).	
	2nd		In Personal Reserve at SAUNDERS Camp. Working party of 160 OR provided. Clearing day for buying cable in forward area in vicinity of DEAN Copse. Wire patching hut in Chips Hill Dugouts, Cannon out. On 2nd Lieut Lt. B.H. HEATON Transport Officer taking over duties of Engineer Transport Officer during cables above mentioned 2nd Lt J.H. HOLDROYD will over duties of T.O.	
	3rd		In Personal Reserve - Work and cable carrying operation this evening of camp during early morning - went during day carried out as above at DEAN Copse and in Camp. 2nd Lt J.H. HOLDRIDGE left Batt. for 17th Div. H.Q. to take over duties of Divisional Officer.	
	4 & 5th		In Personal Reserve - work as above.	
	6th		In Personal Reserve at SAUNDERS Camp. French battalion for penultimate trench Rel. carried out at HERRICK Camp by Batt. during morning - Lt Col. S. DANBY from 9th S. Staffords Batt. and several Other OR. Capt 29 her joined Batt from training Batt. in England. Average age 19. Joining one - well selected Batt. arrived 10 P. Batt. Reserve parade to right Batt. of the right Brigade - secr of Div. Hqrs and moved off from SAUNDERS camp at 5.15 pm proceeding by train from PHIPPS camp at 6 am and arriving at I.32.C.0.5 at about 8.30 pm. At this point Guides met Coys from 10th Sherwood Foresters and we .... from Batt. Cookers, after which Batt. marched to our line. Relay Conference Disposition of Batt. FRONT LINE. OMEN and SHINGLER trenches. "C" Coy right and "D" by left from I.17.B.8.6. to I.11.A.00 approx. SUPPORT - "A" Coy right in SEPP Lane SNAKE and two (J.11. X.C. area). "B" Coy left in SOPP, SNAKE and SEPP trenches (J.16 and 15 X Daens). Batt H.Q.	

A5834 Wt.W4973/M687 750,000 8/16 D.D. & I. Ltd. Forms/C.2118/13

Army Form C. 2118.

WAR DIARY
or
INTELLIGENCE SUMMARY.
(Erase heading not required.)

Instructions regarding War Diaries and Intelligence Summaries are contained in F. S. Regs., Part II. and the Staff Manual respectively. Title pages will be prepared in manuscript.

Place	Date	Hour	Summary of Events and Information	Remarks and references to Appendices
Q. Palestine	10/6 7 (Cont)		on WHITE HILL K.15 B.55.25 (Ref map MOKATTEB 1/3000 Edition 7 H trenches corrected 3/11/17). Quiet - Routine Patrols sent out. In front of trenches. Observed expected extensive M.G. movement at E.28.B all morning Satillery expensed. Quiet - sent Caval out enforcing trenches. Ro Police Patrols sent out - 2 hr warned Jaffa Gate.	W
	8."		In front line quiet. Day dull and poor visibility at 5.45 am. German aeroplane flying on own shot down by rifle fire and landed about 200 yds E of our Battalion Boundary near B.Cy. at K.16.A.55 approx - 10.15 am. Two of our own aeroplanes landed mounting guns over aeroplane. The pilot and observer (an officer) were taken prisoners by F.Cy. and taken over by an officer of 15. Cy. of this Batn to Coy Hg at 2nd Res. Thirty of enemy enemy began shelling the plane attempting to destroy it. During day 30 & 40 enemy seen working at K.28.B about mid day. Artillery expensed, who fired shrapnel rounds at target. Enemy been about 300 5-9 shells at K.17 ace about 10 pm sent in trenches and road, killed enemy carried out at night - Routine Patrols sent out.	W
	9."		Quiet. Enemy shelled D. Coys area with about 20 rounds of 4.2" at 1 am. Enemy seen working at E.28.B at about 5 p.m. and plenty of activity. 1 Material carried. In front line trenches quiet on every following. trenches carried out as before Patrol 1 Officer 2nd K.T.A. MORRIS and 6 men was sent out at night of REINDEER hill opposite OWEN trench and occupied by Enemy. Patrol expected came under fire from position. Enemy shelled area K.16 & K.17 about 7.0 p.m. with about 200 shells. Casualties 1 - Pt killed.	W
	10."		During early morning Enemy s Gun shelled K.16 & K.17 and 200 shells about 20 am.	W

WAR DIARY
or
INTELLIGENCE SUMMARY

Army Form C. 2118.

(Erase heading not required.)

Instructions regarding War Diaries and Intelligence Summaries are contained in F.S. Regs., Part II. and the Staff Manual respectively. Title pages will be prepared in manuscript.

Place	Date	Hour	Summary of Events and Information	Remarks and references to Appendices
R. H. Field	10/10/16		Enemy Artillery fairly quiet during remainder of day. Batt. relieved by 9th R. War. Regt. in the evening and moved into Bde support at L.21 (TMK SUPPORT) arriving by 2 Officers & 80 O.R. from a working party over RE dump near Crucifix. 1 OR. killed by shell fire. 1 OR. wounded by grenade.	etc
	11th		9th Batt ordered "Quiet". Carrying parties amounting to 2 Officers & 60 OR furnished during evening for carrying to front line Batts. Also a 2 Officers & 110 OR. a/c carrying under R.E.	etc
	12th		9th Bde ordered "Quiet". Went as above – also 15 OR. from L as working party under Australian Tunneling Coy Coy. in relief of S. Dept of 6 Officers (2nd Lt. COHEN – W.H. HAYWARD – H. HALL – D.G. KRUGER – R. KEMP – and S.E. HOOTON) and 149 OR. from 23rd Bn. Han. Regt. (8th Cty Bn) Joined our Batt. Quiet.	etc
	13th		Batt. Bde report "Quiet". Went as above except working party under R.E. reduced to 3 Off & 200 OR.	etc
	14th		9th Bde ordered "Quiet". Batt. relieved against trench foot (trench splints) at SLAG HEAP. 7.36.D. Batt. relieved 10th R. Lan. Fus. left Batt in Bde Res sector of Division of front and also took over 500 yds from 9th Bn. area. Relief complete on our right front in the evening. One K.B. team from D Coy was attached to B.B.Coy and one platoon of "C" Coy was attached to "A" Coy. Disposition Front line. (North trench and a return of HUGHES trench on left on a OWEN support & CAREY trench) from K.11.C. 75.45. to K.10.75.3. "A" Coy right (Pluto & Platoon "C" Coy) 7th Coy left (Pluto 1 Lewis Gun team of D Coy Support (SOAR trench) "C" Coy.	etc

WAR DIARY
or
INTELLIGENCE SUMMARY

Army Form C. 2118.

(Erase heading not required.)

Place	Date	Hour	Summary of Events and Information	Remarks and references to Appendices
La Fosse	1916 Feb.		K.R.R., D.Coy, K.R.B. (both accommodated in Bayonets) Line as tactical occupation cleared. Battn H.Q. on WHITEHALL. K.16. D.9.8. Quiet. Our Artillery active, engaged in counter Battery work. "B" Coy sent out a patrol on ratior. "A" Coy sent out a patrol on ratior with orders to approach REINDEER Post to endeavour to ascertain whether any enemy Bat West Riding Regt. (who were out on patrol the previous night over the Bat and were surprised by enemy from above) were at the vicinity trying to find their way in. Casualties 1 Offr. accidentally wounded by a rifle bullet and 1 O.R. wounded at duty accidently wounded by a German bomb lying on ground. 2nd Lt F. KNIBB took over duties of T.O. during K. HEATON attd. as ass TO. for an month.	2
	15th		Quiet. Enemy artillery showed increased activity during afternoon firing on our right and searching for our batteries, with main gun shells at 9.0 a.m. and again at 10 pm at F.R.C. Relation by our Artillery with 300 gun shells after 9.0 pm on be almost and again after 10 gun bombardment went on trenches and enemy CANOE and CANOODLE 1 OR wounded passed by Woolett.	3
	16th		Quiet. A Limited bombardment on Enemy on our right during hours of early morning which diminished after dawn One trench mortar exploded ten loose over our lines at 11.45 am & 7 again at 1.30 pm & 3.40 pm. This enemy of by our A. Gun, Lewis Gun and 1.9 fire. One to late shell at 11.45 am open trellises by US. No enemy action followed. Artillery fire most during day. Relieve patrols out at night and a quiet night however up to REINDEER (K.11.A) for Patrol were taken however our usefulness and actively.	4

WAR DIARY or INTELLIGENCE SUMMARY

Army Form C. 2118.

Place	Date	Hour	Summary of Events and Information	Remarks and references to Appendices
In the Field	1918 Feb. 16.	Between 6-0 & 8-0 pm	enemy carried out M. Kinelia as usual. 2nd Lt. W.H. WISHLADE was over duties of Q.M. pending Hon. Capt. & M.G. J. PITTS absence on his leave.	4
		17th	A few gas shells by enemy on R.16.d. at 8.30 am "Quiet" for remainder of day light - slightly gusty at 9.0 p.m. 2nd Lt. MORRIS 9/D. and another & REINDEER Int. to act as covering party to 6. also dm with the support on REINDEER inc. This was successfully accomplished. 6 to 6.15 Ancroft bucket our circles at 7.30 pm. Converners aide activity at 6 midnight - rest as usual. Converners I.O.R. taken	4
		18th	ill & R. Poste. "Quiet" - Enemy fired Gas shells at R.6.D at 6.15 pm. Batteries were by 6" Power Reg. on enemy and became Bat. Reserve. A.& B. Cys. were relieved by trans- oft relief from O.C. R.45.95 (Ref. MOEUVRES map 1/20000) for HARRICKtamp. and Rep. 67 (1/10000) & R.49. D. Cy succeeded by both march to SLAG HEAP. At 7.30. relieved by Power Reg'. "C" C.o. were Converners aire activity up to 11 pm. and 2 Cy. of Borde Reg. who were being covered by trans were Shot at & were delayed coming to reserve of whole trenches. Relief completed at midnight 18th 19th L. 16 at 6 addition and 15. O.R. Junior Batt. from England.	4
		19th	L. Devisional Reserve - Cleaning up and Bathing.	4
		20-22.	L. Devisional Reserve. Working Party 304 n.c.os and per ried. for burying cable over Gn. Say, daily from 7 am to 11 and from 2 pm. at SLAG HEAP.	4
		23rd	L. Devisional Reserve - Work as above. During Celebration on Devisional Boundary 2 Cys at Beach Camp. moved to Coll. Beaton Line R.32.D. on R. platoon in regiment.	4

Army Form C. 2118.

WAR DIARY
or
INTELLIGENCE SUMMARY.
(Erase heading not required.)

Instructions regarding War Diaries and Intelligence Summaries are contained in F. S. Regs., Part II. and the Staff Manual respectively. Title pages will be prepared in manuscript.

Place	Date	Hour	Summary of Events and Information	Remarks and references to Appendices
L M Palm	23?		2nd Lt. Brown T. and H. Bury joined Batt.	
	24th		2 Personal Parent Ball Period of Reconn Regt on the enemy an front—wl Ball Sapint. Destruction H'& B. Op at SPOR BANK (J85). O.P.D O/P on PACAN Trench (R. 15. A. 7. C.) M. N.G. at LUDGROCHER LANE (R. 13. a. 5. 3).	
			Situation - Quiet. working parties - 6 Officers 234 O.R.	
	26th		Situation - Quiet. working parties - 6 Officers 234 O.R.	
	26th		Situation - Quiet. working parties to source - 37 O.R. emplacements, joined a Batt.	
	27th		Situation - Quiet. working parties to yesterday at 9.0am - large enemy working party at K.4.C.3.9. was disturbed by our 16 Pdrs. Four enemy planes flew over our lines at 9.15am. They were driven off by L.G. and M.G. fire.	
	28th		Situation - Quiet. working parties as yesterday.	

1/3/18.

R W Anington Lt. Col.
Comndg. 12th Battn Norfolk Regt.

52nd Inf.Bde.
17th Div.

12th BATTN. THE MANCHESTER REGIMENT.

M A R C H

1 9 1 8

Army Form C. 2118.

WAR DIARY
or
INTELLIGENCE SUMMARY.
(Erase heading not required.)

CONFIDENTIAL.

WAR DIARY

OF

12TH.(D OF LY). BATTALION MANCHESTER REGIMENT.

From March 1st. 1918.   To March 31st. 1918.

VOLUME XXXlll

WAR DIARY
INTELLIGENCE SUMMARY

Army Form C. 2118.

Place	Date	Hour	Summary of Events and Information	Remarks and references to Appendices
In the Field	March 1.	5.30 AM	Situation Quiet. at 5.30 AM. The enemy put down a heavy bombardment for an hour on a portion of the front reached by the Bn. on our right. Visibility BAD. Aeroplane activity NIL.	—
	2.		Situation Quiet. On the night 2nd/3rd the Bn. moved out of support and relieved the 10 R.Bn. Lancashire Fusiliers in the right sub sector. Half section Lewis C Coy relieved the right Coy with 8 Platoons R & L Teams in HUGHES TRENCH K9. 6YR. 10 a, & 2 Platoons Lewis 2 L G Teams in immediate support CAREY TRENCH (K10 2 3 3). Letter D Coy relieved the left front Coy on NUGENT TR. FRIDA TRENCH & ALBAN Post (K9 a. 3). Letters A Coy relieved the right support Coy in CAREY TR. (K9.d.4.8.). Letter B Coy relieved the left support Coy with a Platoon on ALBAN AV (K9.a.4.2). and 2 Platoons with 2 M.G. on CROSSE AV. (K9 a.6.7). Relief myself 5.5 km. Enemy M.G.S. were active during the night. Our letters were sent out at owing to M.G. fire could make very little headway. Any had nothing to report. Visibility was very poor the whole day.	—
	3.		Situation. Quiet. Patrols were sent out on the whole Bn. front, but owing to deep held mud & M.G. fire they had nothing to report. T M's were active at 5 p.m. on the left Bn front; retaliation was arranged by our Gunners and a chunk of S.A.A. was very heavy was blown up by this shoot. One 2 inch plum was lit on K9.d at 9.55 pm. Aeroplane activity nil. 1 O.R. accidentally wounded until they light pistol.	—
	4.		Situation. Quiet. During the afternoon Letter A Coy relieved letter C Coy in the right front and letter B Coy relieved letter D Coy in the left front. Officers (CO. & Lieut C & by Cos) of the 6th Wiltshire Regt went round the Bn. area with a view to taking over on the night 5/7 inst. At 9.30 p.m. 100 of the enemy were observed carrying large wittle gates from K 3 d 40 80 proceeding towards LOCK 6. Artillery were informed but owing to the mist no observations were possible.	—

WAR DIARY or INTELLIGENCE SUMMARY

Army Form C. 2118.

Place	Date	Hour	Summary of Events and Information	Remarks and references to Appendices
	4 Cont		Enemy T.M's were active, but artillery was very quiet. Our enemy snipers was engaged by 2 Lt Stoddard of the right Coy. The Left Coy reported that they saw one of the enemy carried away on a stretcher from the same place. During the night retrieval was carried to the canal (Lock 4). Protective patrols were out on the whole front, but nothing was seen or heard of the enemy. Aeroplane Activity. Nil.	ditto
	5.		Situation. Quiet. Capt Smith & Lt Monro & 28 OR reinforcements joined the Bn. in the line. Enemy Artillery intermittently shelled K 9 Square. At 10.5 A.m. and 4.30 p.m. several Officers and men were observed to be looking at different trench firm wire. A party numbered 17. One Officer had got board on his hat. also white bands on his arm. His men were wearing white bands on round caps few were observed to be wearing head gear which resembled a Fez. (1st Artillery men appeared with great circles on the Br. of the enemy men observed to be drilling at a distance of 2.000 × N of MIEUVRES (Goat station). This party must have been Bn.! A large working party was observed at E.20.c.20.20 Artillery were informed must of this party must have been Bn.! A large working party was observed at E.20.c.20.20 Artillery were informed must of engaged with H.A × M.G with no effect. At 8.40 p.m. a formation of 12 were action followed M.O's were less active Bn. usual and our patrols were out the whole night. Very bright flares were at our Raw before dawn, but there was nothing of interest to report. Casualties. 1 OR wounded.	ditto
	6.		Situation. Quiet. Enemy. Artillery active. Enemy. T.M's active on K.9 & L & K.10 u. M.G. active during the night. Visibility Good. much movement observed. Targets were given to the artillery & airmen working M.G. with y oh spotting in our approach fort of the enemy were but by to our M.G. Several E.A's flew over our lines at a high altitude without opposition. Protective aerial patrols were out. There was nothing seen or heard of the enemy. Lt. Stallion & 11 OR went out on a fighting patrol to obtain identification from enemy but it being so excellent there some was impossible to obtain.	ditto

WAR DIARY or INTELLIGENCE SUMMARY

Army Form C. 2118.

(Erase heading not required.)

Place	Date	Hour	Summary of Events and Information	Remarks and references to Appendices
	7th		Situation Quiet. Enemy Artillery very quiet. Enemy T.M's very active on K.9.G.d, K.10.a, M.G. active probably was just the whole day, some movement had observed at E.27.G.15.00. 90 of the enemy were engaged by our M.G. Several casualties were caused. Our parties were also engaged with good results. One 2"mm aeroplane slipped two bombs on K.3.a. The enemy engaged Fixed A.H. M.G. & T.M. over bombs. B.H.Q. Particularly heavy batch was at during the night. Intelligence new or report of the enemy. Casualties. 2 O.R. wounded by T.M. fire. (HUGHES TRENCH)	ditto
	8th		Situation Quiet. Enemy Artillery. One 5.9". K.9.a K.10.G received some attention during the morning otherwise quiet. T.M's but 3 bombs on K.9.B at noon. M.G's were very quiet during the night. Rifle was much movement during the day, all targets seen again engaged with good results. At 1.20 pm, one E.A flew thro' NAGENT TRENCH (K.9.4. to 70). The Coy. was M.G. was driven off by L.G. fire. Enemy lights were sent up at frequent intervals during the night, no apparent action followed. As a result 2 L.S. fire from our left Coy. some new land from enemy lines. The projector were to be fired on Coras K.3.a.G. but owing to indifferent being apparent little was cancelled. Projectors & Special Patrols went out. At nothing was seen or sun of the enemy. Casualties. 1 O.R. wounded. 1 O.R. killed.	ditto
	9th		Situation Quiet. Enemy Artillery quiet. T.M's were again active on the night front. Much movement was again observed and engaged by Artillery Putting M.G. during the morning. At afternoon was very quiet. During rotation by 24 Div on our right from 7–7.45pm. our right front outpost area was heavy shelled with 10.5cm × 15cm. Communication wire on the left was cut. Bn. was relieved by 10th Bn. Manch. Yorks, & proceeded via Frognole reserve occupying HERMIES defences between Z.20 on cy (C.Gy) who were accommodated at HEBBURN SPOIL HEAP. 7.34 d. Relief complete 10.25 p.	ditto
	10		Situation. Quiet. A.Gy. and 1/2.C.Gy. Bathed and cleaned up.	ditto
	11		Situation. Quiet. B.Gy. and 1/2.C.Gy Bathed C.Gy. vacated HEBBURN SPOIL HEAP and formed Gdn. at HERMIES. Bn. worked at the defences of HERMIES. Gas shells and H.E fell in the village. 11 o/m × 1.0 a.m. Casualties. 1 O.R. (Gassed)	ditto
	12		Situation. Quiet. D.Gy. Bathed. W.R was continued on the defences of HERMIES. E.A bought down in flames by one of our planes at 2.15pm at J.17.C. Our Artillery active.	ditto
	13		Situation Quiet. Our Artillery was active early morning. Working parties as yesterday.	ditto
	14		Situation Quiet. Working parties as yesterday.	ditto

WAR DIARY or INTELLIGENCE SUMMARY

Army Form C. 2118.

Place	Date	Hour	Summary of Events and Information	Remarks and references to Appendices
	15th		Situation. Quiet. Working parties as yesterday. 2/Lt Hamer, 2/Lt Clarkson & 2/Lt Lippett joined the Bn.	
	16th		Situation. Quiet. Working parties as yesterday. Foot Baths allotted to Bn.	
	17th		Situation. Quiet. Bn. relieved 10th Bn Sherwood Foresters in front line of right Sub. Sector. A Coy in front line, B Coy in immediate support, C & D Coys in Support. A Coy occupying SHINGLER TRENCH, SHINGLER SUPPORT, B Coy SMILE TRENCH, C Coy in SHERWOODS BOULEVARDE, D Coy in LONDON TRENCH - LONDON SUPPORT. Indicative tactics of 1 officer 10 OR went out all night but no sign of the enemy was seen on Road. 2/Lt Barber & 5 OR patrolled to a suspected M.G. emplacement at K.11.5.10 so to ascertain if occupied and if so to what attempt it would not approach but owing to bright moon and enemy working party. Hostile activity practically Nil, except for two rounds of 77 cm fired on front line and after dark. Two Trench Mortar shell fires. Left battalion Sector. Enemy was seen placing number of white flags some yards short at (E 17.0.80. 40. E 22.6 50.00)	
	18th		Situation. Quiet except for two rounds on back area. Protective patrols of 1 officer 10 OR were out all night. 2/Lt Hayward 9 OR patrolled the FLESQUIERES - GRAINCOURT road to a point K.12.a.30.30 where they ran into an enemy patrol and put 5 rifles and 6 Mills bomb and 10 OR patrolled along HAVRINCOURT - GRAINCOURT ROAD to a tank at K.11.5.30.70 where a number of the enemy were seen. Bombs were exchanged and Pte Graham and L/Cpl JTR were wounded. On return of patrol 1 OR was found to be missing. Enemy Artillery quiet except for a number of "Minny" Rounds on front line about 12.30am in reply to a raid by 63rd Div. on the right. Early of 30 men were observed advancing in by artillery with good results. Much movement seen on enemy's back area. Weather very wet and disagreeable rather too fast.	
	19th		Situation. Quiet. Protective patrols of 1 officer and 10 OR out from dusk till dawn. SA 1.30 am at E.23.c.15.50 when 40 of enemy seen and fired on by Lewis artillery with good results. SA at E.25.2.50.70 at 8.10 am 3 officers and 5 men of enemy seen at an emplacement. Weather very wet and disagreeable. bad	
	20th		Situation. Quiet. Enemy artillery active until evening when a few rounds were fired. Many protective patrols of 1 officer 10 OR out. from dusk till dawn, but did nothing to report. In addition all Lewis and 3 men were patrolling to deceive whereabouts of proving man but were not successful. Aeroplanes with very poor, at enemy	

A 5334   Wt. W.4973/M657 750,000   8/16   D.D. & L. Ltd.   Forms/C.2113/13

WAR DIARY or INTELLIGENCE SUMMARY

Army Form C. 2118.

Place	Date	Hour	Summary of Events and Information	Remarks and references to Appendices
	20th contd		was seen placing out about 150 mobile stakes 15' light in groups of 200. From 5pm till dusk enemy was seen coming down from F.23 a to E.23 b.8.80 in single file and warning onwards. He fired 150 to 200 new 5.9s. 23rd Inf. Brigade informed.	Ar
	21st		39 I.F. reinforcements joined Battalion. At 4.30 pm enemy put down heavy barrage on left flank of Bn. front and also shelled Bn. post later. At about 6.30 pm the enemy attacked the left of Bn. and entered a small bomb stop. Much enemy movement observed during day, coming up alongside left Bn. front. Some men carrying wire carrying rolls against what appeared with 3 feet poles in centre. Casualties - about 15 k 20 O.R.	W
	22nd		At about 1.30 pm, orders were received enemy to be driven back. Attacked successfully further N. A. force was to relieve 21st Bn. & occupy HAVRINCOURT trenches. This was successfully accomplished without casualties. Bn. H.Q. kept not too near to leaving. At 6.35 pm enemy attacked the left, after being attacked left Bn. during day along the CANAL. It was driven off. 1 Officer & 35 O.R. and at 8.30 pm the enemy attacked the Bn. 4 coys received success. Many enemy casualties caused by our rifle and M.G. fire and also artillery on SOS signal. Our killed fired SOS as in two occasions. Casualty reported. 2nd Lt. T. Clarkson, killed + about 30 O.R. wounded.	4
	23rd		At about 7.30 am orders were again received that enemy to be driven from better positions N. of our British front line, YORKSHIRE SPOIL BANK (A32.B.A.3.1.D 8.80) & N of HAVRINCOURT WOOD (Rendezvous Pnt 1/8 x 80). Coordinated in left. This accomplished with any 2 casualties. About 11.25 am the HAVRI. Division ordered us[?] [also] seen retiring from their position. On investigation it turned the withdrawal was ordered to disengage our line as orders for the Bn. was received till about 12.50 pm. enemy to the flee troops having seen it, they orders were received that Bn. was to withdraw to RECQUIGNY by 1 pm. O coy & 3rd Bn. and the 13th Lancashire Fus. Bn. arrived at retirement. Although the enemy was about in force with Bn. again, and also in HAVRIN COURT WOOD posting enfilade the hard road to HAVRINCOURT WOOD and M.G. fire all Bn. succeeded in reaching rendezvous	to

A 5834 Wt. W4973/M687 750,000 8/16 D. D. & L. Ltd. Forms/C.2118/13.

WAR DIARY
or
INTELLIGENCE SUMMARY.

(Erase heading not required.)

Army Form C. 2118.

Place	Date	Hour	Summary of Events and Information	Remarks and references to Appendices
at ROCQUIGNY	23rd		By 7 am during the escape our only about 5 O.R. casualties (including 1 man I expect in HAVRINCOURT WOOD where he passed Eng.)	
			About 11.30 pm the Bn. was ordered to move up and occupy an old German line about 500x N running across the RUE-ROCQUIGNY Rd. as the enemy were reported to be on BUS. Patrols were sent out and noted enemy held by our troops. The Bn. returned to Camp at ROCQUIGNY at about 10 a.m. few casualties.	
	24th	About 2° O.R. missing.	Wet weather since midnight 20/3/18. 1 Bd. W.D. 75°R. During morning about 11.0 am enemy was reported attacking on our right. He was observed on ridge at O.33.D and making for O.35.B. Our troops were seen retiring on either flank in connection with situation for covering the withdrawal of part of 63rd Div. and of 2nd Div. on our left. This was carried out on our right by part of the 19th Bn. (the 6 tanks having being in action) at 11.30 am. At 12.30 pm our tanks were observed in action retiring through BARASTRE 0.23.D and enemy seen retiring at 0.35.D and 0.35.B. Six tanks killed. About 1.0 pm proceedings terminated and Corps Regt. informed Bn. Bn. were withdrawing. Just before 1.15pm 2nd Bn. were seen to have come in on the left. At 1.15pm enemy seen again started on ridge at O.35.D. One of our tanks was hit and burnt out. Honour and the 2nd were for our lives. Two enemy aero seen to avoid. To avoid tank.	
		About 2.15 pm the C.O. so the London Regt. returned that Bn. on 6 right had broken and he had had the withdraw. It was on command of the Bn. and had broken also retired on Ridge and passed to orders at this division. Thos C.O. 2 in 2 Bn. London Regt. informed the Bn. I would remain and would open right flank. At 3.45 am 4 enemy guns successed in full view on ridge in front of YPRES Bn. C.O. sent opened fire on our trenches (which had been called especially round Bn. W.D. during most of the noises) Bn. Abos/Grp Trench was also enfiladed by a M.G. on the right. Night (it was in haste) was put in by the enemy and was observed on our rear in ROCQUIGNY as well as noble movement. Tanks again came into action for a short period on our left at about 3.15 pm. Enemy looks begin to appear on our left about. LE TRANSLOY	

WAR DIARY or INTELLIGENCE SUMMARY

Army Form C. 2118.

Place	Date	Hour	Summary of Events and Information	Remarks and references to Appendices
	24th		as well as on our right rear. The position appears critical. The men were very exhausted. P.7.33½ Lt Q.B.R. W. Ridings Regt. informed O.C. Bn., Lt Col Roy, that orders from 19th to withdraw and that 13th could conform. These orders were a few minutes late, reached Bn HQ and arrangements were made for conforming with 19th when at 7.50 P.M. Lt 9 & Bn. W. Ridings Regt. anxious withdrew on our left and was forced at one side the Bn. A Coy stood fast for a short while to cover the retreat and the remainder of the Bn. so soon as Coy could made for FLERS where 19th rendezvous was fixed. Stood the remainder of the Bn. so soon as bayoned and fire. Many missing. At dusk the walked to FLERS and either sniper was there. O.C. 13th around the village. A Hostile artillery experienced into sons and on salvos. Several enemy rifles were observed on the vicinity and on our rear. Downed could not be communicated with and so no orders were received. K 9.0 P.M. It decided to reassemble at MARTINPUICH and endeavour to get in touch with Div. as it acknowled the 19th would have been surrounded in FLERS with hardly any ammunition or rations. The march of 13 near MARTINPUICH where they got into a position in advanced rank for the night arriving there about midnight. On withdrawing from POUZIGNY J.S.M. P.497b 2 B coy finding 2 Lt. L. ADDISON J/40 Coy being wounded & brought in at once, bring M G fire, heavy attacks him in a bad state. He found Bn in a single and finally carry him in so back till he reached some shell-hole at an Obs. post. Night. Quiet. Casualties. 2nd Lt. E. Heatherd. wounded. 2nd Lt P. J. Layron. wounded & missing. 2nd Lt. E. H. Price. wounded. 2nd Lt P.J.W. Jacob. missing. T.Lt M. Liggett. wounded. & missing. and Lut. 120 O.R. wounded, missing, & prisoners.
	25th		At 4.0 A.M. Bn. was ordered to move over the 13th marched to MARTINPUICH. SOURCELETTE HQ. as not met by which enemy were holding L.e.) & Le Crow Rrab South of SOURCELETTE which was strong held & you made to find all trace of Div. It is with them there had been not since 23rd was obtained from there 13th proceeded down BAPAUME-ALBERT road to MEAULTE information was at first obtained that Div. 4.8 was at the latter place. On reaching PUZIERES which the enemy were expected to attack

A 8834   Wt. W4973/M687   750,000   8/16   D. D. & L. Ltd.   Forms/C.2118/13.

WAR DIARY
INTELLIGENCE SUMMARY

Army Form C. 2118.

Place	Date	Hour	Summary of Events and Information	Remarks and references to Appendices
	25th contd		enemy were driven in the edge. As above although R.E. & right on our line orders were received that the scale take up a position at 11.0 am. This also was done as was received that the News Bearer to FRICOURT was ordered as delay in Park in FRICOURT Wood, collecting rations to Bn and to CONTALMAISON at 12.0 pm. The enemy attack ano was delivered efforts that first and Bn was ordered to act to rally near FRICOURT Wood. Being badly in need of sleep. It both it afresh enough attack had succeeded everywhere and Bn was ordered to take up a position in front of FRICOURT at 12.0. The Battalion of 7th Div: Bn HQ on position stayed with R.H.Q. 7 Div HQ. Riding kept in FRICOURT Chateau. Quiet night. Casualties wounded 1 O.R.	Apx
	26th		At 7 a.m. orders were received to withdraw to HÉNENCOURT in 3 Corps reserve. Bn HS was all billeted. Bn was accordingly assembled & the concentration to more at 4.10 am. Via MEAULTE, DERNANCOURT and MILLENCOURT. Bn arrived from about 8.0 to 10 am and rested in little time. At 6.45 pm Bn was ord at 9.15 pm (M) and were under Bn from time to more by 9.30 pm Bn moved off to SENLIS as every was reported to have broken through at DERNANCOURT and advancing N.W. direction. Rations were drawn at SENLIS and Bn bivouaced to Mailly Brouilis included AMIENS- ALBERT Road in a SE direction and took up a position of 2 Ref Road. Bn HQ established at Pt. Edit (say Plat of) ALBERT (40000) Patrols were pushed out and reports to BDE in front and other position. Casualties: Thirteen O.R. wounded + missing	Apx
	27th		At about 4 am Bn was ordered to retire to villages to HÉNENCOURT and HÉNENCOURT and MILLENCOURT Bn. came under orders 14th Div and saw sick. And to am every and relate to live orders through the road wear. LAVIEVILLE and BRESLE and has orders to try and through to ALBERT. To Bn, advanced from Bridge Cullum to Military Brewades. Patrols were pushed out to a distance of about 2 miles. Mailly Richene Ribem, Rasne. Worked into enemy. 1st Military asgo the Div. of 9 Div and 12 35th Div. were in support.	Apx

WAR DIARY
or
INTELLIGENCE SUMMARY
(Erase heading not required.)

Army Form C. 2118.

Place	Date	Hour	Summary of Events and Information	Remarks and references to Appendices
	27th contd		Newhaven troops arrived to relieve the 4 Divn. and as they began to occupy the position held by the Bn., hostile M.G. was ordered to retire to Fellus as all was clear. Our guns were nervous moving forward. Bn. returned to Fellus about 4 a.m. and slept night in HENENCOURT. Casualties. 1 O.R.	
	28th		Bn. in HENENCOURT. Bn. held in readiness during afternoon to move at 1/2 hours notice to occupy position E. of MILLENCOURT with view to counter attack as enemy were reported to have attacked 50th & 51st Bde also W. of ALBERT. As this information proved incorrect Bn. remained at HENENCOURT. Village shelled during day. R.S.B. Quiet. Casualties — During period from 21st when attack started men and officers were returning to Bn. from leave and enjoying a rest at last. Two batches up strength of the Bn. From 21st to arrival at HENENCOURT Bn. in 3rd Bde in addition to fighting also rear guard marched 41 miles. Bn. transport arrived during the period moved from VELU Wood to BEAULENCOURT. THILLOY, LE SARS, LA BOISELLE, HENENCOURT, VADENCOURT, FORCEVILLE, PUCHEVILLERS & CONTAY, at which place it was finally established on 29th, having travelled a distance of roughly 100 miles. The Transport succeeded in delivering rations to the Bn. on each night except one, when the whereabouts of the Bn. was unknown and was supposed to have been surrounded. Casualties. 2 O.R.	
	29th		Bn. in billets at HENENCOURT. Bn. E.G. HENENCOURT at 7.0 p.m. Rest. in front of ALBERT. 'B' Coy. 'C' Coy in front line. 'A' Coy in support. 'D' Coy in reserve with H.Q. & B. Casualties —	
	30th		Very wet day. C Coy out and relieved one of the enemy in the morning. 1 O.R. 'B' Coy recovered 1 L.G.R. 'B' Coy Killed, thick area lightly shelled and area relieved by T.M.T. Columbia whistle pistol. A pistol night was quiet. Draft of 4 men joined the Bn. as reinforcements.	

Place	Date	Hour	Summary of Events and Information	Remarks and references to Appendices
	31st		"A" & "C" Coy sent out patrols to study nature of ground in front. Two enemy M.G. emplacements discovered and reported. Otherwise nothing unusual occurred. The day opened very hot and at 11 A.M. - 2 a.m. area was again shelled. Several scouts very considerable all day by the enemy. Our Coys were shelled by T.M.'s about mid-day and enemy assembled doubtful from wounding 1. L.R. D Coy H.Q. was shelled lightly again. Front areas shelled. P.C. on our "Strong Line" and sent to Bdge H.Q. Enemy attacked 103g on [left] and [western] back [line] front-right [trench] was immediate counter-attack, failed to regain. Bn. End Security shelled by 2 heavy T.M.'s at afternoon and about 5.20 P.M. burst of enemy rifle [musketry] [was] reported on left flank. S.O.S. was sent up by 11st Leics Bn. Ie enemy discovered in [heaping] on our [right] flank but was spotted and [time] again made contact. Military [reports] that 4 Coy in [coming] in reply to S.O.S. [had] working parties came out from field lops to dig trenches [front] in order to consolidate the line. At [evening] of active M.G. [fire] a number of casualties was caused and the work had to be left. Whilst unwilling a working order came through to our in must expect an attack on our front on the morning and in consequence sent to be ordered for 4.30 a.m. and Bn staff were non active. No attack developed. Bn Boundary altered and "A" Coy [withdrew] from their position and dug in behind Batt. H.Q.	
			Casualties { 2nd Lt M.J. Sergant Wounded. From 21.3.18 to 31.3.15 - 14 O.R. Killed. 132. O.R. Wounded.	
			{ 2nd Lt H. Hall Wounded	103. O.R. Missing. + 15 [Officers] [unfit] in [that] [period]
			Various [missing] men having [turned] up meantime for [prior] me in [show].	

Signed: [Stanley]
Lt. Col.
Commdg. 1/8th S.U.W. 11th Manchester Regiment

(Copy)

Operations of the 12th Battalion Manchester Regiment.
21st/25th March 1918.

A little time previous to the 21st March, a certain amount of enemy activity was observed on the Battalion front. The enemy was seen to have placed square boards with a plain black circle in the middle resembling a target, in lines at equal distances apart. The purpose of these boards was never ascertained.

At 4-50 a.m. on the 21st the enemy put down a heavy barrage with flames on the Battalion front and later shelled the Battalion front itself.

At 6-30 a.m. the enemy attacked on the left flank and entered a small bombing stop. Shelling was active during the day, especially in the back areas and the Battalion Transport lines.

At 1-30 a.m. on the 22nd orders were received that owing to the enemy having attacked further north, the Battalion would have to retire forthwith to occupy Havrincourt advance defences. The above orders being received, this movement was successfully carried out without casualties.

Battalion Headquarters had been situated in a large old German dug-out and the Colonel and the writer set the dug-out on fire with a tin of rum when leaving.

At Havrincourt the Battalion Headquarters was taken up in a dug-out close to the front line, but an entrance to the dug-out was found to come out in front of the front line! Another position therefore had to be found for Battalion Headquarters. The first enemy attack came at 6-35 p.m. and between then and 8-30 p.m. there were four successive attacks all of which were repelled with heavy enemy casualties by rifle, machine gun fire, and artillery.

During one of these attacks the writer, who was Adjutant of the Battalion, considered it advisable to burn all documents in case of accidents. Major C.T.Wilks, M.C. did active and valuable work in repelling the enemy attacks and pulled into the trench by the seat of his trousers a yelling German who was caught up in our wire and was taken prisoner.

The Battalion's own casualties were 2nd. Lt.T.Clarkson killed and about 30 other ranks killed and wounded. These were partly accounted for by our Artillery firing short on one or two occasions. As there was no telephonic communication available to the Brigade Headquarters the Battalion was not able to get in touch by this means with the Artillery to deal with this matter.

2.

At 3-30 a.m. on the 23rd orders were received that owing to the line having been broken further North the Battalion would withdraw to the old British Front line Yorkshire Spoil Heap north of Havrincourt Wood. This movement was accomplished with only two casualties.

About 11-30 a.m. the Naval Division on the Battalion's right was seen withdrawing from its position. This it appeared was for the purpose of straightening the line. The Manchesters were still without orders. These did not arrive until 12-15 p.m. owing to the Brigade runner having been hit. The orders were that the Battalion should withdraw to Rocquigny.

"B" Company and the 10th Lancashire Fusiliers covered the retirement. The weather was beautifully fine and some of the enemy were seen on the Slag Heap to the Battalion front. Although the enemy was almost in touch with the Battalion again and was enfilading the flank road to Havrincourt Wood (and was actually, it afterwards appeared, in the Woods to the rear of the Battalion on their left flank), the Manchesters succeeded in reaching the Rendezvous at Rocquigny with only five casualties.

On arrival at Rocquigny the Battalion took over a camp belonging to heavy Artillery who were just on the point of moving and had to leave their dump of clothing, boots and rations. The Battalion Quartermaster was ordered to give the men clean shirts and new boots as required, and fresh meat, which latter as it turned out later was a God-send.

At about 11-30 p.m. on the 23rd. the Battalion was ordered to move up and occupy an old German line running across the Russ-Rocquigny road, the enemy being reported to be in Russ.

Patrols were sent out and reported that the enemy was held by our troops. The Battalion returned to camp at Rocquigny at about 1 a.m. on the 24th. having had about 25 casualties.

After the return to camp the Battalion was ordered to wire the old German trench, and the Battalion took up its position in the trenches in the early morning.

A Subaltern in charge of an 18 pounder reported to the Battalion's Headquarters that his gun was in front of our front line; he was told he had better take up a position behind it. However, he said he had had explicit orders to stay where he was, and to remain there until he had fired off all his ammunition. At about 11-2 A.M. the enemy was reported attacking on the Battalions right. Our troops were then seen operating on either flank in connection with the operations for covering the withdrawal of part of the 63rd and of the 2nd Division on the Battalion's left. This was carried out on the right by the 17th Division (6th Dorsets), at 11-30 a.m.

In this connection, half to three quarters of a mile to the Battalion's right, lines of our men were seen advancing as if to attack, and the Battalion's hopes rose as it was thought fresh troops had come up and were attacking the advancing Huns. However, they were seen to swing round across the Battalion's front about 1,000 yards ahead and disappeared somewhere to the Battalion's left. These were troops to the Battalion's right, who were presumably unable to withdraw as the enemy were behind them, and so had to retire in a north westerly direction somewhere to the Battalion's left.

At 12-30 p.m. our tanks were observed in action moving from Brastre and the enemy were seen to be retiring. The proceedings terminated about 1 p.m. and the Dorsets informed the Battalion that they were withdrawing. Just before 1.15 p.m. the enemy was again observed on the ridge, the lines were shelled and one of our tanks was hit and burst into flames. Two of the enemy were seen to surrender to another tank at about 2-15 p.m. About this time the enemy had been seen to the right advancing in rushes down a slope opposite troops on the Battalion's right flank. The Officer in charge of the 20th London Regiment reported that the Battalion on his right hand was broken and that the enemy was following through. He offered to remain and protect the Manchester's right flank.

A little later Verey lights were seen being sent up by the enemy right to the rear of the Battalions on its right and in Rocquigny; the situation was critical. Meanwhile four enemy guns unlimbered in full view of the ridge in front and a German Officer was seen through field glasses to pull out a map, and began to shell the position.

The line was also enfiladed by a machine gun fire on the right. The position was more critical; the men too were exhausted. At 3-30 p.m. the 9th West Ridings stated that they had been ordered to withdraw. The Battalion was still without orders but a few minutes later the Manchesters received similar orders. At 3-50 p.m. the West Ridings withdrew on the left and the Manchesters followed. "A" Company stood fast for a time to cover the retreat and then followed as fast as they could making for Flers where the Rendezvous was fixed. The shelling from the four enemy guns mentioned above now began at high speed and first laid a barrage across a road which the Battalion had to cross, and enemy machine guns hidden in the right rear of the Battalion swept the men with their firing.

The writer and one or two officers tried to form a covering line of troops, but the targets were too well hidden and the four guns were now at longer range, so that there was nothing for it but to withdraw with all speed for the Rendezvous. As the writer at this moment went over to 2nd Lt.F.F.Taylor whom he saw lying wounded in a shell hole(2nd Lt.Taylor who was captured has subsequently stated that he was wounded again that day) he (the writer) was left to follow some distance behind the Battalion and could see the result of the enemy's fire. Machine gun fire was poor at first and should have wiped out the Battalion, but the enemy Artillery had now got the range and was mowing down with its shrapnel the men who were in its full view in large numbers. Many casualties were suffered from shells and machine gun fire and there were many missing.

At dusk the Battalion reached Flers and outpost positions were taken up by Brigade round the village. A hostile patrol was encountered which after exchanging shots withdrew. At 9 p.m. it was decided that the Brigade should re-assemble at Martinpuich and endeavour to get in touch with the division since to remain at Flers practically would have meant being surrounded. The Battalion moved up to the vicinity of Martinpuich where the Brigade took up a position as defensive flank for night arriving there about midnight.

On withdrawing from Rocquigny 44531 Company Sergeant Major P. Lamb ("B" Company) found Lt. L.Addison of his Company lying wounded but rescued him under heavy machine gun fire first wheeling him in a chance discovered barrow, then on a bicycle, and finally carrying him on his back until he reached the first aid post. The distance covered by C.S.M. Lamb was considerable, and not taking into consideration the exhaustion of all ranks, his feat was one displaying extraordinary strength as well as bravery. For this he was awarded the D.C.M.

The losses had been considerable. 2nd Lts. L.Addison and E.Hines were wounded. Lts. R.B.Hamer and M.Liggitt and 2nd Lts. F.F.Taylor and A.H.Jacob wounded and missing and about 120 other ranks wounded and missing or prisoners.

At 4 a.m. on the 25th the Battalion received orders to move and the Brigade marched a Battalion strong with Brigdr. Genl. Eden, D.S.O. leading personally to the cross roads south of Courcellette (Martinpuich-Courcellette Road) (It appeared that whilst the Battalion was moving down this road the enemy was on either flank only about 400 yards or so away.) Here the Brigade halted and efforts were made to find the location of Divisional Headquarters with whom touch had been lost since the Brigade had been all but surrounded.

As the Battalion Transport had been unable to obtain information as to the whereabouts of the Brigade this was the only day that rations went astray, but even so they had dumped them at the cross roads at the actual spot where the Battalion halted. However, another unit had taken them. Fortunately the men were well provided with food from the Artillery Camp at Rocquigny, and only Battalion Headquarters Officers, who had had nothing to eat since the previous morning at Rocquigny were short, though the Brigade Mess Cart was able to find a loaf and some jam as the Brigade marched down the Martinpuich-Courcellette Road.

From this point the Brigade moved down to Bapaume-Albert Road near Meaulte, information having been obtained that Divisional Headquarters were established in the latter place. On reaching Pozieres where the enemy was expected to attack, evidence of his presence was observed on the ridge. As there appeared to be a gap in our line the Manchesters were ordered to fill the breach at 11 a.m.

A later order directed the Battalion to proceed to Fricourt where it would come under orders of the 47th Division. This was done and the Battalion took up the position as defensive flank in Fricourt Wood collecting rations at Contalmaison on the way. The enemy attack was, however, not delivered opposite the Battalion's front and it was ordered to rest in the valley near Fricourt Wood, the men being badly in need of sleep and utterly exhausted.

A low flying enemy plane flew over the Battalion but did not return, perhaps mistaking our troops for its own, as someone waved, thinking it was one of our planes until overhead when the German cross on the plane was visible.

At this time information was received that the advance attack had succeeded elsewhere and the Battalion was ordered to take up a position in front of Fricourt to cover the withdrawal of the 9th Division. The Manchesters and West Ridings shared Battalion Headquarters in Fricourt Chateau. The night passed quietly. At 3-30 a.m. on the 26th orders were received to withdraw to Henencourt (in 5th corps reserve) where Divisional Headquarters were established. This was successfully carried out, the Battalion moving via Meaulte-Dernancourt Road and Millencourt. Lent for the time being to the 9th Division the Battalion received intimation to be prepared to move at half an hour's notice.

Alan J. C. Singleton
late Capt & Adj'
12th Bn. The Manchester Regt

17th Division.
52nd Infantry Brigade

WAR DIARY

12th BATTALION

THE MANCHESTER REGIMENT

APRIL 1918

Army Form C. 2118.

WAR DIARY
or
INTELLIGENCE SUMMARY.
(Erase heading not required.)

Instructions regarding War Diaries and Intelligence Summaries are contained in F.S. Regs., Part II. and the Staff Manual respectively. Title pages will be prepared in manuscript.

Place	Date	Hour	Summary of Events and Information	Remarks and references to Appendices

CONFIDENTIAL.

W A R   D I A R Y

O F

12TH. (D of L.Y.) BN. MANCHESTER REGIMENT.

From April 1st.   To April 30th. 1918.

VOLUME XXXIV.

Army Form C. 2118.

WAR DIARY
INTELLIGENCE SUMMARY.
(Erase heading not required.)

Place	Date 1918	Hour	Summary of Events and Information	Remarks and references to Appendices
"Field"	April 1		Bn. in front line W. of ALBERT E.2.c. and E.3.A. (Ref. map ALBERT 1/40,000) Great aerial activity all day by enemy. About 10 p.m. heavy T.M. bombardment of Bn. on right took place and shortly afterwards a strong patrol approached the line but was dispersed and driven off by enfilade L.G. fire from B Coy. 1 O.R. wounded in hand in afternoon (S.I.W.) 2nd Lieut W. TURNEY joined Bn.	
	2.		Situation very quiet, except for the enemy registering on valley behind Bn. H.Q. and a small attack on Australian Bn. on our right, which was broken up by L.G. fire from our front line company. Enemy aeroplane bombed our lines in early morning with a number of very small grenades and 1 O.R. was wounded. Our snipers shot at, and hit, one of the enemy in the afternoon. The Bn. was relieved at night by the 4th Suffolk Regt on relief marched into billets at WARLOY	
	3		The Bn. spent the day resting and cleaning up, in the billets at WARLOY. Between 4.0 p.m. and 5.0 p.m. a few enemy shells fell just in rear of the village. Bn. in VI Corps Reserve	
	4		Bn. moved by march route from WARLOY to VILLERS-BOCAGE and was billetted there for the night	
	5		Bn. moved by march route to CANAPLES at 11.30 a.m. and went into billets. Bn. should have moved at 9.30 a.m. but stood by till 11.30 a.m. owing to heavy firing having been heard. Staff of 9 O.R. joined Bn.	
	6		In Corps reserve at CANAPLES. Cleaning up. Bn. carried out: Draft 5 officers and Lieuts. E.S.R. McDOWELL, V.D. DALGOUTTE, A.P. TEARE, J. BRADLEY and W. KNIGHT and 122 O.R. of the 4th Bn. S. James Regt. Late of 4th Div. joined Bn. at mid day	
	7		At CANAPLES. Church Parades. Lieut. A.E. STAITE and 9 O.R. reinforcements joined Bn.	
	8, 9		At CANAPLES. Training	
	10.		At CANAPLES. Training. Draft 23 O.R. reinforcements joined Bn. mostly from New Sug. 45th Bn. Manchester Regt	
	11		At CANAPLES. Bn. moved to TOUTENCOURT at 10.30 a.m. and should was accommodated in tents in the wood. 14th Bn in III Army Reserve and supporting 31st & 4th Corps to meet any extraordinary arising on VI Corps front. An enemy attack on AMIENS being anticipated at an early date. Bn. on one hour's notice to move and take up defensive positions in support to 52nd Inf. Bde if necessary J. Brown joined Bn. 2nd Lieut. K. Sewar sick to Hospital	
	12.		At TOUTENCOURT. Training. Hostile aircraft passed over TOUTENCOURT about 9-0 p.m.	
	13.		At TOUTENCOURT. Training. Draft 9 O.R. joined Bn.	

WAR DIARY
or
INTELLIGENCE SUMMARY.
(Erase heading not required.)

Army Form C. 2118.

Place	Date	Hour	Summary of Events and Information	Remarks and references to Appendices
Field	April 1918 15		At TOUTENCOURT. Church Parades. 14th Div. relieved 63rd Div. in left sector of Corps front and 52nd Brigade proceeded to Divisional reserve in relief of 189th Inf Bde. Bn. proceeding to FORCEVILLE at 9.15 a.m. relieving HOOD Bn. Echelon B and Q.M. Stores at LEALVILLERS. 2nd Lieut. J.A. BROWN left Bn. to join 2/6th Sherwood Foresters. Lieut. C.DRUMSBY joined Bn. at Dixonbring. At FORCEVILLE, in Divisional reserve. Specialist training carried out. Bn. on one hours notice to move in case of enemy attack.	
	16			
	17		At FORCEVILLE in Div. Reserve. Training. Enemy shelled back areas about 11.0 a.m.	
	18		In Div. Reserve. Training. Enemy fired about 2013 shells in neighbourhood of FORCEVILLE.	
	19		In Div. Reserve. Training. Hostile aircraft passed over FORCEVILLE between 1.0 a.m. and 2.0 a.m. Enemy shelled neighbourhood of FORCEVILLE within a few rounds of 4.2 HV at odds intervals during Tuesday. All shells fell outside the village. 1 Off and 30 O.R worked under T.M.B taking guns round ENGLEBELMER. 30 O.R provided for your under Town Major. 6 O.R reinforcements joined Bn.	
	20		In Div. Reserve. Training. 5 O.R joined Bn. as reinforcements. Working party, 1 Off. 60 O.R. salved wire round ENGLEBELMER during day	
	21		At FORCEVILLE. Training carried out and voluntary church services. Working party, 1 Off. 60 O.R. salved wire round ENGLEBELMER. Enemy shelled village about 3-4 p.m. with about 15 H.V shells which landed in the main street by Bn. HQ, killing 2 O.R. and wounding 3 O.R. (and also slightly wounding 2 men who remained at duty) Also killing 2 mules and 1 H.D horses of this Bn. Six of sub other casualties to men of other units were caused and 4 horses in civilian's cart were killed. The 52nd Bde. were ordered to relieve the 50th Bde. in left sector of Air front and Bn. was to move forward abt 3.30 p.m. to relieve 6th Bn. Dorset Regt. located E. of ENGLEBELMER, Q.20 and Q.26. (Ref map 57 D SE) and 6/8 Bn. in Bde Support. At about 8.0 p.m. orders for relief were postponed and finally cancelled owing to the enemy having attacked and captured two posts at Q.29.D which overlooks the valley towards HAMEL in which enemy were believed to be about to mass prior to attack. No attack however developed. Casualties:- 2 O.R killed, 3 O.R wounded.	
	22		At FORCEVILLE in Div. Reserve. Enemy shelled village from 2.10 a.m. to about 4.0 a.m. with H.V. shells (mostly duds). Working party, 1 Off 60 O.R salved wire round ENGLEBELMER. Section training carried	

WAR DIARY or INTELLIGENCE SUMMARY

Army Form C. 2118.

(Erase heading not required.)

Place	Date	Hour	Summary of Events and Information	Remarks and references to Appendices
Field	April 26 1916		day, one falling near transport lines. Casualties - 5 O.R. killed, 11 O.R. wounded. Lieut R.B. HAMER and 2nd Lieut A.H. JACOB reported missing 25th March, now reported prisoners of war.	
	27	6.10 p.m.	In Bde. support. Same working parties ordered as for 26th less 30 men for 52nd T.M.B. At 3.35 p.m. and 6.10 p.m. S.O.S. was sent up on the night of MESNIL on right Divisional front, by the right Bn of right Bde and also by left Bn of Division on the right respectively. As a consequence of above the boys and working parties were ordered to stand fast and later, partly carrying up to front line was cancelled and men ordered to rest, and the two boys working on and manning the Intermediate system were ordered to carry on. Occasional activity during day and evening both of our own and enemy artillery. Branch shells of ENGLEBELMER was knocked down by an enemy shell about mid day. Four or five enemy 8" shells were also fired near ENGLEBELMER in the afternoon. Night quiet. Capt. J.H. BIRLEY of 4th Bn. W.R. Rifles Regt joined the Bn. at 3 a.m. front lines	
	28		In Bde. Reserve. Occasional artillery activity during the day. Working parties provided as follows: 1 N.C.O. and 10 men relieved shift of 50 men working on Bn. HQ. at 3 p.m. and worked during afternoon and 2 officers and 150 O.R. provided at 9 p.m. as usual for four's on reed manning Intermediate line during dark. Enemy fired few gas shells at batteries in Q20a between 8.30 p.m. and 9 p.m. Our own and enemy artillery active on the left during the night.	
	29		In Bde. Reserve. Morning quiet. Three shifts of 15 men each provided for work on Bn. HQ during day. Occasional artillery activity of our own and enemy during afternoon. Enemy aeroplanes flew over Bde. position at 3.15 p.m. and 5 p.m. Enemy artillery again active on left at 4.30 p.m. and 8 p.m. ENGLEBELMER shelled at 8.15 p.m. and 8.45 p.m. Bn. relieved 9th Bn. West Riding Regt in the front line in the left section of Bde. front, in trenches from Q29a.44 to Q23 a 3.3 (W of HAMEL) Right line B Coy right, A Coy left. Support B Coy two platoons between Q22 d 54 - Q22.b.65.90 and two platoons in Sunken Road Q25 a. Reserve C Coy in shelters in Q22 c and d. Bn HQ Q22 d 5.3 (Ref. map 57D SE 1/20,000) Band & Bn. moved from Bde. support at 8.30 p.m. and relieved support boys 9th Bn. West Riding Regt while 'A' and 'D' boys relieved the Intermediate system till relieved by above boys of 6th Bn. West Riding Regt. When 'A' and 'D' boys were relieved, they moved forward to relieve the two boys of 9th Bn. West Riding Regt in the front line. Casualty - 1 O.R. wounded. Relief complete 2.20 a.m.	
	30		In front line. Quiet. Work carried out on improvement of trenches.	

Army Form C. 2118.

WAR DIARY
-OF-
INTELLIGENCE-SUMMARY.
(Erase heading not required.)

Instructions regarding War Diaries and Intelligence Summaries are contained in F. S. Regs., Part II. and the Staff Manual respectively. Title pages will be prepared in manuscript.

Place	Date 1918	Hour	Summary of Events and Information	Remarks and references to Appendices
Field.	April 30 contd		during early morning whilst dark enemy fired at MESNIL with a few shells at noon. Occasional enemy shelling on left of Bn during afternoon and occasional shelling at 8:30 p.m by both ourown and enemy artillery.	

R. Stern Capt for
O.C. 12th (D of L.Y.) Bn. Manchester Regt.

Army Form C. 2118.

WAR DIARY
or
INTELLIGENCE SUMMARY.
(Erase heading not required.)

Vol 37

CONFIDENTIAL.

WAR DIARY
of
12TH B'N. MANCHESTER REGIMENT.

FROM MAY 1ST TO MAY 31ST 1918.

VOLUME XXXV

Army Form C. 2118.

WAR DIARY
or
INTELLIGENCE SUMMARY.
(Erase heading not required.)

Instructions regarding War Diaries and Intelligence Summaries are contained in F.S. Regs., Part II. and the Staff Manual respectively. Title pages will be prepared in manuscript.

Place	Date	Hour	Summary of Events and Information	Remarks and references to Appendices
In the field	May 1st 1918		As result of operations in front, CAPT T.H. DIXON and CAPT F.A. PICKLES were wounded. M.G. and 5 of the M.H. of the front line. Slight local activity on night of 1.30 am and enemy lights sent up. Quiet during day. Heavy gun fire heard about 6.30 PM on night and at intervals during evening. Work carried out at night on deepening trenches and wiring. Night exceptionally quiet. No enemy lights fired at night on Bn front except on frontage of night and left Battn. Bde reported 3 Bde expected gun shelling (Blue Cross) at 10.30 PM - 11.10 PM - 11.30 PM of night. Bde expected gun	G.H.
	2nd		from 12 midnight 1/2nd to 1.30 am. Some sort of Jumbos seen blowing up in R.36 (Ref. map) 5½ D.1/40,000). Our artillery fired organised shoot 3-0 AM to 3.10 AM. Remainder. Night quite as above. Visibility for whole town had been poor as weather mostly up to today which had been bright and sunny. There was consequently some aerial activity of own and enemy. An enemy aeroplane flew at odd intervals during day over Bn area and was engaged by M.G. and L.G. fire. Slight intermittent shelling by own and enemy artillery during day. Night quiet. Intro Coy relief carried out at dark. B Coy relieving A Coy and C Coy relieving D Coy. A Coy becoming Support Coy and D Coy reserve. Work carried out improving and wiring trenches and making 2 new Coy H.Q. Casualties 1 O.R. killed.	G.H.
	3rd		Organised shoot by our Artillery from 3.0 AM to 3.10 AM. Remainder of night exceptionally quiet. Intermittent shelling by own gun and enemy Artillery during day and MESNIL still held. Small and German propaganda balloon sailed over Bn about 4.5 PM. A hostile aeroplane flew away our lines in the morning and 5 about 5.0 PM these were all engaged by	G.H.

WAR DIARY
or
INTELLIGENCE SUMMARY.

(Erase heading not required.)

Army Form C. 2118.

Instructions regarding War Diaries and Intelligence Summaries are contained in F. S. Regs., Part II. and the Staff Manual respectively. Title pages will be prepared in manuscript.

Place	Date	Hour	Summary of Events and Information	Remarks and references to Appendices
			by M.G. and L.G. fire. Aerial activity during evening. Work carried out at night by us on 2nd, and night harassment in main line of resistance handed over to night Bn (10th Bn Lancashire Fusiliers). Night Quiet. Casualties 1 O.R. wounded.	W/
	4th		In front line. A few enemy shells fired on Bn sector - Cart - MESNIL shelled during afternoon. A enemy aeroplanes flew over our lines at 5.0 P.M. Aerial activity during evening. (11- 8.55 P.M. heavy bombardment heard on left. Slight smell of pineapple gas noticed. At 9.25 P.M. enemy signalled one of our aeroplanes own by stream of t green lights. Enemy searchlights at once switched on - Owing to reorganisation of Nul. Frontage, A Coy of 9/18 Duke of Wellingtons Regt. took over B Coy position and a Coy of 11/H.L.I. Border Regt. took over position of two platoons vacated by A Coy at 9.0 P.M. Bn then distributed as follows:- Front Line: C Coy right, A Coy centre, B Coy left distributed in depth from outpost line to close support line. Support: D Coy in support line - Work improving trenches and wiring carried out. D Coy made themselves accommodation. Night Quiet. Casualties 1 O.R. wounded.	
	5th		In front line + front. One hour fired at Bridge crossing stream N. of HAMEL at midday. Usual trench aerial activity during afternoon and evening. Enemy planes engaged by M.G. and L.G. fire. One plane observed to be hit. MESNIL shelled at 9.0 P.M. Work improving outpost line and	W/

A 5634 Wt. W4973/M687 750,000 8/16 D. D. & L. Ltd. Form-C.2118/13.

WAR DIARY
INTELLIGENCE SUMMARY

Army Form C. 2118.

Place	Date	Hour	Summary of Events and Information	Remarks and references to Appendices
	6.		Improving trenches carried out. R.E's were Support Line and party of 9th Bn. West Riding Regt. under R.E. worked on Support line digging. S.O.S tested by lights being sent up at 11.0 p.m. from Right front Coy H.Q. Result satisfactory. Night Unit - Casualties NIL. 2nd Lieut. F.F. TAYLOR reported wounded and missing 5/4.3.18. now reported wounded and prisoner of war. In front line. Slight hostile shelling at 10.0 AM. Much enemy movement and transport observed during early morning. Heavy Artillery informed but two shells fired. May Unit - Enemy aeroplanes flew over Bn. area about midday. Our guns active at 8.30 P.M. HESNIL shelled at 9.0 P.M. Work was carried out and party of 9th Bn. West Riding Reg. dug Support line Northwards under R.E. Two Coys of 9th Bn. West Riding Regt in reserve line placed under tactical command of the Bn. Anson on right and left of Divisions on Battalion's right and left reports hostile tanks seen in the morning. Night Quiet. Casualties NIL.	G/W
	7.		In front Line. - Enemy transport heard during early morning and about 4-6 AM was visible during morning. Day Quiet. Bn relieved by 63rd (R.N.) D.D. on 7/8 and 8/9- Troy and Beaumont Left Sub sector Bn. of V Corps. Bn. relieved by the ANSON Bn. of the 188th Bde and marched to FORCEVILLE billets at N. end of village.	G/W

Army Form C. 2118.

WAR DIARY
or
INTELLIGENCE SUMMARY.
(Erase heading not required.)

Instructions regarding War Diaries and Intelligence Summaries are contained in F. S. Regs., Part II. and the Staff Manual respectively. Title pages will be prepared in manuscript.

Place	Date	Hour	Summary of Events and Information	Remarks and references to Appendices
	8th		Bn. marched at 3-15 pm to billets in ARQUEVES.	6pm
	9th		Bn. marched at 9-15 AM to billets in TALMAS. Attached personnel rejoined Bn. Bn. left support to Corps front.	6pm
	10th		At TALMAS. Cleaning up, bathing and fast inspections carried out. Roll call at 10w² Wing regards Bn and 1 Officer reinforcement 2nd Lt W. FOSTER. 2nd Lt W. TURNEV left Bn. for attachment to S.S.2.T.M.B.	9pm
	11th		At TALMAS. Training. Bn on 1 hours to move each morning between 5.30 AM and 8.30 AM.	9pr
	12th		At TALMAS. Church Parade and shooting competition held.	9pm
	13th		At TALMAS. Training and shooting competitions held.	6pm
	14th			
	15th		At TALMAS. Training and shooting competitions held. 2nd Lt M.E. BARLOW left for England for attachment to R.A.F. Flying Corps. Enemy aeroplane flew high over village at 9.0 AM and also at night. SD9 "A" Bn. marked by V Corps Commander. Bn. in 4th	9pm
	16th		At TALMAS. Training as above.	9pm
			Corps Commander. Bn. in 4th only. Competition won by Bn.	4pm

WAR DIARY
or
INTELLIGENCE SUMMARY.
(Erase heading not required.)

Army Form C. 2118.

Place	Date	Hour	Summary of Events and Information	Remarks and references to Appendices
	17th		At TALMAS. Training as above.	GW
	18th		At TALMAS. Bn. moved at 6.0 A.M to Camp W at LEALVILLERS O.14.B.2.2. (Ref Map 57¹/d 1/40,000) vacated by 10th Bn. Showed gratitudes and took over defence scheme of Bde.	GW
	19th		At Camp at LEALVILLERS. 1 Officer and 400 OR provided for digging PURPLE Line (near MAILLEY-MAILLET and ENGLEBELMER) from 10-0 AM to 4-0 PM under RE. 10th Battn aeroplane flew over camp at 9.30 A.M. Specialist training.	GW
	20th		At Camp at LEALVILLERS. Training and bathing carried out at CDR. LUMBY. Joined Bn from "D" Wing and 30 of reinforcements. Owing to hostile attack being considered imminent Bn on half an hours notice to move daily between 3:30 AM and 4:30 AM	GW
	21st		At LEALVILLERS Camp. Training carried out. Hostile aeroplanes flew high over Camp about 9:30 A.M. Also active at night. 30 of reinforcements joined Bn.	GW
	22nd		At LEALVILLERS Camp. Bn practised attack during afternoon before Third Army Commander (General Byng) and V Corps Commander - Hostile aircraft active at night.	GW

WAR DIARY
INTELLIGENCE SUMMARY
(Erase heading not required.)

Army Form C. 2118.

Place	Date	Hour	Summary of Events and Information	Remarks and references to Appendices
	23rd		At LEALVILLERS Camp. Working party of 1/16 Officers and 400 o.R. proceeded to work under R.E. on trenches near MAILLY-MAILLET during morning - Specialist training and Bn. L.C. competition held during afternoon by Bn. Lt.COL. S. DANBY awarded D.S.O.	9pm
	24th		Training at LEALVILLERS Camp.	9pm
	25th		At LEALVILLERS Camp. 1st M.G. relieved 12th (Sv.) North MAILLY sector of IV Corps front. 11th Sans of f. Bn. relieving the 3rd G.H. Bde. the Bn. moved from Camp at 4.0 pm and relieving the 6th Bn. left in the front line in right sector of Bde front - (night sub-sector) S.E. of AUCHONVILLERS. (Q1 a Central to Q23 a 3.7) Dispositions front line- C Coy right, D Coy left, Support B Coy Reserve A Coy. Bn HQ Q15.c 20.30 (Ref Maps 57. D. SE ¼₀,₀₀₀). An (?) army personnel sent to TALMAS - 2nd Lt R. STODDARD sent to hospital. Personnel to Bde School at ARQUEVES sent off.	9pm
	26th		Established in wood S.E. of COUVENCOURT at O.6.f. Rlwy contain 12-15 am - Morning Quiet. Bn Outpostions heavily shelled from 1.45 pm to	9pm

WAR DIARY or INTELLIGENCE SUMMARY

Army Form C. 2118.

Place	Date	Hour	Summary of Events and Information	Remarks and references to Appendices
	27th		Intermittent shelling of Bn area with gas shells from 2 am to 4 am. Intermittent shelling during day. E.A. fairly active. Night quiet. E.A. brought down by 2 of our planes.	7m
	28th		E.A. flew over our lines at various intervals during day. Quiet night.	9m
	29th		E.A. fairly quiet. A few shells fell near Bn HQ about 3.0 pm. Bn was relieved by 10th Bn Lincs. Australians and became Support Bn. A Coy Q.15 t, B Coy Q.15 a, C Coy Q.15 a, D Coy Q.15 a, Bn HQ Q.15 t 2 1. E.A. brought down by 2 of our planes. 1 of Killed.	6m
	30th		Quiet day. A few shells fell at MAILLY-MAILLET. A+B Coys to 108 Bn found fatigues. Working parties supplied at night by A+B Coys to 108 Bn found fatigue. 5+1 officers 148 oR. West Riding Regt to work in the front line. 5+1 officers 148 oR employed.	9m
	31st		Left Bn Hqrs proceeded to U.W. on horse. Normal quiet. A few E.A. flew over Bn position at intervals during day. Working parties supplies to front line Bns by B+C Coys. 6 Officers 140 oR employed.	7m

G. Milton Major
for OB/IC 12th (S) Bn Lancashire Regiment

Army Form C. 2118.

WAR DIARY
or
INTELLIGENCE SUMMARY.
(Erase heading not required.)

CONFIDENTIAL.

WAR DIARY.
of
12TH (D.L.O.Y.) BATTN MANCHESTER REGIMENT.

FROM 1ST JUNE, 1918 — 30TH JUNE, 1918.

VOLUME XXXVI

WAR DIARY
or
INTELLIGENCE SUMMARY.

(Erase heading not required.)

Army Form C. 2118.

Place	Date	Hour	Summary of Events and Information	Remarks and references to Appendices
Hebuterne	1.6.18		Bn in Bde Support - Bn HQ at Q.10 d 3.4 (Ref Sheet 57 D SE 1/20,000) Quiet day - Little EA activity.	A4
	2nd		Enemy heavily shelled Bn. positions with gas shells and known from 2.0 am to 3.0 am. Remainder of day quiet. A few EA flew over our lines during the day - Bn. proceeded at 10.0 PM to relieve 9th Bn. West Riding Regt in left sub sector of Bde front.	
	3rd		Relief completed 12.20 am - Front line A Coy Q.10 d 33 to Q.17 b 66. B Coy Q.16 b.6.6 to Q.17 a 4.4. Support C Coy. Reserve D Coy. Slight shelling of AUCHONVILLERS about noon. Movement below normal. Weather 10 R wounded.	A4
	4th		About 2.30 AM enemy put down a very heavy bombardment on Bn front line. S.O.S was sent up by night front line (B Coy) - Our Artillery with exception of 18 pdrs was very slow in opening - MGs and certain TMBs opened at once and were kept going well. A party of the enemy approached our lines of a strength of about 20 men but they made no progress after and seemed uncertain. The bombardment ceased at about 3.30 AM - Communications held well and worked satisfactorily. One Lewis Gun was put out of action but was immediately replaced from Bn HQ. Casualties 1/OR wounded. 2 O/R and L/Hudson to hospital.	A4
	5th		Hostile aircraft flew over Bn. at 10 AM - Quiet. Work going out improving line and repairing damage done by shell fire. 2 a junior W.O.	A4

WAR DIARY
or
INTELLIGENCE SUMMARY.

Army Form C. 2118.

(Erase heading not required.)

Place	Date	Hour	Summary of Events and Information	Remarks and references to Appendices
			WISHLADE to hospital. A slight epidemic of a type of influenza occurred in Bn whilst in front line.	
	6th		3 hostile aircraft flew over Bn at 10 AM. Hostile T.M's active at 9.0 AM - Quiet during day. Work improving line and wiring carried out. Casualties 4 O.R. wounded	
	7th		Hostile T.M's active during early morning. Intermittent shelling during day. At 9.30 PM enemy suddenly lit up had also green lights all along the Cotps front and put down a light barrage on forward area and opened with his M.Gs. It appeared that the enemy had put up the S.O.S. Remainder of night quiet. Casualties 3 O.R. June LtCol S. DANBY, DSO, MC, proceeded to England on leave and course. Major G.J. WILKES MC took over Command of Bn.	
	8th	About 3.15 AM	a gas stokes mortar barrage was carried out by the R.E. After the gas discharged enemy made no reply and were very quiet. Hostile T.M's active during morning and at about 3.0 PM. A hostile aeroplane flew over our lines about midday. Remainder of day fairly quiet. At about 10.5 PM two Bns of 30 B.g. carried out a raid on L17 of Bn. The Bn cooperated by keeping certain areas under L.G. and rifle fire and in framing Very light to confuse Casualties	

A.5834 Wt. W.4973/M687 750,000 8.16 D. D. & I. Ltd. Forms/C.2118/13

WAR DIARY
or
INTELLIGENCE SUMMARY.

(Erase heading not required.)

Army Form C. 2118.

Place	Date	Hour	Summary of Events and Information	Remarks and references to Appendices
	9th		the enemy. During the raid which was accompanied by a heavy barrage our front line was thinned. Enemy barrage (minenwerfer) fell on Bn front and support lines about 10.9 PM and lasted 20 minutes. Raid lasted 90 minutes. 50th Bn HQ were accommodated at Bn HQ during raid which was successful. (30 prisoners and 6 MGs captured.) Casualties 10/R wounded.	
	10th		3.45 AM. Remainder of day quiet except 6.45 PM when enemy shelled AUCHONVILLERS and MAILLY. Work improving line and wiring carried out — Casualties 10/R wounded. Quiet. 52nd Bn relieved by 50th Bn. Bn relieved by 6th B Coast Regt. and went to Bn reserve at P15 and 16 (R) N.of 57D. (1/40,000) near ACHEUX	
	11th		In Bn reserve. Bn bathed and cleaned up — 2nd Lieut W. FOSTER to hospital sick — Lieut M. LIGGETT reported wounded and missing 24/3/18 now reported wounded and prisoner of war. 15428 Sgt H GLANVILLE awarded D.C.M. in half yearly honours list.	
	12th and 13th		In Bn reserve — Specialist training carried out and football	

WAR DIARY or INTELLIGENCE SUMMARY

Army Form C. 2118.

Place	Date	Hour	Summary of Events and Information	Remarks and references to Appendices
	14th		Competitions. In Divl. reserve. - Specialist training carried out. R.E. 2 Coy. provided working parties for digging at 10.0 PM to forward area amounting to 4 Officers and 150 OR.	
	15th		In Div Reserve - 2 Coys. handed working parties for 14 hours work amounting to 40 Officers and 200 OR digging at 6.0 AM in forward area. 1st & D Coys. provided 4 Officers and 145 OR for work at 10.0 PM as on 14th. Football competition continued-	
	16th		In Div. reserve - 52nd Inf. Bde. relieved 51st Inf. Bde. in the MAILLY LEFT sector. Bn. moved off at 10.45 PM. and relieved 14th Bn. Argyll & Sutherland Regt. in the PURPLE SYSTEM East of MAILLY MAILLET (Q8 Central to Q2 Central approx) and became Bn. in Bde. reserve. Bn. HQ. Q4 d 1.4. (R4 Map 57D 1/40,000). Working parties amounting to 10 Officers and 100 OR provided for often raids under R.E.	
	17th		In Bde. reserve. Quiet. 12 minute shelling during day. Working parties amounting to 3 Officers 210 OR provided for work with digging with R.E. and carrying for T.M.B. at night and morning. Enemy double shelled towards MAILLY about 16.30 PM	
	18th		In Bde. reserve- Quiet - Area occupied by D Coy at Q8a (approx)	

WAR DIARY
or
INTELLIGENCE SUMMARY.

(Erase heading not required.)

Army Form C. 2118.

Place	Date	Hour	Summary of Events and Information	Remarks and references to Appendices
			bombarded by enemy during the afternoon (2 se note 5.9's) - Hostile aeroplanes flew over about 6.30 PM to observe result of shooting, but were driven off by our planes. Enemy artillery quiet at night. Our guns active at 12 midnight. Cooperating in raid by a Bn of 42nd Div on our left. Working parties wounded as fol. 1/4th - Casualties bat wounded 2 2/Lt Hudson injured from trap door.	
	19th		In B.H. Reserve - Our artillery active at 12.0 noon & 3.30 PM and 8.30 PM. Enemy artillery slight intermittent shelling during day. Quiet at night. Our aeroplanes active. 8 enemy aeroplanes flew over front line 8.0 to 8.30 PM. 2/Lt R.G. Dalgoutte transferred to H.Q. Coy.	
	20th		A front attack was carried out on S. portion of AVELUY WOOD at 2.0 AM. Our artillery active from 12.0 midnight 19/20th to 5.30 AM - Gas projectors were fired on the night at 2.0 AM. Enemy artillery quiet. Intermittent shelling during day. Our artillery active at 10.15 PM - 8 to 10.0 PM Bn. moved off to relieve 9/Bn. West Riding Regt in the front line ("Advanced Forward Zone") from Q.10.d 20.30 to Q.4.a 40.46 - front line A Coy right, B Coy centre, and C Coy left. Left flank (W. defence) D Coy - Bn HQ Q.3.D.4.4. (Rf. Mab. 5/D 1/20000) - Night quiet. Work improving posts and wiring carried out.	
	21st		Raid carried out on night Q.35.t and Q.23.a by 38th Bde at 2.5 AM - Our artillery active - Remainder night and day quiet. Our aircraft active	

WAR DIARY or INTELLIGENCE SUMMARY

Army Form C. 2118.

(Erase heading not required.)

Place	Date	Hour	Summary of Events and Information	Remarks and references to Appendices
	22nd		Few enemy shells fell round Bn HQ at 1.30 P.M. Work at night warning and improving huts carried out. Road at Q3d 90.15 blown up by R.E. as Tank Trap, and gunny concealment to passes lay-hazardlies. 1 O.R. killed and 1 O.R. wounded. Bde relieved by 190th I.F. Bde 63rd Division. The Bn being relieved by 1/1st Bn Royal Fusiliers—casualties 1 O.R. wounded.	
	23rd		After relief Bn. moved to ACHEUX WOOD when breakfast was served and Bn and Transport moved to Camp in TOUTENCOURT WOOD at 4.15 A.M. Bn assumed duties of Bde to man the BROWN LINE between P 28 A 5.0 and N1 a 5.0 (Right supporting two Coys) from 12 o noon from 23rd P. Personnel rejoined Bn from Bde School party attached to R.E. and Army Reception Camp (1st Div Wing) also 9d kill R/t DEWAR, Hospital and Army reinforcements. 2nd Lt F. HALLIWELL and 8 O.R.	
	24th		Cleaning up and bathing carried out at TOUTENCOURT. Orders issued that the Bn is on 5 hours notice to move to XXII Corps in case of hostile attack to lift in G.H.Q. reserve. Mobile detachment of 6 Lewis Guns Teams (1 Officer, 18 O.R.) detailed in case of emergency to move off by lorries at once.	
	25th		Training and bathing carried out at TOUTENCOURT. Orders received that Bn to be prepared to occupy BROWN SYSTEM V.14 d.15.00 to V.3 Central.	

WAR DIARY or INTELLIGENCE SUMMARY

Army Form C. 2118.

Place	Date	Hour	Summary of Events and Information	Remarks and references to Appendices
	26		(Ref Map 57D 40/500) at 2 hours notice and 1 hours notice between midnight and 5.0 P.M. in case of emergency whilst R.is in Right Support, to V Corps at to be ready to counter attack on any other portion of V Corps front.	
	27		Training at TOUTENCOURT. Hotel bombing about midnight.	
	28		Training at TOUTENCOURT. Bn Sports held in afternoon for game. Hostile Bombing Planes active about 11.0 P.M. in neighbourhood of TOUTENCOURT.	
	29		Training at TOUTENCOURT. Church Parade in morning and training in the afternoon. TOUTENCOURT Wood bombed by hostile aircraft at 11.0 P.M. Casualties caused to X of James two and 9th Bn West Riding, adjoining Bns Camp, but no bombs actually fell in Camp occupied by the Bn. 2nd Lt W.W. WISHLADE rejoined Bn from Hospital. 20 o/r reinforcements joined Bn. Influenza of a mild type prevalent in Bn whilst in TOUTENCOURT. Lt/Col Birchall D.S.O. M.C.	
	30		reigned Bn from leave & took over command of Bn. D.Bn now on an hour notice between 6.0 A.M. & 3 hours after an warning of 3 hrs duty to move to XXII Corps. Namely 12th (D of L) Bn Manchester Regiment.	

Army Form C. 2118.

WAR DIARY
or
INTELLIGENCE SUMMARY.

(Erase heading not required.)

CONFIDENTIAL.

WAR DIARY

of

12TH (D.L.OY.) BN. MANCHESTER. REGT

FROM 1ST JULY, 1918 to 31ST JULY, 1918.

VOLUME XXXVII

WAR DIARY or INTELLIGENCE SUMMARY

Army Form C. 2118.

(Erase heading not required.)

Instructions regarding War Diaries and Intelligence Summaries are contained in F.S. Regs., Part II and the Staff Manual respectively. Title pages will be prepared in manuscript.

Place	Date 1918	Hour	Summary of Events and Information	Remarks and references to Appendices
Suzanne	July 1		Bn training at TOUTENCOURT. Major G.T. WILKES, M.C. proceeded to England for Senior Officers course at ALDERSHOT. Major E.R. THOMPSON, M.C. takes over 2nd in command of Bn. during his absence.	
	2		Training at TOUTENCOURT	
	3		Training at TOUTENCOURT. Lt Col E.R. PILKINGTON, C.M.G. late Bn Manchester Regt joined Bn for 1 month's attachment.	
	4		Training at TOUTENCOURT. 2nd Lieut (A/Capt) P. DICKINSON, 5th Bttn R. Manchester Regt joined Bn	
	5		Training at TOUTENCOURT. Capt BTNLEY MORO, U.S. left Bn to join U.S. forces and Capt T. SCOTT, R.A.M.C. joined Bn in his place.	
	6		Training at TOUTENCOURT. 2nd Lieut W.H. HAYWARD transferred to 52nd L.T.M. Bty. At TOUTENCOURT Church Parade. 2nd Lieut E.T. SUTER rejoined Bn from England.	
	7		Alarm practised by Div. and Bn ordered to man BROWN LINE V.14 (Ref map 57(D)) at one hour's notice. Bn moved off at 12.25 a.m. and returned to camp at 8 a.m. Bn wounded at 9 a.m.	
	8		Training at TOUTENCOURT. 1st and 2nd platoons of A Coy despatched to HARPONVILLE for carrying under R.E. during Div tour. Personnel despatched B Bn Reception Camp at 2nd Lt E.T. SUTER (details)	
	9		At TOUTENCOURT. Whilst at TOUTENCOURT a mild type of influenza was prevalent. Bn rejoined 125th Div. in the line. Bn moved off at 4.30 p.m. to relieve 17/18 W R & Stafford by 5/2nd Suff Regt on right sector of SUZANNE. Bn moved forward 3000 (advanced bound) in the night and rested of Bt. Bde Front, East of BOUZINCOURT Bn halted on the way up to the trenches, at WARLOY where tea was served and from where Bn moved off at 9.30 p.m. Dispositions:- Front line W.15 d 3.1 to W.15 a.7.9. C' Coy right D Coy left Support A Coy (east Hutton) Right B Coy left. Bn HQ W.13 a 3.6. (Ref map 57 D 3 E	
	11		In front line. Quiet. Our Arthl. activity few over our lines at 8.30 pm. Shelling in the evening. Day intermittently shelled in GAUDRIE during which there was one of which	

WAR DIARY
INTELLIGENCE SUMMARY
(Erase heading not required.)

Army Form C. 2118.

Place	Date	Hour	Summary of Events and Information	Remarks and references to Appendices
Authuille	11/8/16		had to be destroyed. Wiring and work on bars carried out. (2 platoons worked under R.E. wiring. Casualties :- 1 O.R. wounded.	
	12.		Sn. front line. Quiet.	
	13.		Sn. front line. At 4.15am our howitzers open fire on BEINGCOURT and finished at daylight. Quiet. Our aircraft active. Enemy aircraft active. Observer sighted during afternoon fired over our lines at 8.50pm. Having brought down two of our balloons. Much artillery active during the day. During evening our howitzer batteries fired salvoes into enemy front line. Casualties :- 3 O.R. wounded.	
	14.		Support line S.E. of NOOTE Au HUT left at about 1.0am. Both Bns. to bivouacs near M.G. school rifle and Zn. tents. S.E. of NOOTE Au HUT left at about 1.0am. Both Bns. to bivouacs near M.G. school rifle fire. Obtained Russian shelling during morning. Our aircraft active. On my arrival Bn. requested by 4th Bde. to be behind Regt. and after being seen moved for work under R.E. ab 10.0pm. the number of my offices and under V.13c - V.12 - V.12.6 central and PURPLE systems and became Bn. in (the number of my offices and Vs.13c - V.12 - V.12.6) have also 2 O.R. wounded.	
	15.		W.4a and 6, By. HQ V.12c (Rf map 57D 1/40,000). keep for a while about 4.0am hostile in the Piozière. Relief complete 2.30am. arbitrary quiet. Our Observers reported when hostile in 3 lines 100 yds apart and 200 yds distance stretching in south westerly direction from N.30a 40.80 (part of ALBERT). These were similar to those observed on March 18 when first enemy offensive. Enemy also observed gathering in forward area. 25 were observed. At 10.30am a fighting patrol (left behind in line on relief consisting of 2 Lt. R.DEWAR and 15.0R of D Coy went out to endeavour to raid the enemy trenches to obtain a prisoner. The owing to enemy raids and tendency and could not return to trench. Working party of O.R. plays and others proceeded under R.E. at 10.0pm. for digging. Casualties 3 O.R. wounded.	
	16.		On the Reserve Quiet. Our artillery active at night. Hostile aircraft active during morning up to 10.0am and engaged by A.A. and L.G. fire. Our aircraft active. Observers reported column of (start of column) being led N towards AVELUY Wood Arn. Bns. relieved by 3rd Bn. H.L.I. Bn. being relieved by 10th West Yorks Regt. Bn. proceeded down to R.18 camp. On relief representated by W.9 Mdr. Reg. at V.14.6, V.15a and V.8a, N.E. of WARLOY (A map 57D 1/40,000). Bn HQ V.14. N.B.5. (Others)	

WAR DIARY or **INTELLIGENCE SUMMARY**

Army Form C. 2118.

Place	Date	Hour	Summary of Events and Information	Remarks and references to Appendices
In the Field	18		In Divisional Reserve. Cleaning up and kit inspections.	
			In Divisional Reserve. At 1.0 p.m. enemy aeroplane observed to have been hit by one of our A.A. guns. A Coys 2nd two detailed for fatigue reported. Bn. During to re-organisation of Coys & spent the day. Bn. was ordered to relieve the 37th in the MESNIL right sector on the re-adjustment of front. The 52nd Bn. relieved parts of 114th Bn. and 115th Bn. 10th Bn. in the MESNIL right sector the Bn. relieving them the NELSON R. (less 2 Boys) and the 2nd Royal Welsh Fusiliers (less 2 Boys) occupied the area Q2b.0 and Q2d.0 in the intermediate System and ENGLEBELMER trench. PURPLE SYSTEM Q.25.a and 0 in Bn. Support. (many forward Coys). Front - A Coy right. B Coy left in intermediate System. Support - C Coy right. D Coy left in PURPLE System. Bn. HQ P.30.a.29.	
	19.		In Rt. Support. One of our Scouting aeroplanes observed to shoot down by enemy A.A. fire after his having brought down one of enemy Kite balloons. He landed W. of MARTINSART. Quiet day. At 12.15 a.m. Bn. Bn. in the left raided the states near BEAUMONT-HAMEL. Our artillery active. Quiet day. Occasional enemy shelling (counter battery) during day.	
	20.		In Rn. Support. Quiet. Enemy attacks S. of ENGLEBELMER at such a few burning flares from his shell search up for transport in the brewing. 2 hostile aeroplanes flew low over our lines (P.M.) at 8.30 p.m. our aeroplanes return. Wireless entries enumerated to 2 Boys provided at night (P.M.) with us on R.E. Remainder of Bn. worked on support trenches - 2 o.R. killed.	
	21.		In Bde. Support. Quiet. One of our aeroplanes shot down enemy kite balloon near POLIERES at 11.45 p.m. and at 2.20 p.m. an enemy aeroplane driven up in flames near VARENNES. O.Pirs gas shelled by enemy at 10.30 p.m. P.34.6 and P.30 at 11.30 p.m. as above.	
	22.		In Rn. Support. Quiet. Occasional shelling in afternoon (counter battery). Intermittent hostile shelling during night. (S.3.2) At dark C Boy moved forward to new positions as follows:- two platoons at Q.24.c.9.0 and two platoons Q.24.c.6.0.b. Boy HQ at Q.26.c.0.5. Bde. at about C.26 dug themselves in. Lieut. D.E. MORGAN joined Bn. A few officers and N.C.Os of U.S.A. Army attached for two days for instructions. Casualties:- 2 o.R. wounded.	

WAR DIARY or INTELLIGENCE SUMMARY

Army Form C. 2118.

Place	Date	Hour	Summary of Events and Information	Remarks and references to Appendices
Julia Field	July 24 1918		In Bde Support. Quiet. Bn relieved 6th/8th West Riding Regt in the Left Bde. sector. Advanced Headquarters, S.E. of MESNIL. Dispositions Q3c.d. 5.1 to Q29.c.0.1. Brigade on Right, "A" Bn Left. Supports "D" Coy right, "C" Coy left. B"HQ Q2a. 95.30 N.W. of MESNIL. (Ref. 57. DSE 1/20.000). Bn relieved by about 5 p.m. Infantry fairly quiet. Hostile aeroplane over our lines at 5.30 a.m. and 3.30 p.m. Night quiet.	
	25.		MESNIL shelled fairly heavily from 9 to a.m. to 2.20 p.m. A hostile T.M. fell about 5.30 p.m. on one of B Coys posts on Eastern Flank causing one casualty. T.H. COWEN and 3 N.C.O.s wounded 1 O.R. as follows: 6 nights in 1st line, 6 nights in support, "D" Coy right centre, "B" Coy left centre, "C" on left, "A" reserve. Individual hostiles were observed to work in 2 & 3's. Enemy appears keen out Patrols sent out on night and hefts. A second party of hostile was seen to work in U S A Enemy appear keen for two days. Something of Rifles (Pvt. T.H.COWEN) 3 O.R. killed, 12 O.R. wounded.	
	26.	1.30 p.m.	In front line. Hostile M.guns very active at 10 a.m. Hostile T.M. barrage at 4.30 p.m. on our front line. A number officers were observed at 4/10 a.m. crawling towards our line. Our BANK Post (Q35b) about 450 ... 25 hm. BANK. was shelled. Hostile T.M. and 4.2cm. shells. Some of the enemy were post and front line was bombarded by hostile T.M. and 4.2cm. shells. Some of the enemy were observed crawling up to ourselves of BANK post and was fired at by our shells. One was wounded and the other 3 was knocked out and the remainder were driven off but to back to their lines. A platoon went up in by the our flanking and to BANK Post and our artillery was asked for in front of BANK Post at 5.45 p.m. thus of the B'NK Post. Our artillery was asked for in front of BANK Post during the evening and night. Patrols sent out on night and left. Casualties 14 O.R. wounded and working parties carried out.	
	27.		Rather quiet. Hostile artillery during day and about 9.30 p.m. 2nd Bn H.Q. Our artillery active during day and night. Wind stock enveloppe patrols sent out. One special Patrol sent out to reconnoitre enemy post (Q36a, 1.4.) with view to raiding same at a later date. Casualties: 3 O.R. killed, 8 O.R. wounded.	
	28.	2.15 p.m.	Our artillery active, between 2.15 p.m. and 2 a.m. Much enemy movement (M.T.& Artillery) observed, but kept up engaged by our M.Guns. Bn being drawn from army groups above moving during night. Even Infantry Brigade M.Guns and men MESNIL but during the M, 29. Front 5.25 p.m. Path to dig out overnight at 6.a.m. Work as usual. Following accounting to it	

WAR DIARY
INTELLIGENCE SUMMARY
(Erase heading not required.)

Army Form C. 2118

Place	Date	Hour	Summary of Events and Information	Remarks and references to Appendices
In the Field	1918 July 28		Officers and 320 OR of 3rd Bn. 318th Regt. of the American Army joined Bn. for two days instructions. Night quiet. Casualties: 2 OR wounded	
	29		Our enemy aeroplanes flew over our lines at 9.30am but driven off by S. fire. Enemy artillery quiet. No enemy movement observed. Night usual.	
	30		At 9.0am a sham attack was carried out on Bn. dumps. Eleven projectors from Bn area (Q3rp) Smoke barrages sent up from left Special by R.E. discharged HQ at 9.25a.m. and repeated at 10.50 a.m. for 5 mins. Outposts line was cleared for this operation and manned again by 11.0am. Hostile shelling normally very slight and no enemy lights signals observed at ZERO HOUR. At 10.0pm + enemy aeroplanes over our lines and dropped some bombs on Bn. right (Q33central) Thus the attack and dropped two of our planes one of which fell in flames near ENGLEBELMER. Hostile TM's active during day also his artillery. Our artillery active. Work as usual and active patrols sent out. Casualties - 1 OR of U.S.A. Army attacked killed and 1 OR killed and 1 OR wounded.	
	31		At 11.30am hostile transport heard in AUTHUILLE. At 5.20am + 5.40am + 6.12am. At 6.15am enemy fired 4 + 2 trench mortars on our outpost line in AVELUY Wood. Slight hostile intermittent shelling and usual TM activity. Our artillery active. Attacked enemy trench returned to their usual at 4.30pm. A special light signal sent up at 10.0pm by last SOS. Night quiet. Work and patrols as usual. Hostile aeroplanes passed over Bn. 10 to 10pm. During the Bn tour in this line 16 OR reinforcements joined Bn and various reinforcements and following officers joined Bn. Reception Camp for Bn. 2nd Lieuts. S. SURKITT, H. CODE, J.A. CORLEY, J.W. BARTON. 2nd Lieut S. SURKITT and 19 OR reinforcements joined Bn. from Our Reception Camp. Casualties - 1 OR wounded.	

Capt. for
Lt. Col. (D of L.Y.) 12th Bn. Manchester Regiment

52nd Bde.
17th Div.

12th BATTALION,

MANCHESTER REGIMENT,

AUGUST 1918.

Army Form C. 2118.

96 35
52/17

WAR DIARY
or
INTELLIGENCE SUMMARY.

(Erase heading not required.)

CONFIDENTIAL.

WAR DIARY
of
12TH (D.L.O.Y.) BATTALION MANCHESTER REGIMENT.

August 1ST 1918 — August 31ST 1918.

VOLUME XXXVIII

WAR DIARY
INTELLIGENCE SUMMARY

Army Form C. 2118.

(Erase heading not required.)

Instructions regarding War Diaries and Intelligence Summaries are contained in F. S. Regs., Part II. and the Staff Manual respectively. Title pages will be prepared in manuscript.

Place	Date 1918	Hour	Summary of Events and Information	Remarks and references to Appendices
In the field	Aug 1		In front line. Intermittent hostile shelling. Our artillery active. German propaganda shot down in our lines and found to carry French literature. At 9.30 p.m. a raid was carried out by Bdes on our right. Bn. relieved by 10th L'pool and moved into Bde. Reserve to man PURPLE line occupying area at P.303. and d, Q.25.a and Q.31.a. Bn. HQ. P.30.C.4.0. Casualties 3 O.R. wounded.	App.
	2.		Raid carried out on our right at 1.30 a.m. Relief complete 1.45 a.m. Twenty reported to have evacuated his position and to be withdrawing E. of ANCRE. Quiet day. Bn ordered to sulleys 9th & 13th Riding Regt and became Bn in Bde support (adjusting forward gans) occupying sunk positions in Letrunecel System as an 24th July with D.A and O. Coy work westing and J Bn in support. Rn HQ remained P.30.c.4.0. One Coy (H) did fir work over dug-outs under tunnelling Coy by day and wiring parties amounting to about 111 platoons provided for 414th Fld. Coy. R.E. at night. Hostile shelling of Backareas at night. 1 Aeroplane driven off by A.A. fire.	App.
	3.		In Bde support. Hostile artillery quiet during day. 5 hostile aeroplanes flew over our lines at 8.9 p.m. but HEDAUVILLE at night. Very little hostile movement observed. Our aircraft active. Intermittent shelling of HEDAUVILLE at night. Work parties as above (one platoon under 414th Fld R.E.)	App.
	4.		In Bde support. Hostile artillery very quiet except few shells fired at a battery near ENGLEBELMER. Working parties as above. R.A. Observers reported no enemy seen this side of POZIERES.	App.
	5.		In Bde support. Quiet. Working parties as above. 2nd Lt. E.E. KNIBB to hospital from Aid Pott. Casualty during morning from very long range Rd. shell fired on area occupied by A Coy. Bn relieved by 16th Bn Royal Welsh Fusiliers of 113th Bde 38th Div. Afterrelief Bn proceeded to camp at V.4.a and b. (near HEDAUVILLE - WARLOY road) Bn HQ V.14.b.2.4. (Ref map 57D 1/40.000) Casualties 2. O.R. killed.	App.
	6.		Bn. became night support Divn. in reserve, in G.H.Q reserve ready to move at 2 hrs. notice. Cleaning up and kit inspections carried out. Personnel from 51st Reighton Carnp rejoined Bn including reinforcement of 2nd Lieut. H.CODE, J.A.CORLEY,MM, J.W.BARTON and F.G.CORKER. Working parties equivalent to about 2 Coys provided under 123 Fld Coy R.E. during the day.	App.
	7.		In Camp V.14.a and b. (Ref map 57D 1/40.000). Work as above. Owing to our troops having broken through the enemy lines on the AMIENS front Division ordered to be on two hours notice to move. All working parties recalled at noon and Hd. Bde. ordered to be ready to move at any time from 1.0 p.m. to 4.0 p.m. for QUERRIEU area. Bn warned, march south to billets in BUSSY-lez-DAOURS, at 4.45 p.m. in VI Corps Area (IV Army)	App.
	8.		Bn. arrived at billets in BUSSY at 2.0 a.m. 5.20 Inf. Bde. ordered to move to billets at HEILLY in the evening. Bn. moved off at 9.0 p.m. for HEILLY in III Corps Area (IV Army). Battle surplus	App.
	9.			

A5834. Wt. W4973/M687. 730,068. 8/16. D.D.&L.Ltd. Forms/C.2113/13

WAR DIARY or INTELLIGENCE SUMMARY

Army Form C. 2118.

Place	Date 1918	Hour	Summary of Events and Information	Remarks and references to Appendices
In the field	Aug 9 (contd) 10.		personnel left Bn. for DAOURS and afterwards returned to BUSSY. Bn. arrived at billets in HEILLY at 12.30 a.m. and rested during day. Aerial activity at night.	
	11.		At HEILLY. Aerial activity at night. Hostile aircraft dropped a few bombs in vicinity of HEILLY on night 11th/12th.	
	12.		At HEILLY. Division ordered to relieve the 3rd Australian Division in the left centre sector (immediately S. of SOMME) of the Australian Corps front, IV Army. The 52nd Inf Bde. (to be in Reserve) embused at HEILLY on the HEILLY–BONNAY road at 4.30 p.m. and debussed at HAMEL to relieve 9th Australian Bde. Bn. marched from HAMEL to area Q.23.d. SE. of MORCOURT (Ref map 62 D S E 1/20,000) in relief of 3rd Australian Bn. in Divisional Reserve. Dispositions:– C. Coy right A. Coy centre, D. Coy left, B. Coy support, B'n. H.Q. Q.29.b.85.45. Relief completed 10.45 p.m. Hostile aircraft flew over Bn. at 9.10 p.m. and dropped bombs. They were very active. Hostile shelling negligible. Transport moved from HEILLY by road and echelon B. established at POH 6.0.8. (Ref map 62 D S E 1 20,000).	
	13.		In Divisional Reserve. Occasional enemy shelling during night and at 3.30 a.m. Our artillery active during night (especially on left shore and operation was commenced at 12.45 a.m.) and at 3.0 a.m. Few hostile shells fired at 10.30 a.m. and quarry near B. H.Q. was shelled intermittently throughout the day. Our aircraft active. Bn. ordered to move to the left and for proceed to take up positions at 5.0 p.m. as follows: A.B.C. D. Coys in line finding own supports from R.19. C.29 to R.13 o 65.90. Bn. H.Q. Q.24 central (Ref map 62 D S E). Hostile aeroplanes flew very low at 6.30 p.m. Enemy fired few shells at B. Coy H.Q. Hostile bombing planes active 9–10 p.m. 1 o/r. killed, 4 o/r. wounded.	
	14.		At 3.30 a.m. hostile shelling was considerable. Occasional hostile shelling during day. Hostile aircraft active during early part of night. Casualties 2 o/r. wounded.	
	15.		In Divisional Reserve. Hostile shelling from 2 a.m. to 5 a.m. Day quiet. Occasional enemy shelling. Bn. to be relieved by 59th or 60th Australian Bns. of 15th Australian Bde. Hostile barrage fell 8 o'c to 8.30 p.m near PROYART. Hostile artillery active at night, also usual hostile bombing. 3 o/r killed, 16 o/r wounded	
	16.		Owing to non-arrival of relieving unit who had taken up a fresh position. Bn. marched to bivouacs and billets at FOUILLOY near CORBIE and at 3.0 p.m. Bn. marched to fill to at VECQUEMONT and DAOURS	

WAR DIARY
INTELLIGENCE SUMMARY

Army Form C. 2118

Instructions regarding War Diaries and Intelligence Summaries are contained in F.S. Regs., Part II. and the Staff Manual respectively. Title Pages will be prepared in manuscript.

Place	Date 1918 Aug.	Hour	Summary of Events and Information	Remarks and references to Appendices
In the field	14th (contd)		where Bn. accommodated at the chateau. Division in G.H.Q. Reserve. A large amount of enemy material was salvaged by the Bn. during this tour. Casualties:- OR wounded.	
	14.		At VECQUEMONT. Division being transferred from Australian Corps to Vth Corps III Army, the Bn. moved off at 8.30 p.m. for billets at HERISSART. 2nd Lieut. P. DICKINSON to hospital. Battle Surpluses rejoined	
	18.		At HERISSART. Bn. moved at 2.30 p.m. for billets in BEAUQUESNE.	
	19.		At BEAUQUESNE. Cleaning up and resting. Reinforcements joined Bn. from Div. Reception Camp. - Lieut. J. HEATON and 16 OR.	
	20.		At BEAUQUESNE. Training. Bn. moved to ACHEUX area at 10.0 p.m. Battle Surplus remained at BEAUQUESNE for time being. 2nd Lieut. H. JAMESON took over Adjutancy. 2nd Lieut. R. KEMP to Bn.H.Q. for Liaison work between Bde. and Bn.	
	21.		Bn. moved at very short notice to BROWN line (12.30 p.m.) behind MAILLY-MAILLET and ENGLEBELMER. Quiet day. 2nd Lieut. MARSH to Bde. on cycle for Liaison which 50th Bde. 2nd Lieut. HUDSON went on Special Leave.	
	22.		Quiet day. Bn. moved at 10.0 p.m. to PURPLE Line just in front of MAILLY-M. Lieut. J. HEATON as extra Liaison Officer at Bde. 1.0 a.m.	
	23.		19th Div. attacked (THIEPVAL) 1.0 a.m. Bn. moved 10.30 a.m. to THIEPVAL RIDGE and again at 2.0 p.m. to Regt. behind and in touch with forward advancing troops. 2nd Lieut. MARSH rejoined from Liaison work and 2nd Lieut. KEMP continued as such. 2nd Lieut. F. HALLIWELL to leave.	
	24.		Battalion attacked at 4.0 a.m. "A" and "C" Coys in front. Band "D" Coys in support. Advanced very well, took and cleared MARTINPUICH, after which we were held up by heavy M.G. fire for rest of day after advancing 4,000 yds. 21st Div. on left. 38th Div. on right. Latter slit no down badly during day by returning from HIGH WOOD. Our casualties were severe during their absence. Casualties: — Killed: — Capt. T.H. DIXON M.C., 2nd Lieut. H. CODE, 2nd Lieut. S. COULTER, 2nd Lieut. Wounded: — Capt. F.A. PICKLES M.C., 2nd Lieut. S. SURKITT, 2nd Lieut. J.H. HOLDRIDGE, (Lieut. L.L. BOARDMAN, 2nd Lieut. W. KNIGHT, 2nd Lieut. W. MARSH, M.M. OR Killed 28, OR wounded 112, OR missing 1.	
	25.		Bn. advance resumed 5.0 a.m. Started badly but owing to most excellent work by our remaining officers, especially 2nd Lieut. C.T.L. McDOWALL, of position (M.G.) Bn. overcame and during day advanced a further 2,500 yds. and was again relieved to Bn. (3rd Div. late in town again.) C.S.M. LAMB was badly wounded and died same day. He had been in charge of "B" Coy for 30 hours and did excellent work. 2nd Lieut. R. DEWAR took charge of "B" Coy. 51st Bde. passed through Bn. at night and it became Support Bde. Casualties: — Killed: — 2nd Lieut. R. KEMP, 2nd Lieut. A. MORRIS wounded, 2nd Lieut. C.T.L. McDOWALL OR Killed 19, Wounded, 82. Total casualties for the 2 days: Officers killed 5, wounded 4, OR killed 47, wounded 194, missing 1. WAR BOOTY 43 hostile M.Gs., 5 hostile T.Ms., 150 prisoners	

WAR DIARY
INTELLIGENCE SUMMARY
(Erase heading not required.)

Army Form C. 2118

Place	Date 1918	Hour	Summary of Events and Information	Remarks and references to Appendices
In the Field	Aug 27th		Quiet day for us in support. At dusk we reorganised and took area for accommodation a little further back (300yds) and became Reserve Bde. Casualties - 2. OR wounded.	
	28.		Still Bde. in Reserve. Heavy hostile shelling (with sweeping gas) for an hour at 9.30 p.m. 2/Lieut. J. HEATON rejoined B Coy from liaison. Reinforcements from Div (Reinf) arr.Camp arrived in early morning - Capt. J.A. BIRLEY, Lieut. C.D.R. LUMBY and 55. OR. Capt. BIRLEY took A Coy and Lieut. LUMBY 'B' Coy. 2 Officers and with each Coy. 50th Bde went behind us and we became Support again. Casualties - 5. OR wounded.	
	29.		2nd Lieut E. WINDER rejoined Bn. HQ from Liaison with 50th Bde. Bn. moved to E. of FLERS early in afternoon (2 cookers and batman up) Casualties - 1. OR wounded.	
	30.		Quiet day. 10.0 p.m. Bde took over from 51st Bde. Bn. relieved 4th Lincolns in front of GEUDE COURT as Reserve Bn. Bn. HQ in Quarry with boys rather behind. Capt A.J.C. BINGTON (adjutant) detailed to proceed to England for bone-outshiours of duty. Casualties - 8. OR wounded.	
	31.		Bn. did not move, though owing to rather persistent hostile shelling, B Coy moved by HQ and two Matrons from trench into Bn. HQ sdp. 2nd Lieut. W.H. HAYWARD (attd. 52nd T.M.(B)y) killed low plank Rd. and buried there. C.O.'s conference at Bde. at 4.30 p.m. Coy Cmdrs conference at Bn. H.Q. later.	

O.C. 12th (D. of L.Y.) Bn. Manchester Regiment.

Capt. for,
Bn. Manchester Regiment.

Army Form C. 2118.

WAR DIARY
or
INTELLIGENCE SUMMARY.
(Erase heading not required.)

Instructions regarding War Diaries and Intelligence Summaries are contained in F. S. Regs., Part II. and the Staff Manual respectively. Title pages will be prepared in manuscript.

Place	Date	Hour	Summary of Events and Information	Remarks and references to Appendices

CONFIDENTIAL.

WAR DIARY
of
12TH (D. of L.Y.) BATTN MANCHESTER REGIMENT.
from
1ST SEPTEMBER to 30TH SEPTEMBER 1918.

VOLUME XXXIX.

WAR DIARY
INTELLIGENCE SUMMARY.
(Erase heading not required.)

Army Form C. 2118.

Place	Date	Hour	Summary of Events and Information	Remarks and references to Appendices
Somme	1/9		Tanks with 4 Coms Hundson at first. Tanks cld. cars had difficulty in getting on to road at M/6 for men. LE TRANSLOY. ... P. Rivington CMG. at GC10 for ting school Richaching of Railway Command of Div. old the M/G P. (P. Wm.) cars are now casualties.	A
	2/9		4.5 Howitzers of 5 A.D. made ground as well as full Day battle M.G. fire both intelligence. A/P. Courtyell Bar on our ? - they would use little dark sent to hostel the track. The 3rd retired near CAPPONIE PERONNE. On ? were again relieved with Roverge at the School adjacent only Patrols on our Tanks attacked by men cats in went forward. Casualties Gausts. E of ROCQUIGNY & Hon. E. Morlan lost over B Coy ? were ? only 1 officer and each by ?. A/Cpt. S. BRITON C.S.E. DEWAR D GH WRLEY. Major C. Hunt. 10 O.R. J.A Gaughlin; Exit. To BIRLEY Killed. G.C.DRUMMY, R.J.HATON, E.R.C. WITZ. 2.L.P. CONGHN, wounded. 2.L.P. CONGHN and 30 R. Field in front line at 5 Pde support. 1hr. Tagused on O3 B & D pit S.W.	A
	3/9		ROCQUIGNY. Pdr. mto moved ups. Pound ? field. Cage draft joined us. ? (1 Officers + 218 O.R. Order to be received to move on inward at any time. at present is to ? to the ROCQUIGNY line.	A
	4/9		Orders rec'd P.m. to be out of brestile Junction G. 4.30 a.m. and to occupy ROCQUIGNY line. No orders had been done. Bn. ROCQUIGNY & entrenched were shelled - 5. O.R. Casualties (4 Pr. + Q.) C.O. went to Pde. and aft. the actions were used back again in French S.W of ROCQUIGNY (O32B-D) by 5 p.m. Where we had an understanding night. Cookers and ?cart came up, also drew rations for the men. then Ford cooked.	A
	5/9		Quiet day. Nothing of importance during day. Form ordered ? 6/9 (Billy at P.M.) Q. Hum. Pane's stores again on morning at night. Try ahead of Road. and Company Commanders called at HQ at P.m. Ads west Road of Pn. attend ? Pole on Cove left ? at dark. C.O. left with or ahead of Pn. ?. ?. 2000 Nk ahead on Duck? being in trenches on P86 (PRICKLY PEAR TR) Con. Two or orders of well. Behind us Pn. ? 93 came right up. and 5am. Bank Stunt was expected ahead C (?) HEATON killed of tarkest? fire. del not take effect till 6 a.m.	A
	7/9		1 ? attacked and Bn's Lewisgun ?mobiles thy before you ? + one 3 Cp. on rear ? in before 7000 in order to follow our R. Coy ? when the advance commenced. the attack went will	A

WAR DIARY
INTELLIGENCE SUMMARY.
(Erase heading not required.)

Army Form C. 2118.

Place	Date	Hour	Summary of Events and Information	Remarks and references to Appendices
	8th		Subalterns only to overlook M.G. fire. T.O.C. (Bn) arrived Tr. H.Q at 9·00 + 5. The C.O. but already gone forward with one of the two Orderlies (Trench O.R.) gained with ease (DESSART WOOD) though two visitors sent that it was fairly full. C.O.R. reappeared abt 2 hrs in font and spected (A.C.R.) D (Right) F and B with supart with C b. T. Report. Cas Pos were detailed to rifts at DESSART WOOD. Tr. H.Q moved up to Sunken Rd Q.7.c and road about 1/2 was called at Q.22.c 40.75. T.a and July save the with Plant: numbers. Brigadier & many Gunner officers called. Bn was & have attacked again at 3 p.m but this was cancelled over the phone. DESSART WOOD was heavily shelled by battle guns of large calibre. In evening Tr. H.Q moved into to a dug out on FARM at Q.21.D.21 4.5. Casualties were eight. 2-Lt CARTWRIGHT and slowed (N.Y.O.N)	A
	9th		The Battn W. relieved us at night. Bn moved to trench in V.6.B – P.36.A.Q.7.C. Pa.T.Q at P.36.0.5.7 Raining till noon. When G.S.O.I called Battn training order came for Bn to attack next morning. C.O. Col. made a reconnaissance also for officers. At dusk the W. Yorks took our our positions and the Bn. moved & starting off line where it was in relation to 9 p.m. starting off line for Bn was Sunken Road. We 2. to 10.35 to N.T.A.I. Right (boundary Q.9.A) & near the Reno. & N and (right boundary the light railway. Cas Pos were on our Right. Coys S.W. to Support. C.O. saw all Coys of as starting line & passed Tr. H.Q in new position in trench N.J.C. & P. H.Q & later moved to N.J.A.2.0. F.O.B. Sent post north of day moth up.	A
			Batte fan Pos attacked 4 Am with Creeping Barrage. Very dark morning & at least 160 in the fore-direction very difficult. White Canvas cups show down and endured a good deal of the direction were no two leading Coy HEATHER TRENCH – the right Coy HEATHER SUPPORT. Coy were thin & were supposed al ARICON TR – SUPPORT. Objection gained, Lut ARICON TR – SUPPORT are strong held by every as also trench in Q.14.C & B. Enemy did not extent guns way in a hurry & were discovered from bushes that we had clear & the German strew against us & he put in a little later our another attacks from this & our Right were had exception in Q.14.C & were repulsed discussing	A

WAR DIARY
INTELLIGENCE SUMMARY.
(Erase heading not required.)

Army Form C. 2118.

Place	Date	Hour	Summary of Events and Information	Remarks and references to Appendices
	10th		the day. each time the enemy appeared to advance on AFRICAN TR's SUPPORT in a S.W direction Batt 4" were sent up to assist Coys at a time, we had to evacuate AFRICAN TR. Line top open holding took place during the day. men fighting with fixed Bayt. according Comparatively few of our men were employed to our men. Col. A. Bt. enemy. The Bn. put up a splendid fight, and acted itself with glory. H.Q. Coys came in for the worst time and E.C. R. DEWAR 2-Lt. I.H. BRETON did some excellent work. Fighting continued up to dusk all day unsuccessfully. Coys were still somewhat disorganised at night when we were relieved by elements of 17 Yorks and Dorsets.	
			Bn. H.Q. Rest moved up to N4.a.1.6 where Relief Completed between ourselves and 17 Yorks was completed by 11.30 p.m. The Dorsets did not appear to make an effort to relieve at all, so at 7 a.m. next morning the Adjt. went out to look for a Coy. of Dorsets who had not been seen at all. They were found there. Relief was completed at 10.30 a.m. on 10th. Own Evacuation during the 9th were heavy - Two officers were Killed :- 2-Lt. HODGKINSON & 2nd-Lt. LAIDLAW. Relief Completed no later. Bn H.Q learned had already moved away. C.O + Adjt joined Bn. in N.P34.D.10 with Pte HQ. P25c.2.5. 32nd Bde was now in Div Reserve. Cookers had Rations ready for all men. Col. A was only 500 away. 9.O.C. Stag Capt. called in evening.	KA
	11th		Quiet day. Reorganisation of 10 WELSH (7th DIV) called for purpose of taking over at night as were relieved at 4.0 p.m. 1st Bn. marched to Bde. area. (LE TRANSLOY.) Vn. ROCQUIGNY. Pte. actually billetted at MEAULENCOURT in N.ogen 34.5. N.11.c.D (Bn. H.Q N.11.c.75.50) 2 Rifles from Pte. H.Q. Lt. E.F. HUDSON 2-Lt. F. HALLINELL. joined Bn. from Base. Draft from Div. Reception Camp. Div. M.Q. at LECHELLES. Orders. Major R.W. J.E. WOSTON. Comdo. ad Closing Deficiencies Paraded in morning - all except a Few Corporals bathed during afternoon at ROCQUIGNY BATHS and in draft of 60 joined up from 10th L. Range Regt. O.C. and Q.R. of 2 met. Lo Horatio. C.O. attended Conference at Div. M.Q. at	KA
LECHELLES	12th		Bn. C.O. Nilson Major Riddell, O.O.C. 1st Bde Major called "ODDS" Informed at SUGAR FACTORY Sale O.S.O.C. 1st C. went to DOULLENS.	KA
	13th		Constance Paraded and completed deficiencies returns. Two or three officers to DOULLENS. 1 each by 2 of 9 4 m. Col. N & PARIS (1330) Car from Div took him to AMIENS. Capt. J. THOMPSON assumed command	KA

WAR DIARY
INTELLIGENCE SUMMARY.

(Erase heading not required.)

Army Form C. 2118.

Place	Date	Hour	Summary of Events and Information	Remarks and references to Appendices
	14th		of the Bath. 2/Lt F. HUDSON & 2 Agricult. OR's to Div. Signals for 5 days course. Capt. H. AUSTLEY M.O. reported from extended leave in U.K.	A
	15th		FODEN LORRY at disposal of Bn. left 5pm. All OR's kits were permitted. Pte. Browne undertook all & Officers & Revr. Gunn from Officer to DOULLENS. Orders received from Officer that Bn. was in Corps Reserve should be treated at short notice to occupy trench system N. of EQUANCOURT. 52nd Bde. would be in Div. Reserve & Bath. would occupy position in VIC Officers VR.9.03 reconnoitered at daylight. The Brigade Commander was to have available the Bath. at 10.a.m. (minus Transport) but this was audacied as vehicles in view of "Urgent engagements." It was too late to arrange Church Parade. Pm. Rapid ... makes burns some French & Capt. Gen. S.I. Coles. Bn. march also Religion. A & B Parading Coles at 5pm. to move to VALLULART WOOD. Advance party sent off at once. Packs, Blankets & more dumped with Q.M. at once. all prepared to move to 1 upon Orders received that Bn would move after dark. Bn. would have Bde. H.Q. at F.5pm Coles of Bde. March. Date of W Ban. & M.R. to accommodation in VALLULART WOOD. but there was no barracks or parking in the wood - Transport (exclusive baggage wagons) accompanied us. Oreless were made for the Coys. Settled down in early hours Much Rattle (rattling during night, but no casualties in Bn.	A
	16th		O.P. attended Confce. at Div. H.Q. (LECHELLES) at 9pm did not return till 7.30pm having made reconnaissance of front. Bath Coys. came to 3rd Q.M. & Adjutant. Orders received for Bn. to move at dusk. Before 5th Lieut. & Rifles. (77 OR's) in front line trenches W11.6 - W15a (LOWLAND SUPPORT) first move to rearrive the Bde. Commander called & spoke to all Offrs. so the war. Bn. two parties from VALLULART WOOD left about 8.30pm the Adv. of W.O. 7.50pm & M.R. first went in string Transport (Wagons) followed in rear. Battle Swillso. Pte R. Smith, R.C.O. Director, C.S.M. Rainey. & M.Cookery.	A
			Comp. Hall (I Capt. for Cornawer) to Div. Reception Camp at BEAULENCOURT. 2/Lt. D.E. MORGAN detached to take charge of Unposted Pack Mules 2/Lt. WELCH off to intermediate	

WAR DIARY
INTELLIGENCE SUMMARY

Place	Date	Hour	Summary of Events and Information	Remarks and references to Appendices
T.M.B.	14th		P.M. rather late on 13th both gas & Bn was going past SOREL-LE-GRAND and HEUDECOURT.	
			Bn HQ established with Duke of Wellington Regt jointly at W9d 7.0. Heavy storm just after relief finished.	
			Sunken Road in which were our HQ, was a hive of industry all night. Q Battery of 4.5 Hows in road itself with 18 pounder Battery on top of reverse bank. Another Battery of 18 pounders 200x in front in open.	A
			2nd Lt PHILLIPS attd Bn. HQ (from B Coy) as Signalling Officer.	
			Situation quiet all day, but any amount of work going on our own side of line, guns coming up, ammunition etc.	
			Dispositions of Coys till 12 midnight were - 3 Coys (B.C.D) W.11a.6.9 — W.18a 3 8 with A Coy in Sunken Rd W.16a 4.9. R.A.P. quite close to A Coy. Rations taken right up to said Sunken Rd & A Coy provided carrying parties to 3 other Coys, after which they returned to their own position & moved up to front line between C + D Coys.	
			Orders of Coys was then for lift to night - B.C.A.D. These were ASSEMBLY positions for attack next morning & the movement was completed in good time. In addition to this "Joy" bridge came up with rations. These were placed across the trenches occupied by B + C Coys for use of troops following our attack.	
			Bn HQ moved forward to W.10.a.9.0 will forward R-E- in line at W.11.B.9.4. Wire Int. + Signalling Officers were will have to B^de + Bn HQ	A
16th		Zero 5.20 A.M. 6 minutes after which (from left to right) 5.38, 17, 21 Divs attacked - 17th Div had 52nd Inf. Bde in front line with 50.3 Bdes in line	

WAR DIARY
INTELLIGENCE SUMMARY.
(Erase heading not required.)

Army Form C. 2118.

Place	Date	Hour	Summary of Events and Information	Remarks and references to Appendices

L.F. on Left, M.R. centre + D. of W. on right, latter covering CHAPEL HILL.) 50th Bde followed us at short distance, with 51st Bde behind them.

Attack started to time, with wonderful barrage of all calibres 500x deep. Then rain commenced before the attack + continued for about 2½ hours - this, coupled with smoke barrage, made visibility + work of runners very difficult -

B. objective was LOWLAND TRENCH from W.11.B.8.2. (Rly level) to W.12.C.9.9. (C.T wood.) This was gained up to time, but not without opposition. The Bosche had erected a certain amount of wire + groups of unnerved (detailed infantrymen) was necessary in order to make necessary gaps for the platoons - In addition, CHAPEL HILL - part of which our Right Coy (D) covered, gave some trouble to our right until Coy (A) by enfilade fire. This did not last long however as the D. of W. and our right Coy (D) carried the hill frontally. Various C.T.s also had to be cleared to ourselves the enemy -

Having firmly established ourselves on the 10m 1st objective, the 50th Bde passed through us. W. Yorks actually going through on Bn. Patrols previously detailed from our Coys followed to Yorks till they had gained our 2nd Objective, when our patrols withdrew, and the Bn reorganised and consolidated in trenches of 1st objective. 4 Coys in line as for assembly.

At 6.35 AM 51 Bde passed through 50 Bde. BORDERS passing through M.R. Our flares were not able to come over before 7.30 AM on a/c of mist, and by this time our batteries had already started moving forward.

Our casualties were:- 4 Officers 114 OR

WAR DIARY
or
INTELLIGENCE SUMMARY.
(Erase heading not required.)

Army Form C. 2118.

Place	Date	Hour	Summary of Events and Information	Remarks and references to Appendices
			Officers:-	
			Killed - 2nd Lieut. W.F. GOODALL. Buried at WE 16	
			Wounded and Died of Wounds - Lieut. C.W. WHITAKER M.C	
			Wounded - Capt. H. BUCKLEY M.C.	
			2/Lieut. F.A. HARROP	
			(Estimated) OR 5 Killed, 32 Wounded, 114 Missing (these were reduced in 2 days	
		6.31 of M using)		
		2-15-9 Estimated Prisoners of War.	
		2-104 Recruits to -do-	
			Brigade now in Div: Reserve - 11.0 P.M. Enemy reported advancing S.W	
			from GOUZEAUCOURT. L.F.s then formed a defensive flank W to E and Bn had	
			orders to close on our left Coy (B) & be prepared to support defensive flank. Nothing	
			came of this -	
			In afternoon Bn spread out again with intervals between Coys, so as to allow our	
			Right Coy (D) cover the front of CHAPEL HILL, the B of W having taken over positions forward	
			from Dorsets.	
			At 6.10 PM our SOS went up, but Artillery dispersed away attempted counter	
			attack. -	
			9.0 PM 14 and 35 Divs attacked again, but the Bn was not affected.	
			Rations and Watercart arrived 9.30 PM & were taken right up to Coys.	
			Quiet day for Bn. Brigade Commander called in afternoon - 3.0 PM W.O	19A

WAR DIARY / INTELLIGENCE SUMMARY

Army Form C. 2118.

Place	Date	Hour	Summary of Events and Information	Remarks and references to Appendices
GOUZEAUCOURT Road	20th		Received to move at dusk + occupy AFRICAN SUPPORT on each side of FINS – GOUZEAUCOURT Road. We and R of W shared HQ again at W4 a 1.6. Coys in new positions by 1.0 AM. Bde now had L.F. in front line, D of W in Suffolk + M.R. in Reserve. 2nd Lieut F. HUDSON and two Signallers Ottos rejoined Bttln B from 6 days course at 10w HQ. 2nd Lieut E.J. SUTER and 2nd Lieut A. CORLEY to Hospital, and in consequence 2nd Lieut J.W. BARTON took over C Coy from the former. Heavy hostile shelling of our front + support line in afternoon. C Coy had 1 Killed and 9 of wounded. At dusk the Bn. side slipped again + relieved elements of 38 U Div. 2nd R.W.F. were relieved by our A R and D Coys in AFRICAN SUPPORT and QUEENS CROSS from Q.28 d.9.5 to Q.35 c.15 80, + our C Coy occupied AFRICAN Support from Q.35 c.15 80 to FINS-GOUZEAUCOURT Road incl. This position had been just vacated by some of the 10th S.W.B. Bn. HQ remained in same location. Ration and water cart came to Q.34 c 35.45. Pioneers and R.E. worked during night on Posts + trenches recently in front line.	(A)
	21st		Quiet morning + afternoon. Bde Commander called to C.O.'s + altered our dispositions slightly. B Coy vacated Queen X and went to support in front Q.34c. A Coy held Q.28 d.q.5 to Q.29 c.1.b with 2 platoons incl. road	(A)

WAR DIARY
INTELLIGENCE SUMMARY.
(Erase heading not required.)

Army Form C. 2118.

Place	Date	Hour	Summary of Events and Information	Remarks and references to Appendices
	22nd		of LFs & placed the other 2 Platoons in & about Q ness X - 9.45 PM mobile messg from Brigade to effect that than had been reported to have evacuated certain parts of trenches on Bde front. Officer patrols sent out reported very much otherwise - 2nd Lieut RETAYLOR from A Coy took out own patrol - T.Ms active on our front & supports in morning and afternoon - They were located as far as possible, & our Batteries opened on small areas several times during the day. At noon orders received for Bn to relieve LFs but night in front line. B & C Coys to relieve 3 Coys LFs between Q 36 c 1045 and W 6 B 0.5 - Our A Coy to occupy shell holes in W 5 d & W 6 c after being relieved by A of LFs and our "D" Coy (after being relieved by A Coy of LFs & own "D" Coy (after being relieved by D Coy LFs) to relieve A Coy D d W intend W S B 2 Y - W S B 2 5 9 0 - Q 3 5 d Y 5.00. Bn HQ did not move - Relief completed by 1.30 AM (2 front Coys earlier) Special "K" Coy R.E. released gas on to suspected T.Ms at 1.30 AM and 3.30 AM. don at least & hour at each — affect our 2 front Coys had to wear Box Respirators, but the other 2 Coys were not affected. Lieut Col. S. DANBY D.S.O. MC rejoined Ech B from Paris leave. W.O. that Bn would be relieved at night by 50d Bde Brigadier called, & representatives of the relieving Bn ie 4/5 Yorks Bn advance party (R.S.M. Cpl Cooper + Police) to view area, ie e accomodation of HQ & Yorks in HEATHER and LOWLAND SUPPORTS in W 11 a + c with Bn HQ W 10 B b 6. 2nd Lieut F. HUDSON went there from Ech B & made necessary arrangements. Relief went well - 2nd Lieut WINDER met incoming Bn will guides and Police guided our Coys into new areas - Good deal of Bombing during relief, but no casualties.	AJ AJ

D.D. & I. London. E.C.
(A8504) Wt. W777/M2031 75000. 5/17. Sch. 53 Forms/C2118/14

WAR DIARY
INTELLIGENCE SUMMARY.
(Erase heading not required.)

Army Form C. 2118.

Place	Date	Hour	Summary of Events and Information	Remarks and references to Appendices
	24th		Relief complete by 11.0 P.M. but word did not reach C.O and Adjt. till after midnight. Coys soon settled down in new area. Code word for Relief and Entry of Battalions sent also to 51st Bde as in addition to being in Gw. Reserve, we (as a Bn) were at tactical disposal of 51st Bde in case of hostile counter attack.	A)
			Glorious day and Coys when rested in morning cleaning up etc. Company Officers called in evening. Quiet day and no shifting in our area. Some hostile Bombing at night.	A)
	25th and 26th		C.O and Adjt (21 Qw) went round Coys in morning. Representatives of Wilts Regt (21 Qw) came up to mess accommodation, but they were not actually relieving us, merely occupying part of our trenches. 1st Wilts took over our HQ and our Coys left their trenches at 10.0 pm (A,B,C,D. HQ). L.G. Limbers came up befriend for guns &c. A long march and lovely frosty night. Bn. collected at rendezvous (BEET ROOT FACTORY N 22 c. 9.1. 57.c.s.e. 50,000) and men had hot vegetable soup + a short rest. Marched from there as a Bn. + reached new Camp (T8 e + T9 a LES BOEUFS) at 5.30 AM. Breakfast ready for men. All rested during morning. Sick parade 3.30 PM. C.O. Orderly Room 7.8 PM.	
	27th		2nd Lieut R DEWAR, 2nd Lieut J BRADLEY and 213 OR joined from Dw Reception Camp, also Lieut G.E.H. PARKES.	A)
			Baths (LES BOEUFS — MORVAL Rd) allotted to Bn from 8am — noon — Draft had bath a couple of days before joining us — 2nd Lieut HUDSON and 2nd Lieut BRADLEY busy with L.G and Musketry Instructor respectively — Coys paraded	

WAR DIARY or INTELLIGENCE SUMMARY.

Army Form C. 2118.

Place	Date	Hour	Summary of Events and Information	Remarks and references to Appendices
	28th		for reorganisation and deficiencies. Guard dealt with under R.S.M, also Coys & Coy- 2nd in Command checked Charge Sheets with Part II orders. Officer Platoon Commanders instructed in Map Reading by 2nd in Command in afternoon. The C.O spoke to all Sgts in afternoon, after which he and Adj: made round to find suitable ground for Bn parade + Rifle Range. 11.38PM WO to effect that Bde and F.A would move next day about 3.0PM to ROCQUIGNY. In view of W.O Coys paraded under own arrangements for reorganisation only. 2nd Lieut WINDER and 1 N.C.O. per Coy went off 10.0AM as Billetting Party. Packs and Blankets drawn and Battle Surplus details got ready. Bn moved off behind Bde HQ and passed starting point (X Roads in LES BOEUFS) 3.43PM. Reached new Camp in ROCQUIGNY (O.33.B) at 5.45PM March casualties 9/d. Officers had tea on arrival. Bath allotment for Casuals from 7-8 km to town of this given to W.O.s & Sgts	K.9
	29th		C of E Church Parade at 10.0AM jointly with 10th L.F. on ground near Q.M. Stores. Brigade Commander present & addressed the 2 Battalions beforehand. Duke's had been affected. Bn under 2 hours notice from 11.0AM Blankets + Packs therefore were dumped with Q.M. and Battle Surplus marched off under 2nd Lieut J.W BARTON (5 f. off) to BEAULENCOURT. Soccer match in afternoon – M.R. v L.F. 10 nowl.	K.9

Army Form C. 2118.

WAR DIARY
or
INTELLIGENCE SUMMARY.

(Erase heading not required.)

Instructions regarding War Diaries and Intelligence Summaries are contained in F. S. Regs., Part II. and the Staff Manual respectively. Title pages will be prepared in manuscript.

Place	Date	Hour	Summary of Events and Information	Remarks and references to Appendices
	30th	3.0 P.M.	news received that Bulgaria had surrendered unconditionally - Troops had a quiet day - Corps did a little P.T. and L.G. firing before dinner -	

Stanley
Lieut. Col.
Commdg. 12th (D. of L.V.) Bn. Manchester Regiment

Army Form C. 2118.

WAR DIARY
or
INTELLIGENCE SUMMARY.
(Erase heading not required.)

Vol 37

CONFIDENTIAL.

WAR DIARY
of
12TH (D.O.L.Y.) BATTN MANCHESTER REGIMENT
from
1ST OCTOBER to 31ST OCTOBER 1918.
VOLUME XL

Army Form C. 2118.

WAR DIARY
or
INTELLIGENCE SUMMARY.
(Erase heading not required.)

Instructions regarding War Diaries and Intelligence Summaries are contained in F. S. Regs., Part II. and the Staff Manual respectively. Title pages will be prepared in manuscript.

Place	Date	Hour	Summary of Events and Information	Remarks and references to Appendices
In the field	1/10/18		Bn still under 2 hours notice. Usual training, range etc. Advanced Guard scheme by Coys and 2 hour Ceremonial Parade in the morning. Afternoon each man trained in his own arms for 1 hour. Bn concert in Y.M.C.A at 19.00 hrs.	A) A)
	2/10/18		Parades as on 2nd. Football match with Lancashire Fusiliers - Bn won 6-2. Bn open air concert 18.00 hrs. Bde under 3 hrs notice.	A)
	3rd		Warning Order received that Bde would probably move during the day. Parade as usual. Baths allotted. Bn sports held during afternoon. W.O. cancelled at 18.00 hrs.	A) A)
	4th		Parades as usual during the morning. W.O re move received at 11.00 hrs. Bn moved to EQUANCOURT area, Bn being billeted in area V.11.c+d and V.17.a+b. Bn HQ V 17.a 90.55. Winter time came into force at 01.00 hrs. W.O re further move cancelled at 02.00 hrs. Owing the morning Bn paraded for P.T. - MAJOR G.T.WILKES MC rejoined the Bn.	A) A) A)
	5th			
	6th			
	7th		Bn paraded during morning for P.T. etc. At 19.00 hrs W.O. to move to GOUZEAUCOURT area at 06.00 hrs 8/10/18 received. Advanced party paraded at	A)
	8th		Bn moved at 06.00 hrs to GOUZEAUCOURT area and was billeted in area Q.36.c, W.6.a+d. Bn HQ W.6.35.80. At 14.30 hrs Bn began	A)

WAR DIARY
or
INTELLIGENCE SUMMARY.
(Erase heading not required.)

Army Form C. 2118.

Place	Date	Hour	Summary of Events and Information	Remarks and references to Appendices
	9th		wounded forward and was killed in BLEAK TRENCH R.28.c.4.8 with Bn HQ R.28.c.4.8. Orders passed through 21st Division. At 02.05 hrs Bn. moved forward to M.30.b.d (sunken road) with Bn. HQ M.30.d.5.9. At 09.00 hrs as the Bn moved forward again to Bank N.20.c. with Bn. HQ N.30.b.3.4. At 18.30 hrs Bn moved again to sunken road. O.8.a with Bn HQ O.8.a.5.8. MAJOR G.T. WILKES he left the Bn and took over command of 1/4 Bn East Yorks.	A)
	10th		Bn. moved to Q.100.r.e + ordered to be in position by 08.20.hrs. Kept in touch with 50th Bde and finally formed defensive flank facing North 12.a.5.8 - S.16.c.2.1 - S.23 central (North of INCHY). Bn. HQ S.23.6.5.3 (QUARRY) Casualties 2nd Lieut J.TAYLOR passed 1 OR wounded, 2 OR gassed. Bn. still North of INCHY. The C.O. attended conference at Bde HQ at 16.15 hrs after which he held Coy. + Platoon Commanders Conference in connection with attack following morning.	A)
	11th			A)
	12th		The C.O. + Adjutant attended Bde HQ at 01.00 hrs + received orders for attack. Coy + Platoon Commanders again met for final instructions from the C.O. 52nd Bn attacked at 05.00 hrs with 2 Bns in front line (each Bn with 2 Coys in front + 2 Coys in support) 12th Manchesters on left, 1 of Duke of Wellingtons on right. 10th Lancashire Fusiliers in support to mop up the village (NEUVILLY). The Bn lined up on east side of River SELLE	A)

WAR DIARY or INTELLIGENCE SUMMARY

Army Form C. 2118.

Place	Date	Hour	Summary of Events and Information	Remarks and references to Appendices
	13th		the small trench where they had consolidated. This unfortunately involved a withdrawal to the level of the troops on our right (9th D.of W.) who had still failed to cross the Rly owing to enemy snipers in the village + along some parts of the Rly. Many casualties were caused during this withdrawal and previous bombardment & three Officers unfortunately were wounded & left in enemy hands. A line was now taken up at the new SEHE, a little east of our starting point that morning + the enemy did not cause further trouble. During the day we took 1 Officer + 49 O.R. prisoners + our casualties were 11 Officers + 269 O.R. In the evening 4th Bde was relieved by 51st Bn (Sherwood Foresters) relieved H.R.) + the Bn went back to INCHY, to billets, where hot food, blankets, greatcoats & supplied the men, who were very needy for any small comfort after one of the most strenuous days in the history of the Bn. The strength of the Bn was then had a good rest and fur clean up. 4 Officers and 230 odd men.	A1
	14th		but 4 Officers (the Colonel, Adjutant & Medical Officer) . Orders were received Cleaning up was continued + deficiencies taken. from the Bde for a Defence Scheme in case of an enemy counter attack on our front. The Bn was at ½ hours notice + would move (at) between J19 central + J23B (Queeny) 51°B/40,000. The village was shelled during the day and we had 1 OR. killed + 2 OR. wounded — 1 Divn Officer reinforcements joined us in the evening.	B1 A1

WAR DIARY or INTELLIGENCE SUMMARY

Army Form C. 2118.

(Erase heading not required.)

Place	Date	Hour	Summary of Events and Information	Remarks and references to Appendices
	15th		Bn still in INCHY. Reorganisation still being carried on by the new Officers + deficiencies completed. 1 Officer + 41 OR Draft joined Bn from D.R.C. — 50th Bn relieved 51st Bn in line. 52nd Bn to remain in Support Bde. INCHY.	AP
	16th		Village (INCHY) consistently shelled from 0001 to 2630 hrs. a good deal of gas with it — No casualties in Bn. Officers reconnoitred forward ground during day — 400 men bathed under Bn arrangements + L.G. Lectures carried on.	AP.
	17th		W.O. of relief received 1190 hrs. 52nd Bn relieved 51st Bn in line in NEUVILLY sectr at night — Bn took over by 2015 hrs from 1051 W Yorks in Support Bn HQ J.22.c.5.6 (51B N.E. 1/20,000).	AP.
	18th		A good deal of hostile shelling intermittently during th early hours. Bn had 1 OR Killed + 7 OR wounded Fairly quiet day but a fair amount of shelling by both sides — Capt R.E. Cox D.S.O. rejoined + took over C Coy again.	AP
	19th		Quiet day. 51st Bd took over own HQ about 1600 hrs. 51st Bd relieved 52nd Bn at dusk — Own Bn not actually relieved but withdrew to INCHY (51B N.E. 1/20,000). Some shells as before but fell over short. the night in cellars where they were able to sleep after a hot meal + rum.	AP.
	20th		Division attacked 0200 hrs in conjunction with flank divisions. 50th Bde in front and 57th Bde passed through. 32nd Bde called out at

Army Form C. 2118.

WAR DIARY
or
INTELLIGENCE SUMMARY

Army Form C. 2118.

Place	Date	Hour	Summary of Events and Information	Remarks and references to Appendices
	21st	06.00 hrs	and Bn moved to J18 central. We remained on "the Blue" all day and at 14.00 hrs withdrew to our cellars again in INCHY.	A.1
			The attack was quite successful, the final objective being the high ground N.E. of AMERVAL. K4 5YPN6 /30000. Good number of Boche killed and a goodly capture.	
		1700 hrs.	52nd Bde relieved 51st Bde in the line at night. Bn relieved the 9th Lincolns and left INCHY at 1700 hrs. Bn distributed in the line in Platoon Posts in E29 and K4 with D Coy in support as counter attack Coy. Enemy artillery pretty active during relief and all night mainly with HE and Gas. We had 1 Officer wounded and 6 OR casualties.	A.1
	22nd		Very quiet all day with no hostile shelling at all. A few H.E. active now and again. 21st Div relieved 17th Div at night and our Bn being relieved by the 6th Bn Lincoln Regt, 2 of whose Coys took over certain posts of A B & C Coys. D Coy and posts not actually relieved and withdrew on completion of relief. The Bn returned to INCHY where billets had been arranged by Rear under difficult circumstances the place being actually packed with Troops, Echelon B's & everything, ready, meals, cooks, blankets etc.	A.1
			Draft: 2nd Lieut to C. R. McGregor, 2nd Lieut A.J. Thorn and 115 O.R.	
	23rd		21st Bn continued the attack and advanced successfully. Two of our Bn's had left INCHY by 11.00 hours and one (from this place) came under 3 an hours notice. Draft inspected and posted to Coys. Draft contained a number of old soldiers.	

WAR DIARY
or
INTELLIGENCE SUMMARY

Place	Date	Hour	Summary of Events and Information	Remarks and references to Appendices
	24th		but were mostly men with a few months army life also a few from Labour Corps in England. Bn the attached to Bn from 12:00 to 15:00 hrs. 2nd Lieut R. Thomas Evelyn posted to L.T. Group in a Lewis Gun Course. Bn still in INCHY and under 4 hrs notice. Everything ready to move at short notice. 10th Bn Lancashire Fusiliers concentrated in the village (from Richmont) with rest of Bde. Notice received that Bn would not move tonight. A few hostile shells fell in village during night.	K.1
	25		Bn parade had been arranged (in spite of 4 hrs notice) in order to continue some training but the Bde moved at 08:00 hrs to ORVILLERS area. Bn in tents and bivouacs in E.23.a., Bn J.H.Q. E.23.a.5.5. and Transport in adjacent paddock. We took over from Y Borderers whose Bde (51st) went back to INCHY. 52nd Bde now became forward Bde of 14th Div. with 21st Div. still in line. 14th Div. relieved 21st Div. in the line; 52nd Bde relieved 110th Bde and the Bn relieved 6th Bn Leicestr in front line with Lancs Fus on our left, and 9th Duke of Wellington Bn in support. 50th Bde in support in POIX area, and 51st Bde in reserve in VENDEGIES area.	K.1
	26th		Bn marched from camp at 15:50 hrs and marched through ORVILLERS to F.4.c. where Bn Hqrs was in a field. March continued through VENDEGIES and POIX du NORD on the eastern side of which our guns were situated in A.B.D. Corps occupied front line in subby trench along road in K.18.C.&.D.	K.1

WAR DIARY
or
INTELLIGENCE SUMMARY.

(Erase heading not required.)

Army Form C. 2118.

Place	Date	Hour	Summary of Events and Information	Remarks and references to Appendices
	24th		and X 24 b 3, road with Platoon posts out in front. C + B Coys were in support, but C formed on right a defensive flank towards 38th Division (Welsh) Bn HQ in Cane House at X 28 & 3.4. Relief completed by 20.30 hours. A very good one. 51 (A SE) 1/20,000	A/1
	28th		A good deal of hostile shelling (mostly H.E and gas) during early hours up to 06.30 hrs. Gas consisted of Phosgene and Sneezing. The rest of the day was quiet. Bn had 1 light T.M attached to left flank post of left Coy + one 6" Newton in support. Bn called also G.S.O T and several others. H.E & gas shelling by enemy in early hours but from "stand down" till late afternoon everything was very quiet. Major Lionel Vaughan GSOI and others called. W.O received 16.30 hrs that 21st Div would relieve 19th Div tomorrow.	A/1
	29th		Quiet day - C.O + Coy Commanders of 4th Yorkshire called during the day to reconnoitre full relief. "At night 21.00 relieved 11th Div, 110th Bde the 52nd Bde, and 4th Yorkshire the 12 NF. Quickenhuf + the Bn marched to billets in OUVILLERS.	A/1
	30th		Men had tea and then slept the morning + hot meal & assembled in billets. 2d Lieut J.O Plumpton joined Bn from Bde. 5'18 N.E. 1/20,000. Cleaning and refreeness parades + reorganisation.	A/1
	31st		Rept of 2 officers Capt P H "Ruff M.C Wolf Lt fm "HQ and 2nd Lieut E.J S.Le + 31 o.R joined Bn from 1/5 DRC 3rd joined took over "A Coy[x]. Major G.T.O Alex M.C. having was having from Command of "A" Coy, 1.8. Yorks + proceeded after P. Deven DSO went on leave. 7 Capt Dukes oo 2nd in Command	A/1

WAR DIARY or INTELLIGENCE SUMMARY

Army Form C. 2118.

(5gB/40.000) + the objective was the high ground in K.34 +10 - there was no frontal attack on the village the 1/4 F's being West of NEUVILLE until the two flank Bns had crossed the river and Rly. The attack went well on the left and our Bn forded the river, crossed the Rly and reached its objective on the high ground in good time, under very difficult conditions. Our m.g.s came into & and bombed by the enemy whilst crossing the river — Small parties of Bosch had to be overcome before objective was reached. The Bn had not tackled the village & enemy snipers in NEUVILLY fired on our rear from behind. Consolidation was carried on at once and complete under shell fire & M.G. fire. On the night the D of W did not get further than the Rly; thus our right flank was hung much in the air all day and we were in great danger of a serious counter attack. The Division on our left (3rd/4th D) had done well and were up to ug. The Bn detailed to mop up the village were not able to clear it of the enemy entirely, and the first made our position more delicate. In addition the enemy accurately shelled our forward positions and made things very uncomfortable. 2 Coys of 1/4 East Yorks were placed at disposal of our C.O. as well as one Coy of 10 L.F's. The latter had already been placed in position on left of the village & the former was on their way to a position East of the village when the enemy put down a very heavy Box Barrage of some depth. Our troops in front of these were no longer able to retain their hold of the hill crest & were literally blown out of

Army Form C. 2118.

WAR DIARY
or
INTELLIGENCE SUMMARY.
(Erase heading not required.)

Instructions regarding War Diaries and Intelligence Summaries are contained in F. S. Regs., Part II. and the Staff Manual respectively. Title pages will be prepared in manuscript.

Place	Date	Hour	Summary of Events and Information	Remarks and references to Appendices
			W Barton (who reported from rest camp) took over C Coy. Bn. handed at 2.00 hrs and marched to NEUVILLY to see H.S. Scouring the 21st Div Concert party. G.O.C. Bde + Bde Major also went.	AP
			Afternoon party to fight Col. Commdg 12 (D of L) Bn Manchester Regiment	

Army Form C. 2118.

WAR DIARY
or
INTELLIGENCE SUMMARY.

(Erase heading not required.)

Vol 3

CONFIDENTIAL.

WAR DIARY.

of

12th.(D.of.L.Y.)BN. MANCHESTER REGT.

From. 1.11.18.   To. 30.11.18.

VOLUME. XLI.

Army Form C. 2118.

WAR DIARY
or
INTELLIGENCE SUMMARY.
(Erase heading not required.)

Instructions regarding War Diaries and Intelligence Summaries are contained in F. S. Regs., Part II. and the Staff Manual respectively. Title pages will be prepared in manuscript.

Place	Date	Hour	Summary of Events and Information	Remarks and references to Appendices
November	1st 1918		1Bn. harassed as strong as possible and [illegible] Commander came at 11.15 hours to report [illegible] to their respective [illegible] to N.C.Os and men who had been awarded [illegible] since 25th Aug. Officers and men of Batts. who had been awarded (as to above date) 1.D.S.O. 6 M.Cs 2 D.C.Ms 1 Bar 6 M.M. & 1 M.M Also [illegible] Batt. in afternoon to village under the arrangements of [illegible] 2nd Lt F. Dickinson (O6 D Coy) & Lt F.D. Bowes. At 6.0 went up the line to arrange [illegible] & relief with [illegible] who relieved M. Small advance party under an officer [illegible] cook of B + D Coys went up early in [illegible] to quickly use dispositions.	[initials]
	2nd		17th Div relieved 21st Div. 5/2 Brig the 110 Bde. 2 SMR the Leicesters. 17th Bn 6 OVILLERS 1/2 20 hours and into the line via VENDEGIES and POIX du NORD, 10 L 23 on our left 9 S.O. 11 in support on left. 8th Bn Commander came to Bn. H.Q. Bn with HQ attached Battalion at Bde H.Q. at 10.00 hrs.	[initials]
	3rd		Commander remained at Bn. H.Q. at dawn where Bn. got same slack [illegible] the attack to [illegible] morning Grenades and two days rations came up by pack, and taught to the Coys in the [illegible] [illegible] day in the fore - End. [illegible] a good deal of intermittent shelling. Bn Hr + H the Bottle Posn at X.70.a.9.1. which we occupied by midnight.	[initials]
	4th		17th Div attacked. Companies given the 2 days rations prepared the in early morning then formed up on [illegible] tart. D + B Coys in line & Head Sdn + B to Sqrs. Y.O. with A + C releasing ½ in [illegible] support. Two Coys one 95 yards of which [illegible] + Bde had formed up about 500 in rear of [illegible] Private. 10 YBn B Coys 10 MG barrage. Attack started to take [illegible] up arrival & made & Vickers through [illegible] attached M&S + [illegible] the objective (blue line) roughly 330.55 - 3263 39 40 which 37.4 the Lanes Change as to 5th (Leic) Guards. On right with the none Leice an [illegible] (MG Nos.3) One Coy was reaccord. Bn Bn Mo reached their objective in time. J. L Ride [illegible] [illegible] + [illegible] approached more or rather cost just 13/5 hrs 5 Coys stood [illegible] + assault & Henry many lost some wounded in put out Coys tooke were better with a certain 30/[illegible] [illegible] the Heads in the [illegible] [illegible] [illegible] [illegible] [illegible] [illegible] [illegible] [illegible]	[initials]

WAR DIARY
INTELLIGENCE SUMMARY.
(Erase heading not required.)

Army Form C. 2118.

Place	Date	Hour	Summary of Events and Information	Remarks and references to Appendices
			attacking The Germans up to 3 p.m. in early afternoon our artillery returned to our old ground. Our casualties were (estimated) 6 officer 100 O.R. about 10 Batt: M.G. 3 T.M's. Captured to Br. our M.O. Capt R. Scott (R.A.M.C.) all the Staff went to Hospital suffering from Mustard Gas.	appxII
	5.9		21st Brigade continued the advance (17th Bn: being pushed in all directions) with very slight opposition. cleared the rest of Maniel Forest. Practically no opp: on either side all day. The Bn: remained in same place near FOTOY, BELL A.B. joined us - Gratopain Blank to Bio same day men were put under cover for night as far as possible East Hanover RAMC joined us vice Capt R. Scott.	appxII
	6.9 7.9		Very wet day nothing doing Lt: H.Q. Coy into Tois, a casualty due precaution. 5 more received all bonos. The Brigade passed forward to BERLAIMONT.	appxII
			FUTOY opoo hours. H.Q. A.B.C.D. Coys marched via BERLAIMONT. to the moved from LA TETE NOIRE, reaching billet about 1700 hrs. Maroc Eveang's LOCQUIGNOL and on one or two craters flown to the enemy placed the night in BERLAIMONT.	appxII
	8.9		Bn. moved from BERLAIMONT at 3600 hrs. via D.E. of Maroc SAMBRE & 3630 Bn. marched (Lieut: Co: Hudson O.C.) to AULNOYE into Billets there. An advanced billet party found in the Coys & marched from AULNOYE to the Bn. to the next town ? today 21st Route. We go led at 1600 hrs our new Bde at Rte 112 and Coy at 1850 hrs went to St Cde. M.O. Turner met Bn. Patrol at the Quarry at V.3.C.B.3. 9.9 We trapsfaced Etheriau & Cordin continues to advance the Attack at 0576 hrs. No attuhrs of any kind and everything very quiet. Objective reached, consolidation back Bde on kept inward W. 16 Central.	appxII appxII

WAR DIARY
or
INTELLIGENCE SUMMARY.
(Erase heading not required.)

Army Form C. 2118.

Instructions regarding War Diaries and Intelligence Summaries are contained in F. S. Regs., Part II. and the Staff Manual respectively. Title pages will be prepared in manuscript.

Place	Date	Hour	Summary of Events and Information	Remarks and references to Appendices
			N.28 Central. Two Ptns of Pt Platoon worked enemy Right Bank area covered outlook 2 hrs and HQ concentrated on BEAUFORT leaving "A" Coy under Capt H.J. Highfield and N.C. as Outpost Coy in touch with R.Es on left. O Coy became enemy Airfield in NEWPORT. Very quiet day no enemy bodies or M.Gs.	MRJ by
	10			
	11.30		Officials reported that the Russian Coy arrived at a ground of very offensive position by country to a point many miles away. "A" Coy reached "A" Coy on the outpost line during the afternoon. The Division ceased as from 11.30 hrs. Reserve front and employed on the village just after the train and two the Base Pit. Ten places at Maxwells. Permits. M.O. Details yelling of Division at BERLAMMONT about midday. "A"s now in bridges by 19.30 hrs at Division.	MR J by
			relieved 19.0 hrs	MR J M
	12.00		Pat. reached to VENDEGIES AU BOIS an effect staying area.	MR J M
	13.30		Pat. reached to INCHY where Pat. HQ was closed. Division. HQ received from Nouvion Coords.	MR J M
			Moved as	MR J M
	14.00		W Coy, H Company, Parade at day	MR J M
	15.30		Conducted parades for Pt. Base Ball Drill. Coy. transformed in fire arms drill.	GR J M
	16.30		Sector and Museums of moves in P.T. all day	
	17.30		Patrol attended part Band Parade with 2/D.L.C. 2d Bn. "Rugby" Plat. INFHY.	MR J M
	18.30		A Coy Cayuga and Nehoga. Nota. usual experiment H.M.G.s Cadona. B.O.I.Q. b/p Sunday to 19.7	MR J M
			"B" Coy Draw Drill to Pat. Class on Pan bravest of Browning Small and Lt. Cpl. Insect.	
	19.30		"B" Coy Parades at Nehoga 10.00 Lunch training. L.Cp.T. & G.T. Rapid. A.C. C on heard in P.T.	
			and effect order drill, Class for draw on Lt. Boulange Staff.	
	20.30		"C" Coy based at Nehoga had human. Lt. R. Riddol. A.R.+.D. Class Parade in Pt. Art and Nehoga	MR J M
	21.30		"D" Coy in Valage Thos under Lt. P. A. Maples. A.R.+.D. Coy. Operated in PT. + Gas Order Drill	MR J M

WAR DIARY
or
INTELLIGENCE SUMMARY.

(Erase heading not required.)

Army Form C. 2118.

Place	Date	Hour	Summary of Events and Information	Remarks and references to Appendices
	26th		Followed by Ceremonial Drill	
	27th		A Coy carried out Platoon under B.R.C. Kendal. B.C. & D Coys attended Educational Lecture by O.C. B. before P.C. Coy Cadt. Afternoon Baths. Coy A Coy paraded for Ceremonial Drill	
	28th		B Coy carried out Platoon No.4 under B.N.C. Radford. A.C. & D Coys and Coyd paraded for Route March.	
	29th		Part of Batt. paraded in Bye Pass N.C.H. in English with the 18th Batt. Canadians C & D Coys carried out Salvage Work under B Wood. A B Coy paraded Percukedia and then P.O. and to Tactical Exercise. B Coy carried out PT, & Lewis Gun Drill.	
	30th		Maths paraded for Ceremonial Parade & themselves formed up on Brigade Paid & four Companys at AUDENCOURT in the afternoon. Baths and Recreation Awards paraded to Brigade by same. Lecture at TROISVILLERS all day. A.B Coy carried out Salvage Work in the morning. Bathed in the afternoon.	
	31st		C.O. Coys paraded at 08:30 for L Salvage Work and to B Wood. A.B Coy paraded at 8.30 for same for inspection of Lectures. Afternoon A.D Coy carried out Rifle Exercise. A C Coy carried out PT. Gas Order Drill. Afternoon Games & attention. C & D Coys marched for Battalion under etc oo hrs	
	29 E		A.C & G Coys paraded with Brand for Rest Route March. B Coy carried in Salvage Work throughout carried during afternoon.	
	30 E		A Coy carried out Salvage Work. B.C. D Coys carried out PT and Glass Order Drill. B.C & D Coys then paraded at half Ceremonial Drill.	

Commdg 11/2(1/7) Br. Manchester Regiment.

Major
11/2(1/7) Br. Manchester Regiment.

Army Form C. 2118.

WAR DIARY
or
INTELLIGENCE SUMMARY.

(Erase heading not required.)

WO 39

CONFIDENTIAL.

WAR DIARY.

of

12th (D. of L.Y.) BN. MANCHESTER REGT.

VOLUME. XLI.

From. 1st December 1918.   To. 31st December 1918.

Place	Date	Hour	Summary of Events and Information	Remarks and references to Appendices

Instructions regarding War Diaries and Intelligence Summaries are contained in F. S. Regs., Part II. and the Staff Manual respectively. Title pages will be prepared in manuscript.

Army Form C. 2118.

WAR DIARY

Instructions regarding War Diaries and Intelligence Summaries are contained in F. S. Regs., Part II. and the Staff Manual respectively. Title pages will be prepared in manuscript.

(Erase heading not required.)

Place	Date	Hour	Summary of Events and Information	Remarks and references to Appendices
	1/12/18		Joint Church Parade with 10th Lanc Fusiliers in Dub. Stee Incby	A/
	2/12/18		Batt paraded for the inspection of H.M. the King.	A/
	3/12/18		Batt with Band Paraded for Short Route march.	A/
	4/12/18		A Coy on Rifle Range (30 yds) Lewis Gunners of A Coy also paraded for range work. B Coy on palong work. B & D Coy paraded for Close order drill.	A/
	5/12/18		B Coy Lewis Gunners on Range. D Coy carried out palongs work & A+C Coys paraded for close order drill & P.T.	A/
	6/12/18		Bolt. commenced march to demobilization area. Batt. marched to Maurices where whole of Batt was accomodated in huts for night.	A/
	7/12/18		Batt. marched from Maurieux to Hennies where Batt was accomodated in tents	A/
	8/12/18		Batt. marched from Hennies to Lavieril where Batt spent the night under canvas.	A/
	9/12/18		Batt. marched to Albert were accomodates for night under canvas.	A/
	10/12/18		Batt marched from Albert to Buoy were accom. in billets	A/
	11/12/18		March Continued to La Chavre. Batt accom. in Billets	A/
	12/12/18		Last day of march. Batt. marched into demobilization area was billets in Warlus.	A/
	13/12/18		This day was allotted to justing + cleaning up	A/
	14/12/18		Cleaning up under Coy arrangements all day Co. Coy + transport billets in Avelesgers.	A/

Army Form C. 2118.

WAR DIARY
INTELLIGENCE SUMMARY.
(Erase heading not required.)

Instructions regarding War Diaries and Intelligence Summaries are contained in F. S. Regs., Part II. and the Staff Manual respectively. Title pages will be prepared in manuscript.

Place	Date	Hour	Summary of Events and Information	Remarks and references to Appendices
	15.12.18		Batn. with 52nd & 1 tank paraded for open air Church Parade	A
	16.12.18		Batn. paraded for close order drill. Guard mounting & Recreational Training	A
	17.12.18		Coys cleaning up the ground in vicinity of their billets	A
	18.12.18		Coy. in Rifle coy. I.S.C. paraded for Guard Mtg, Lea Training	A
	19.12.18		Coys paraded for close order drill, Guard Mtg drill & Rec Trg, Educational classes started under 2nd Lt Barton, Lewis Gun class under 2nd Lt Thomas. Evelyn D.S.O. Commenced H.	A
	20.12.18		Batn. and Band paraded for short Route March	A
	21.12.18		Joint Open air Church Parade w. 52nd F.A.	A
	22.12.18		Coys paraded for close order Pt & Rec Training	A
	23.12.18		Coy. paraded in parade ground for Rec Trg & close order drill	A
	24.12.18		Bat. provided a fete for the children of the village of Aarlus	A
	25.12.18		Xmas Day. Tol. Church Service in Village School	A
	26.12.18		Boxing Day. Bn. Race meeting at Keyencourt. No Parades	A
	27.12.18		Coy paraded for Rec. Training	A
	28.12.18 29.12.18 30.12.18 31.12.18		Coy. Coy in close order drill & Rec Training Bn. Church parade Service Village School Coy paraded. Rec Training and Coy arrangements in Coy parade ground	A A A A

Army Form C. 2118.

WAR DIARY
or
INTELLIGENCE SUMMARY.
(Erase heading not required.)

CONFIDENTIAL.

12TH.(D.OF L.Y.)BN. MANCHESTER REGT.

WAR DIARY

FROM JANUARY 1ST, 1919.   **TO**   **JANUARY 31ST, 1919.**

VOLUME. XL11.

WAR DIARY
INTELLIGENCE SUMMARY

Army Form C. 2118.

Place	Date	Hour	Summary of Events and Information	Remarks and references to Appendices
Jany 1919	1st		Authorised holiday. 10th Race Meeting	
	2nd		Lectures to men on Coy arrangements. Lecture on "Influenza" & spot on Character good attendance	
	3rd		10 "B" and "C" boys under Coy arrangements. Lectures & talks allotted to D. Coy.	
	4th		Road & Coy Baths. Baths & D. Coys Recreation training and Educational Drill	
	5th		Voluntary Divine Service. Baths allotted to D. Coy	
	6th		Company PT Recreational Training and Educational Drill	
	7th		Company with D. Coys "B" & D. Coys. Recreational Training, Educational Scheme meeting of teachers	
	8th		Battalion in D. Coys "B" & D. Coys "B". Platoon Drill, Ed. work	
	9th		PT. Recreational Training & Educational Drill	
	10th		PT. Recreational Training & Musketry. Drill + Bld marching	
	11th		Recreational Drill, 3 Coys Lecture by Col Burch C.B. & S.O. on "the achievement of the British Empire during the war." 1 Coy and 2 R.B. Bart.	
	12th		Voluntary Divine Service. A Field Day attended by regimental orchestra. Concentration Camp.	
	13th		PT and Recreational Training. 3 Coy Lecture Range. D. Coy under Coy arrangements	
	14th		Musketry. Bath as the personnel Coys	
	15th		PT Recreational Training and close order drill	
	16th		PT Recreational Training. A Coy on Range. B+C under Coy arrangements	
	17th		Battalion parades & Military & Employment returns. Inspection of Colours	
	18th		9th Battalion of the Brigade	
			Great pageant for Exhibition of returns to Base and a R.F.M by Maj. General Sir Richardson Lopay	
	19th		Recruits Returns were dismissed	
	20th		Voluntary Divine Service. Coy allotted. PT+ Divine Service provided to Concentration Camp	
	21st		PT. Recreational Training "B" and "C" Coys kings and D. Coys Company training	
	22nd		letters by Capt. Nicholson of the Unique	
	23rd		PT. & Recreation training. C Coy on Range. 175 and signalling classes preparing for	
	24th		3 Coys. Foot march PCh Dickison army	
	25th		PT and Recreational training. D. Coy on Range. A & C Coy small boy arrangements and Recreational Training. "A", "B" and "D" Coys Lecture. "C" on duty	
			3 Coys Education	

Army Form C. 2118.

WAR DIARY
or
INTELLIGENCE SUMMARY.
(Erase heading not required.)

Instructions regarding War Diaries and Intelligence Summaries are contained in F. S. Regs., Part II. and the Staff Manual respectively. Title pages will be prepared in manuscript.

Place	Date	Hour	Summary of Events and Information	Remarks and references to Appendices
Santy Laiz	1919		Voluntary Divine Service.	
	27th		P.T. and Recreation in the morning. T.C. Coy. "Jailty Baths". D'Coy. Kit Inspection.	
	28th		P.T. and Recreational training. Close by Medical 3 Coys. Returns of Kit in Smaller Kits.	
	29th		Coast by inspection of kits seen.	
	30th		P.T. and Recreation at Gym. 2 Coys. Jailty Baths. "C" Coy. Under Coy own arrangements. 3 Coys at Mach. E. Coy Mty.	
	31st		P.T. and Recreational Training & Coy. Training.	

J. Mills Lieut Col.
Commandg. D. of 2.9 Battn. Manchester Regt.

Army Form C. 2118.

WAR DIARY
or
INTELLIGENCE SUMMARY.

(*Erase heading not required.*)

Instructions regarding War Diaries and Intelligence Summaries are contained in F. S. Regs., Part II. and the Staff Manual respectively. Title pages will be prepared in manuscript.

Place	Date	Hour	Summary of Events and Information	Remarks and references to Appendices

CONFIDENTIAL.

WAR DIARY

OF

12TH (D.L.O.Y.) BN. MANCHESTER REGIMENT.

FOR

1ST FEBRUARY 1919 TO 28TH FEBRUARY 1919.

VOLUME XLIV

Vol 41

Army Form C. 2118.

WAR DIARY
INTELLIGENCE SUMMARY.
(Erase heading not required.)

Instructions regarding War Diaries and Intelligence Summaries are contained in F. S. Regs., Part II. and the Staff Manual respectively. Title pages will be prepared in manuscript.

Place	Date	Hour	Summary of Events and Information	Remarks and references to Appendices
Wailles FRANCE	1.2.19		P.T. + Recreational Training. Kit Inspection	
	2.2.19		No Divine Service. Consignment of Demobilizers proceeded to Divne Concentration Camp.	
	3.2.19		A + B Coys Tailly Baths + Recreational Training. C + D Coys Recreational Training + Company Training. Battn. organised into Two Coys. for parade purposes only. Amalgamation of A.C. Coys & B.D. Coys.	
	4.2.19		P.T. + Recreational Training. Battn. lectured to by Capt. W.T. Monckton, on the "Value of History."	
	5.2.19		The 17th Divnl. Military Advisory Board visit this Unit.	
	6.2.19		P.T. + Recreational Training. Two Coys. Tailly Baths. Two Coys. Close Order Drill + Coy. Training.	
	7.2.19		Battn. Route March.	
	8.2.19		P.T. Recreational Training + Coy. Training.	
	9.2.19		" " " + Kit Inspection	
	10.2.19		C of E + Non. Conformist combined voluntary service.	
	11.2.19		P.T. + Recreational Training. Coy. Training. Lewis Gun + Signalling Classes.	
	12.2.19		" " " "	
	13.2.19		" " " "	
	14.2.19		Battn. Route March.	
	15.2.19		Divine Voluntary Service.	
	16.2.19		P.T. + Recreational Training. Two Coys. Baths. Two Coys. Company Training.	
	17.2.19		" " " Kit Inspection.	
	18.2.19		" " " Two Coys. Baths. Two Coys. Coy. Training. Transport Inspected by	
	19.2.19		G.O.C. Brigade.	
	20.2.19		P.T. + Recreational Training. Coy. Training. Brigade Race Meeting.	

Army Form C. 2118.

WAR DIARY
INTELLIGENCE SUMMARY.
(Erase heading not required.)

Instructions regarding War Diaries and Intelligence Summaries are contained in F. S. Regs., Part II. and the Staff Manual respectively. Title pages will be prepared in manuscript.

Place	Date	Hour	Summary of Events and Information	Remarks and references to Appendices
Warlus FRANCE	21.2.19		P.T. + Recreational Training. Coy. Training. Lewis Gun Class.	
	22.2.19		" " Cleaning Scrubbing of all accoutrements	
	23.2.19		Divine Voluntary Service. Batln. find Supply Train Guard.	
	24.2.19		Coys Baths. P.T. + Recreational Training	
	25.2.19		P.T. Recreational + Coy. Training. Baths.	
	26.2.19		P.T. + Recreational Training + Coy Training.	
	27.2.19		" " "	
	28.2.19		" " "	

Cmdng. 12th (Df L.y) Bn. Manchester Regiment.

G. Mills Lieut. Col.

Felbry 28th 1919.

CONFIDENTIAL.

WAR DIARY

of the

12TH (D.O.L.Y.) BN. MANCHESTER REGIMENT

FROM

1ST MARCH 1919 to 31ST MARCH 1919

VOLUME. XLV.

Army Form C. 2118.

WAR DIARY
INTELLIGENCE SUMMARY.
(Erase heading not required.)

Instructions regarding War Diaries and Intelligence Summaries are contained in F. S. Regs., Part II. and the Staff Manual respectively. Title pages will be prepared in manuscript.

Place: Wailly France

Date 1919	Hour	Summary of Events and Information	Remarks and references to Appendices
Mar. 1		P.T. Recreational Training. Kit Inspection.	
" 2		Voluntary Holy Communion. Evening Service.	
" 3		P.T. Recreational Training. Platoon + Company Training.	
" 4			
" 5		Batt. Route March.	
" 6		Baths for Whole Battn.	
" 7		P.T. Recreational Training. Company Training.	
" 8		Div. O. Race Meeting in afternoon	
" 9		No Church Parade.	
" 10		P.T. Recreational Training. Company Training.	
" 11		Kit Inspection.	
" 12		Baths for whole Batt.	
" 13		Battn. Route March.	
" 14		P.T. Recreational Training. Platoon Training.	
" 15		Company Training.	
" 16		Voluntary C of E Service. 10.30 hours.	
" 17		P.T. Recreational Training. Kit Inspection.	
" 18		Battn. Route March.	
" 19		Baths for whole Battn.	
" 20		P.T. Recreational Training. Company Training.	
" 21		Cleaning thoroughly all equipment preparatory to Supply Train guards.	
" 22		Supply Train guards. Remainder of men collecting R.E. Material.	
" 23		No Church Parade. Supply Train Guards.	

Army Form C. 2118.

WAR DIARY
INTELLIGENCE SUMMARY.
(Erase heading not required.)

Instructions regarding War Diaries and Intelligence Summaries are contained in F. S. Regs., Part II. and the Staff Manual respectively. Title pages will be prepared in manuscript.

Place	Date 1919	Hour	Summary of Events and Information	Remarks and references to Appendices
Marles France	Mar. 24		Supply Train Guards. March order inspection for remainder.	
	25		Supply Train Guards.	
	26		" "	
	27		Fatigues for remainder of Battn.	
	28		Baths.	
	29		Baths.	
Quesnoy	30		Battn. moved to Le Quesnoy when whole of 92nd Brigade Group concentrated.	
	31		Kit re inspection for draft proceeding tomorrow. 3 Officers + 80 o/R. proceeded by lorry to 2.5th Prisoners of War Coy. Villers Bretonneux.	

J. Miles Lieut. Col.

Cmdg. 1/2 [Dep]L.F. Bn. Manchester Regt.